Literature
and Capital

ALSO PUBLISHED BY BLOOMSBURY:

For the University, Thomas Docherty
Literary Criticism in the 21st Century, Vincent B. Leitch
Literature After Globalization, Philip Leonard

Literature
and Capital

THOMAS DOCHERTY

BLOOMSBURY ACADEMIC
LONDON · NEW YORK · OXFORD · NEW DELHI · SYDNEY

BLOOMSBURY ACADEMIC
Bloomsbury Publishing Plc
50 Bedford Square, London, WC1B 3DP, UK
1385 Broadway, New York, NY 10018, USA

BLOOMSBURY, BLOOMSBURY ACADEMIC and the Diana logo are trademarks
of Bloomsbury Publishing Plc

First published in Great Britain 2018

Cover design by Levy Associates
Cover image © Getty Images

A catalogue record for this book is available from the British Library.

Library of Congress Cataloging-in-Publication Data
Names: Docherty, Thomas, 1955–
Title: Literature and capital / Thomas Docherty.
Description: London ; New York : Bloomsbury Academic/ Bloomsbury Publishing
Plc, 2019. | Includes bibliographical references and index.
Identifiers: LCCN 2018002199 (print) | LCCN 2018010788 (ebook) |
ISBN 9781350064652 (ePUB) | ISBN 9781350064669 (ePDF) |
ISBN 9781350064645 (hardback) | ISBN 9781350064638 (pbk.)
Subjects: LCSH: Economics and literature. | Capitalism and literature. |
Culture–Economic aspects. | Politics and literature. | Education–Social
aspects. | Values in literature. | Privatization. | Literature and society.
Classification: LCC PN51.D63 (ebook) | LCC PN51.D63 L58 2018 (print) |
DDC 809/.93358–dc23
LC record available at https://lccn.loc.gov/2018002199

ISBN: HB: 978-1-3500-6464-5
PB: 978-1-3500-6463-8
ePDF: 978-1-3500-6466-9
eBook: 978-1-3500-6465-2

Typeset by Newgen KnowledgeWorks Pvt. Ltd., Chennai, India

To find out more about our authors and books visit www.bloomsbury.com
and sign up for our newsletters.

For George Donaldson, who knows many things,
and especially the meaning of friendship

Contents

Preface and Acknowledgements   viii

Introduction: Literal Capital   1

PART ONE Land and Literature   21

1 Capital and the Embrace of Letters   23
2 On the Credibility of Writing: Material Promises   37
3 The Career of English   63

PART TWO Culture and Capital   99

4 Governing the Tongue   101
5 Inequality, Management and the Hatred of Literature   127
6 Cultural Capital and the Shameful University   153

PART THREE Institutions and Human Capital   173

7 The Privatization of all Interests   175
8 Radical Geography   211

Notes   235
Index   265

Preface and Acknowledgements

This book has had a long gestation, and was growing and developing through my writings over some years without my properly noticing that it was a discrete and large-scale argument, worthy of a full monograph study. I owe the realization to friends and colleagues with whom I have discussed the contents, in various ways, over those years, and also to the many institutions that have kindly hosted me when I have presented work in progress.

I would like in particular to thank my hosts and audiences in the following university institutions: Alberta, Brighton, Cardiff, Lausanne, Leeds, Manchester, Oxford, Portsmouth, St Gallen, Trinity College Dublin, Queen's Belfast, Wolverhampton, York. Many colleagues have commented helpfully on my work in the field or have supported and encouraged me in various ways. I would like to thank: Emmanuel Alloa, Sourit Bhattacharya, Bob Brecher, Birgit Breidenbach, Aidan Byrne, Norah Campbell, James Christie, Ben Davies, Dominic Dean, Cormac Deane, George Donaldson, Michael Gardiner, Ranjan Ghosh, Andrew Gibson, Lyn Innes, Daniel Katz, Katja Laug, Neil Lazarus, Alice Leonard, Angus Love, Leo McCann, Graeme Macdonald, Stuart Macdonald, Paulo de Medeiros, J. Hillis Miller, Pablo Mukherjee, Claudio Murgia, Michael Neu, Carol Rutter, Carolyn Sale, Joe Shafer, Stephen Shapiro, Barry Shiels, Christian Smith, Nicholas Taylor-Collins, Peter Taylor-Gooby, Dieter Thomä, Claire Westall, Julian Wolfreys. For more personal support, I thank Martin Read-Jones and Maureen McCreadie. I would be nowhere without Bridie May Sullivan and Hamish Docherty. I am enormously grateful to David Avital in Bloomsbury for his support for me and for this project, and also to the anonymous readers who reviewed the text and made excellent suggestions for improvement. The errors and infelicities that remain are mine.

Introduction: Literal Capital

1

On 15 October 2013, the UK Coalition government privatized the Royal Mail. The erstwhile public service that had delivered letters in one form or another for centuries – at least since the 'Postage Act' of 9 June 1657, during the Interregnum – became the private property of shareholders. The Coalition's sale of this public asset was a political action that, in some ways, stands as emblematic for the work of my entire argument in the present book. It was, in short, a clear exercise in capitalizing on letters.

There is something of fundamental significance in this. That significance affects us all, and not just those of us who are actively engaged in reading and writing texts that we now call 'literary' texts. 'Literature' – that specific form of writing whose significance is determined by its cultural institutionalization, especially in our educational systems – has become a valued commodity in our time. Likewise, literacy is deemed to be a desirable intellectual capability, and a nation's rates of childhood and adult literacy in the population are often used as an index of national well-being, as well as of cultural and economic wealth.

Many people are engaged in the literary aspects of the culture industries, buying and selling books, journals, newspapers; and many are keen to profit from literature in the commercial market place. Equally, the same institutions that work to produce specific cultural and political values and norms through their endorsement of literature and of literacy can also become complicit in worsening the condition of those who stand excluded from the values that the institutions of literature endorse. The recent history of literary studies over the last half-century is testimony to our recognition of the fact that 'literature' – as an institutionalized scheme of values – conspired, knowingly or not, in the continued oppression of so-called 'minorities'. As a consequence, we have had to work to redress the wrongs that this specific inflection of institutionalized Literature ('Eng Lit') has done to women, people of oppressed races, those with sexualities that have differed from a supposed norm of heterosexuality, those from nations and cultures that have stepped out from colonial and imperial subjection and so on.

The cultures of letters have had many kinds of interplay with various movements of capital in this. As those examples show, this is not just a question of capital in Marxist terms, nor is it related to any steady or stable conception of literature. In this book, I will be exploring how capital has been composed, constructed and construed historically. That will involve a broad trajectory in which we can consider capital in relation to the ownership of land, first of all; and here, a poetry that is itself concerned with patronage and with the dependency of writing on a near-feudal relationship with landowners is important. Next, in the emergence of modern capitalism, this relation shifts and we start to understand capital in terms of commercial transactions and labour exploitation; and, with this, there emerges an idea of some forms of writing as demarcated by the same kinds of value that we find in paper money. We see the gradual shifting of an understanding of capital as it moves, first, into finance, and then into what we now recognize as 'cultural capital'.

Such cultural capital exists and is itself produced only thanks to the various ways in which some forms of writing are institutionalized as being of significant general and public value; and it is in our institutions of education that we find this happening most insistently. It follows that we must seek to understand not just the shift from commercial capital to cultural capital, but also the conditions in which cultural capital is itself formed, through our institutions. Some of those institutions are central to the polity; and this will take us into a consideration of what we can call 'institutional capital'. At this stage, the relation of literature to the State becomes important; and, when the State takes an interest in how its institutions operate to cultivate social and political norms, then we have a potential politicization of letters as such.

That will lead, in due course, to the ways in which a society 'manages' its capital in all forms: land ownership, commercialization, commodification, institutional power as vested in cultural capital or learning, and State power. The final turn in this trajectory is one whereby cultural capital itself moves into some fundamental evaluations – through literature and its institutions – of the managing of 'human capital': the business of capitalizing on private individuals. The fundamental issues that dominated the moment at the start of our history – that quasi-feudal structure of dependency of literature on land – returns here in modified form. What we might call 'capitalized letters' will yield us a form of human capital that witnesses the consolidation of power in land, this time shaped by globalization and servitude rather than by a medieval feudal localism. This changes everything; and capitalized letters now need to attend to the ways in which our institutionalized forms of writing and reading – that is, our forms of criticism – will shape our relation not just to the local land, but to broader ecological survival.

2

Communication – in all forms and not just in oral cultures, chirographic cultures, or in letter-writing during the age of print – is of the essence of *publicity* in its most basic form: the construction and constitution of 'that which is public'. Such public acts of communication make each individual subject a participant in shaping a public domain, and in establishing a relation that allows the individual to exist in relation with others. In normal terms, we would think of this as 'ethics' or as 'politics'.

The 1657 Act, which essentially established the Royal Mail as an official service, linked the sending of letters directly to the concerns of *economics*: trade and business. Its opening prospectus states that 'the Erecting and Setling of one General Post-Office, for the speedy Conveying, Carrying, and Re-Carrying of Letters by Post, to, and from all Places within England, Scotland, and Ireland, and into several parts beyond the Seas ... is the best means ... to maintain a certain and constant intercourse of Trade and Commerce betwixt all the said Places, to the great benefit of the People of these Nations'.[1] This was an establishment not just of the several nations here as a unified entity, but also as an entity shaped by trade and commerce. The Act legitimizes this by making it clear that such trading and commercial activity is managed by the Post Office for the public good. The Coalition's 2013 privatization of the Royal Mail disturbs this, in that the very machinery that enables such a public domain to be realized or to have an existence is essentially disabled through an act that atomizes 'the public' into a series of discrete 'private lives'. Furthermore, it does this for reasons that are fundamentally related to the movement of capital and wealth.[2]

The rationale for the sell-off of this public asset that was advanced – by the then Chancellor of the Exchequer, the Conservative George Osborne, and his partner, the Liberal Democrat Vince Cable who was Business Secretary in the Coalition administration – was that the sale would raise billions that would help to pay down the UK's national debt. The fundamental – and as yet basic – opening proposition of this book is thereby made clear: there is capital to be found in letters; and the State has an interest in that fact. The questions that arise from this proposition, however, are many and complex, perhaps even more so when we institutionalize the act of writing letters into a form that we first of all call *belles lettres* – fine writing – before settling eventually on the identification of some modes of writing as 'Literature'.

The process of 'the privatization of letters' – this mechanism of communication – was one whereby, according to Vince Cable, the future of the Royal Mail would become more sustainable as an enterprise. The ideological claim was that it would be less dependent on government and public funding, because the processes of privatization would ensure the making of profit. A small percentage of the shares in the business would be handed over to the workforce, in the attempt to ensure buy-in from the existing workers by giving them an 'interest' in the business that would be different from and other than the simple fact of working for it to earn a salary. This interest would now be financialized, realized as monetary capital.

As it happened, history staged things differently. The government massively undervalued the shares. Within days they were trading at somewhere close to 190% of their initial offer price. Poorer individual investors capitalized on this, by selling their shares to large-scale investors, mainly hedge funds and pension funds. In short, what had once been owned by all of the general public was now the private property of a small number of interested private parties and globalized corporates. The generally shared or public capital that was invested structurally in letters had been transferred into private hands, and now existed primarily as either private capital or as assets (privately or corporately owned).

Assets are not just monetary. We think of our assets as being related tightly to our property, for example. Land, housing and the like are all fundamental assets. If we own any such property, we consider it our own basic capital. Public assets are different, in that they are not owned and sequestered away by private individuals. In principle, access to them is equally distributed and shared. Public space, for example – the space or domain that you create whenever you try to communicate something to me, say – belongs to no one individual: it is actually constituted as *public* precisely through our sharing of the space in communicating with each other.

There is a third category with which we have now become familiar; and this is an asset that is ostensibly intangible, but no less real for that. We have come to call it 'cultural capital', and it is associated with learning, with literacy, with 'knowledge' in its various institutional forms, and with letters. In short, the financial capital that was initially invested in the commercial economics of the Royal Mail has now ceded place – in terms of public capital – to the cultural capital of letters in the form of literature. In all cases, however, the expectation is that investment (as in the establishment of the Royal Mail, and also in its sell-off) will lead to a return of that capital investment, enhanced by interest.

Interest is itself interesting. It suggests, at least in this context, a coincidence of curiosity and profit. It involves curiosity because letters operate as the sealed 'containers' of information that – precisely because it is tantalizingly concealed behind a seal or an envelope – we would like to see. The letter is intrinsically the site of a temptation: it stimulates desire. It involves profit because, in both writing and reading letters, something new is made or produced. That, indeed, is the fundamental premise from which Marx and Engels started their re-thinking of the nature of human being under capital, when they opened *The German Ideology* with the observation that no matter how we might try to describe human individuals, we must start from the premise that we are 'producers'.[3]

Furthermore, once we start to think of some writing as being different, thanks to its institutionalization as an example of 'literature', a similar desire constitutes the critical reader. We see this typified in, for a simple example, those eighteenth-century epistolary novels of Samuel Richardson. When Richardson decided in 1739–40 to write *Pamela*, the first of his three major novels, he was a successful 51-year-old businessman, whose previous experience of writing as a profession came through his activity as a printer and publisher. The most interesting fact with respect to the present argument is that he saw the writing of his novels in financial terms, as a profession to which he could turn to make money. This, in fact, is where his two most successful novels, *Pamela* and *Clarissa*, begin.

Consider the opening of *Pamela*, in which Pamela sends a letter to her parents. One of the matters she reports to them relates directly to money. She tells her parents about the death of her mistress, following which Mr. B has inherited the house and estate. Seeing Pamela's anxiety about her own position, Mr. B intervenes to tell her that he will keep her on as a servant, thus assuring her of income, and he gives her four guineas and 'some silver' from his now deceased mother's pockets. Pamela tells her parents that she is sending the four guineas home to them.[4] This in itself is 'of interest', financially. Of further interest – this time culturally and related directly to the writing of letters – she adds a postscript. In this, Pamela tells us that Mr. B has already read this letter (though presumably not the postscript). He had intervened not just financially, with the four guineas, but also in the activity of letter-writing itself. He exercised his curiosity in asking to see how she writes, asking to see her hand (the hand that he had already physically held, before all the other servants). She has to open the letter to him, in order to satisfy his curiosity and interest. This initial 'transgression' of a personal communication – his intervening in the space between Pamela and her parents – immediately serves to establish a fundamental economic relation not just between Pamela and Mr. B, but, more fundamentally, between capital and letters.

In a similar manner, Richardson also opens *Clarissa* with letters in which capital is of central interest and concern. The opening letters are not just about Lovelace and the duel that inaugurates the action, they are also about the financial position of Clarissa and her family. As in *Pamela*, that position is affected by an act of writing. In this case, the writing in question concerns the will left by Clarissa's grandfather with its determination of the inheritance of estates and capital. In the postscript to her first letter to Clarissa, Anna Howe asks for a copy, so that her Aunt Harman can assent 'to the preference given to you in that will'. That preferential treatment has driven a wedge between Clarissa and her siblings; and we hear also of her brother 'busying himself in viewing the condition of the considerable estate' that had been left to him in Scotland by his godmother.[5]

Richardson published *Pamela* from his own printing shop in 1740. He was thus able to control the marketing of the text as well as its written content. This is one of the ways in which the marketization of letters begins to intrude into the realm of what we come to identify as the literary. Mary Poovey is extremely clear on how this operates. In her account of *Genres of the Credit Economy*, she argues that in the early days of what became known institutionally as 'the English novel', one determining structural characteristic of the texts was the way in which they inhabited a specific psychological terrain. The ability 'to inspire belief in events that were, strictly speaking, neither true nor false ... was essential to the work we call *fiction*'. In this new construction of the arena of the fictional itself, as an ambiguous terrain between truth and falsehood, we find a parallel with what was happening in the early eighteenth century in financial terms as well.

Credit, after all – along with its realization in forms of credibility – is itself organized by a kind of ambiguity: it works on the assumption that money is there where in fact it is absent. The new idea of 'fiction' as a mediating ground of similar ambiguity between the true and the false is intimately related to this, for it 'was essential to the working of liberal governmentality and the credit economy in particular'. In this way, credit itself can become 'a function of print', which is to say that 'printed texts might be able to generate belief *even when* a reader could not determine whether the events they narrated were true'.[6]

We can observe a similar phenomenon in the emergence of the epistolary form in France, some two decades before Richardson turned to the novel. Capital shapes Montesquieu's *Lettres Persanes* of 1721, especially in its satire on the figure of John Law. Law was the Scottish economist who established the 'banque générale de France' in 1716. This came about twenty years after the similar economic experiment of making a national bank in England, and Law envisaged an institution that would be even more successful than the Bank of England had been. The facts did not match the theory, however; and, in the *Lettres Persanes*, Montesquieu savaged Law's economic ideas. In letters 132, 142 and 146 especially, Usbek and Rica, Montesquieu's Persian sojourners in France, reveal to the French that Law's banque générale has depleted the economy, and left people without any capital at all. The result is the corruption that has been revealed more generally in the whole of the national culture in the rest of the letters.

In Letter 132, Rica visits a coffee-house, where he overhears the other customers discussing their finances, and lamenting the fact that they had invested in paper money instead of keeping their wealth in estates. The key letter, however, is Letter 142, again from Rica to Usbek. Rica tells of how he has himself received a letter from an unnamed correspondent. The correspondent asks Rica if he has any Persian manuscripts, and offers to buy them and also to add to the purchase a number of his own manuscripts: 'je vous le paierai tout ce que vous voudrez, et je vous donnerai par-dessus le marché quelques ouvrages de ma façon, par lesquels vous verrez que je ne suis point un membre inutile de la République des Lettres' ['I'll pay you whatever price you ask, and I'll also throw in some works of my own, from which you will see that I am not a totally useless member of the Republic of Letters'].[7] This letter-within-a-letter, proposing a financial transaction, also envelops the first of the manuscripts that is offered by Rica's correspondent; and it is this – the 'fragment of an ancient mythologist' – that contains the satire on Law.

The basis of the satire is that Law substitutes imagination for reality. Essentially, paper money operates as an imaginary symbol of something that is more tangible and more substantial: material wealth in gold or other precious metals, and in estates. In the fragment, a Scotsman offers wealth advice to the people of Betica: 'Peuples de Bétique, voulez-vous être riches? Imaginez-vous que je le suis beaucoup, et que vous l'êtes beaucoup aussi; mettez-vous tous le matin dans l'esprit que votre fortune a doublé pendant la nuit;

levez-vous ensuite; et, si vous avez des créanciers, allez les payer de ce que vous aurez imaginé, et dites-leur d'imaginer à leur tour' ['People of Betica, so you want to be rich? Imagine that I am very rich, and that you are very rich: get yourselves into the belief every morning that your fortune has been doubled during the night; rise, then, and if you have any creditors, go and pay them with what you'll have imagined, and tell them to imagine in their turn'].[8]

That was written in 1721. It could equally well have been written as a satire on the financial system in 2007–8 when, as Michael Lewis and others have shown, the world's 'wealth' was imaginary and built on precisely the same kind of exponential inflation of imaginary funds, as trading grew and multiplied credit-default swaps and other financial derivatives.[9] When Usbek writes to Rhedi, in Letter 146, he asks a fundamental question about Law's banking system: 'Quel plus grand crime que celui que commet un ministre lorsqu'il corrompt les moeurs de toute une nation, dégrade les âmes les plus généreuses' ['What crime can be greater than that which a minister commits when he corrupts the morals of a whole nation, and debases the most noble spirits'?].[10] This banking system, alleges Montesquieu, is one in which capital corrupts not just individuals, but the public space in which those individuals find their moral and spiritual realities. It is a corruption of the systems of communication that shape a national identity, and something that warps the relation between works of imagination (or literature) and the material conditions of life and history.

3

Arjun Appadurai has characterized the crisis of 2007–8 as 'primarily a failure of language', because 'the derivative is above all a linguistic phenomenon, since it is primarily a referent to something more tangible'.[11] The failure of the system of finance, he argues, is actually a failure of language systems; and the key linguistic flaw is the same as that which Montesquieu satirized. The derivatives that caused the crisis were based not on the material reality of real estate (that 'something more tangible'). Derivatives are based instead on a system of linguistic promises; and the system of linguistic promises exponentially increases its distance from any firm ground, becoming a self-supporting quasi-autonomous system, built only on the premises of language itself. Appadurai calls it 'the monetization of promises', through which 'every link in the promissory chain was built on greater risk, as distance from the underlying asset was increased'.[12] When the value of that underlying asset fell, the whole promissory system was revealed as a pure act of imagination: people had got wealthy by imagining themselves so.

That is the shape of contemporary capital. It is not just related to language; it is also related, as I will show, to that specific mobilization of language that allows us to institutionalize letters as 'Literature' – capital L – as a source of capital itself.

This is at the core of the present book, which will address the ways in which capital intercedes in and informs the 'space of communication' that we identify as literature. I will trace a steady shift in the relation between capital and the institutions of literature (especially the educational institution of the university). Capital here moves from allowing us to see a basic relation of value to the land itself; this mutates into financial capital – money for its own sake, as it were; and then on into cultural capital before finally assuming its contemporary position in terms of the various shifts in forms of labour that we identify as human capital. At the core of all of this is the way in which literature is formed, invented, and above all institutionalized as a form of writing that sits at the core of our human being, our humanity or humanities.

The book is not about the book-trade, although that is an occasional important reference point; and nor is it an economic treatise. What I seek to do is to show the fundamental interplay in which the forms of capital shape the forms and functions of literature and of literary study. Wealth and value will be disentangled, so that we can see the many and various contradictions that their linkage involves.

Why might this be of especial interest at the present time? My contention is that some fundamental economic relations that shape our advanced societies have changed since the financial crisis of 2007–8; and that this has had a major impact on culture and, within that, on literature and on how we evaluate those forms of languages and letters that we identify as 'literary'. The economic collapse, starting in the US housing market, reveals some fundamental political flaws in the organization of societies, and in how we consider the value of wealth, and the cultural authority of wealth – and also what we once were taught to call 'cultural capital'. It seems obvious that cultural capital has itself become subject to capitalization, and that it has capitulated to the market. Market fundamentalism, as Sandel and many others have argued, has contaminated areas that should have been inoculated against it.[13] Appadurai's 'monetization of promises' is in fact just one aspect of a much larger financialization of aesthetics as such. Were Keats to be writing in today's so-called post-truth culture, it would be difficult to write that 'beauty is truth, truth beauty'; rather, he would be struggling to work against the identification of beauty with wealth.

Literature, of course, has nearly always had some relation with money. Writers need to make a living, and only a blockhead would write for anything less, as Samuel Johnson noted. However, the inquiry in this book is more specific than this. My concern is the relation between different modes and forms of capital and the *institutions* of literature; so the main quarry here is not just specific works of literature (although these will be central to almost all of my particular arguments), but also and primarily the institutionalization of literature, especially considered as a source of wealth or less obviously material forms of capital. In our time, this implicates the institutions of education, and especially that of the university. It is in the university that literature becomes institutionalized as a phenomenon marked by cultural value. It follows that our inquiry must consider the value of literature in relation to the operations of the university in our societies. At the core of this is the relation between the university and capital. Literature is a fulcrum point in that relationship, for it brings together the value system that we associate with culture and the value system that we associate with monetary wealth.

The 2007–8 crisis starts in a question of land ownership – fundamentally in real estate. However, that becomes critical when the instruments that were used by the banks to capitalize on real estate turned out to be based instead on imaginary financial fantasy. It was the story of the American dream coming true, and revealing in that truth that it was, indeed and after all, a dream and not a reality. As with Law and the financial corruption of France as Montesquieu saw it, so also here with the banks and the corruption not just of the

United States but of the entire public sphere as a place of human interaction, communication and politics.

For Georg Simmel, money was a mechanism whose operations affected all social relations, in various ways. It permitted all sorts of transactions to take place, certainly; but it also tended to allow the abstraction of impersonal exchanges to supplant real human involvement in all social relations. The individual becomes dissociated from others, using money as a kind of virtual substitute for her or his 'real presence' in a market. I indicated above that the letter-form of the early novel constructs us in terms of desire, because of the sealed nature of letters. As Simmel has it, 'We desire objects only if they are not immediately given to us for our use and enjoyment; that is, to the extent that they resist our desire'.[14] Yet this desire – given the fact of resistance as the fundamental principle of its realization – must also meet its opposite desire, precisely the desire to resist. Thus, for Simmel, the 'philosophical significance of money' lies in its ability to realize, in external if symbolic form, that way in which 'things receive their meaning through each other, and have their being determined by their mutual relations'.[15] Money is the realization of the different values that we ascribe to things as we exchange them; and this applies to those things we call letters. This is as true of letters as it is of commodities; and money thus becomes 'the pure form of exchangeability'.[16]

The exchange of capital and of desire that constitutes the act of reading and writing letters entails the establishment of an increasing distance between real individuals and subjects, and their replacement with tools for calculation. Human interaction and communication become instrumentalized and mechanized, as an activity factored in terms of a calculation of profit and loss.

Money allows calculation to take place and to supplant other forms of direct human social engagement. The perceived benefit of this is in the predictability and thus security of the outcomes of our engagements. If I tender this fifty pounds, euros or dollars, I can be sure I will receive that shirt in return, say. However, this security and predictability are gained at the cost of the intimate social bond between individuals as human subjects: the abstract logic of transaction replaces human interaction. Obviously, this becomes even more pronounced in the credit-based business of online transactions. Thanks to money, our relations become less human, more instrumental, and thus more open to further financialization. Should I invest in you? What will it mean for me to invest time in this activity, and so on? We can take this back to a fundamental act of calculation that was designed to redeem humanity. Pascal's famous wager says that we should calculate a profit-loss cost-benefit analysis of our position with respect to the existence of God. For Pascal, the Jansenist who believes that humanity is corrupt because fallen, there can be no rational proof of the existence of God: it is a matter of faith. Yet that does not settle the matter, especially for the human who is endowed with reason and who has no other mode of argumentation and rhetorical persuasion. So, as he puts it, 'il faut parier' [you need to make a bet one way or another]. 'Cela n'est pas volontaire, vous êtes embarqués' [it's not a matter of choice, you're already committed]. You need to measure your interests here, he writes: 'voyons ce qui vous intéresse le moins' [let's see what will cost you the least]. He then follows with a quasi-mathematical form of economic reasoning:

Pesons le gain et la perte en prenant croix que Dieu est. Estimons ces deux cas: si vous gagnez vous gagnez tout, et si vous perdez vous ne perdez rien: gagez donc qu'il est sans hésiter.

[Let's do a cost-benefit analysis in betting that God is. Let us estimate the two possibilities: if you win, you win everything, and if you lose you lose nothing: so bet that he is without hesitation][17]

This is rationalist economics; yet Jansenists believed that since human nature is essentially corrupt, reason cannot be an adequate basis for moral judgement. So the wager is not designed to persuade, in fact; rather, its point is simply to excuse or explain an already pre-existing belief – an apologia showing that, *given faith*, belief in the existence of God becomes rationally explicable. As a process of reasoning, it thus becomes irrational and tautological: given the fact of belief, one will believe. The key point, however, is that the apologia is cast in the form of an economic reason.

The contradiction lies not just in the fact that one needs to have faith in order to believe in the wager at all; rather, it lies in the fundamental contradiction between the proto-capitalist calculation of profit-and-loss, or 'investment' in belief, set against the entirely different economy of the 'gift' of belief, or an economy of 'grace'. In his *Ecrits sur la grâce*, Pascal had already posited that our choices of action are themselves determined by the will of God that acts through us. This 'will' is either realized by us, or thwarted by us; and, if it is thwarted, then that is due to the exercise of a human will, an exercise that will mean that we have damned ourselves. That is to say: grace is something that disrupts a calculative proto-capitalist economy, for the simple reason that its source lies beyond secular life itself.

This, indeed, is part of the substance of Pascal's greatest 'literary' work, *Les Provinciales*, letters published clandestinely between 1656 and 1657. The letters are a series of satirical arguments that focus centrally on issues of grace: on whether grace is given to all people equally and on whether it is efficacious or not. It is grace that threatens the kind of economics at work in the wager. And in the *Ecrits sur la grâce*, Pascal asks fundamental questions about human will, and the freedom of individual agents to take responsibility – and reward or punishment – for their actions on earth. Grace complicates economics – the relations of 'crime and punishment', action-and-reward, 'measure for measure' – for the simple reason that it is *gratuitous*, not a 'necessary' or intrinsic condition of our human engagements with each other or with the world.

There is a fundamental contradiction in Pascal's thinking here: he argues that reason is inadequate to an understanding of God, yet he does so by means of a reasoned bet or calculation. This is also the fundamental failure and self-contradiction of capitalism itself in our times. Contemporary capitalism, especially in its neoliberal market-fundamentalist form, assumes that the ground of all human agency is the operation of the free and rational agent, making rational choices for her or his own private benefit. The benefit in question is not just always fundamentally financial, but even if it were not so, the choice would nonetheless be made on the same rationale as a choice made in terms of capitalist investment.

In all of this, we see why the arguments here are important. Capital and its discontents are fundamental to our modes of communication and, importantly, to a consideration of the institutionalization of literature – paper credit – in our time.

4

What, then, is the relation of these economic issues to the institutionalization of literature? Start from the operations of criticism. Critics, we say, 'give' a reading of a text; in our universities, teachers 'give' a lecture on a literary text. Criticism, in general, 'gives' offence (or 'offers' approbation); and sometimes such offence is 'taken' without being 'given' in the first place, especially in social settings.[18] The question concerns the relation of these acts of 'giving' – these gifts – to grace, and to the economy of literature as such.

In the reading that Derrida gives of Baudelaire's *Counterfeit Money*, he points out that the gift has a tendency to undo itself, and thus it becomes extremely difficult to 'realize'. The gift is the site of 'the impossible', in a specific sense. A gift undoes itself whenever it is reciprocated; for, at that moment, it enters into an economy of exchange, of measure for measure, of debts incurred and repaid (with or without interest). Furthermore, the gift undoes itself in exactly the same way even when it is acknowledged *as* a gift, even when its recipient simply or minimally experiences it as a gift, because to conceptualize it as something that is thus given unconditionally, one again brings it into the domain of a specific understanding that senses the gift as that which breaks with a capitalist economy. To negate such an economy, by the giving of a gift, is also to sustain that economy precisely because that economy shapes our understanding of the gift as such.

If this is so, then the kind of grace that I discussed above also becomes a manifestation of 'the impossible'. Yet, at the same time, how can literature – as literature – be something that is caught up in such a capitalist economy? We might buy a book, certainly; but do we thus also buy 'literature'? Is it not the case that part of the point of the institutionalization of letters is itself an attempt to circumvent the idea that literature and the literary are commodities? There must be a politics to this, just as there is always a politics to the gift in Derrida, a politics that becomes clear when he turns to his second volume on the gifting of time, *The Gift of Death*, which opens with a consideration of Jan Patočka in 'Secrets of European Democracy'.

'Politics excludes the mystical', writes Derrida,[19] yet it surely includes the demand for a specific 'responsibility'. In this, there is a clear intrinsic link between the political and the critical, given that any critical engagement is, at least at a basic level, informed by a 'response' to a situation, a predicament or a text. Given that such a response is itself always situated, the response itself also calls for a response in turn. Furthermore, the institutionalization of some writing specifically as 'literary' is itself an act of criticism; and it takes place always within an institution that makes the act of critique valid, comprehensible and valuable. That is to say: critical responsibility is the condition of the legitimization of literature, of instituting letters as literature. Critical responsibility must therefore also lie at the very core of those institutions that legislate for literature: schools and universities.

The political dimension of this is related to capital, and to how an institution capitalizes on its institutionalization of literature. For Derrida, 'it takes very little to envisage an inevitable passage from the *democratic* (in the Greek sense) to the *totalitarian*'.[20] This turns us to the other dimension of the present study, as we seek to understand the conditions of culture and of cultural capital.

Matthew Arnold famously sets culture against wealth. He sees, in 1869, England, a country where the broad consensus holds the view that England is 'great', because of its wealth, especially in the form of natural resources, such as coal. Culture, he says, asks us instead the question 'what is greatness?' In doing so, it calls such financial wealth, such capital, into question, inviting us to consider 'love, interest and admiration'. 'Interest' is being considered, paradoxically, in terms precisely of 'disinterest'. It is an interest that is specific to culture, and that does not demand financial return. Indeed, 'culture begets a dissatisfaction which is of the highest possible value in stemming the common tide of men's thoughts in a wealthy and industrial community'. In doing this, the 'investment' is in the unpredictability of a future, and culture 'saves the future ... from being vulgarised, even if it cannot save the present'.[21]

The rhetoric here is telling. On one hand, Arnold sees the positive in culture in its rejection of the idea that all value, including that of a national identity, is wrapped up in monetary or resource-based wealth. At the same time, he dreads vulgarity. He would be fully aware of the etymology here: he dreads the 'common people', the *vulgus*. Arnold was certainly aware of social class; but he tried to transcend its divisions by proposing an entirely new class, the class of those who are neither barbarians, nor philistines, nor populace. This is that class of 'aliens', as he calls them, 'people who are mainly led, not by their class spirit, but by a general *humane* spirit, by the love of human perfection'.[22] Aliens like this exist in all classes, for Arnold; and, if there is to be hope for the future, it lies in these. These aliens, however, have a system of value that is utterly independent of financial capital. Their interest is in cultural capital.

This is as much as to say that, for Arnold, there is a kind of democracy available to the future, and one that is not based on the commonplaces of the vulgar (or what we might today call 'populism'). It is an amalgam of an aristocracy (of manners) and democracy (of shared manners). It is exactly what Bourdieu will much later identify as 'the aristocracy of culture' in his 1979 study of taste, *Distinction*.[23]

E. M. Forster follows in a similar vein to that sustaining Arnold's argument. In 1944, Forster wrote an essay on the tercentenary of Milton's *Areopagitica*. There, he contrasts the utilitarian language of governmental politics with the value of uncensored literature. He argues that the rationing of paper has led to the prioritization of 'officialese' over literature. The economic condition of a country at war has led to a mode of censorship, and a determination of what counts as our fundamental values. These are decidedly not literary values, if in situations of economic difficulty we relegate literature and prefer the political and cultural authority – the status – of government documents over those that figure and celebrate the literary.

Orwell had also written on the tercentenary and, like Forster, also wrote against censorship. So, when Forster comes to write about Orwell, it is not surprising that he finds much to commend. He especially commends the link that Orwell makes between literature and liberty. For Orwell, 'Liberty ... is connected with prose, and bureaucrats who want to destroy liberty tend to write and speak badly, and to use pompous or woolly or portmanteau phrases in which their true meaning or any meaning disappears'. Forster goes on to point out that many critics attack 'officialese', but that Orwell is 'unique in being immensely serious' in his connecting of 'good prose with liberty'.[24]

Forster is also noted for his famous claim that his own political priorities are not given to beliefs, but to persons. A culture that rests on the generalities of 'belief' is one that will put politics before personal relationships. As with Simmel on money, the personal becomes distanced from reality in such a culture; and essentially, economic investment and exchange supplants personal relationships. A money culture, which Forster refers to as an 'efficiency-regime', is one that displaces human and humane trust and co-operation onto the system of money and of political efficacy.

Forster takes a different view of responsibility. The human realization of responsibility – a fundamental ethics – depends on our willingness to place our trust in persons, who will nonetheless often let us down. However, all this means is that we must graciously extend yet more trust, because 'reliability is not a matter of contract – that is the main difference between the world of personal relationships and the world of business relationships. It is a matter for the heart, which signs no documents'.[25] It is this that lies behind his celebrated proposal that 'I hate the idea of causes, and if I had to choose between betraying my country and betraying my friend, I hope I should have the guts to betray my country'. It is extremely important that, although some will find this shocking, Forster claims a source for it that is of the essence of cultural capital, the *literary* source of Dante's *Inferno*.[26]

Once more here, we have a 'gracious' literary culture set against the value of the capitalist efficiency-regimes that run the State. Forster's claim is that 'Love and loyalty to an individual can run counter to the claims of the State. When they do – down with the State, say I, which means that the State would down me'.[27] Here, too, is the further overlap with Orwell, who in *Nineteen Eighty-Four* sets the personal relation of Winston and Julia against the demands of the political and totalitarian State, the State that sees every element of personal life – and of culture and letters – as being reducible to a political status. In Forster, these considerations lead to a concept of democracy whose characteristic is that it 'does not divide its citizens into the bosses and the bossed – as an efficiency-regime tends to do'.[28]

5

Forster offers two cheers for democracy, 'one because it admits variety and two because it permits criticism'. In permitting variety and criticism, it provides also the grounds on which literature, as institutionally valued writing, is constituted. The only capital involved in this, for Forster (as for his predecessor Arnold), is cultural and human, based in what he calls (after Swinburne's 'Hertha') 'Love the Beloved Republic'. Forster replicates Arnold's class of aliens, but has fewer qualms about describing them as an aristocracy. 'I believe in aristocracy', he writes; but immediately he nuances this stance, meaning it is 'not an aristocracy of power, based upon rank and influence, but an aristocracy of the sensitive, the considerate and the plucky. Its members are to be found in all nations and classes, and all through the ages, and there is a secret understanding between them when they meet. They represent the true human condition'.[29] The political problem, for Arnold, was to make the best self of the alien class prevail; for Forster, it is a tragedy that 'no device has been found by which these private decencies can be transmitted to public affairs'.[30]

If literature does indeed condition and constitute 'the public', then we will see how important literature is to this politics, a politics that does not rest on the priorities of financial capital or monetary wealth, but on the institutionalization of literature as the very space of the possibility of human exchange and of human sociability. Forster knows, realistically, that material history is unforgiving and that 'all society rests upon force'. However, the progress of history is not simply the same as the progress of force, as there are intervals – spaces, moments, instances – when force is not to the fore. In those moments, we get creativity, he claims, and 'I want them to be as frequent and as lengthy as possible, and I call them "civilization"'.[31]

Culture, we might now say, is something that happens; and, therefore (pace Williams) it is only ever extraordinary, never ordinary. It is not a commodity, and insofar as it takes the form of a substantive 'event', it cannot therefore be for sale in a market: it is not one stable entity, but is instead a process. We might now describe politics as the duty that we have to keep force or mere physical violence (the expression of a political will by crude and brute power) in check; and literary culture – the culture of letters – is one of the key mechanisms by which we can do this. This is the capital that is vested in letters.

I close this introduction by adverting to a letter that is marked by restraint, provisionality, and the uncertainties given by any text that can be properly characterized as 'literary'. Forster claims that 'The more highly public life is organized the lower does its morality sink'. A political philosopher, such as Hannah Arendt, might well endorse such a view. Forster acknowledges that for some, redemption from such immorality and corruption lies in Christianity. The more clear-sighted would agree with him when he writes: 'I think that such influence as it [Christianity] retains in modern society is due to the money behind it'.[32] That would be a monetization of faith itself, and thus also a contradiction in terms if faith is understood to be inimical to capitalization. 'Believers', like Pascal, 'have Faith, with a large F. My faith', writes Forster 'has a very small one',[33] one that is therefore 'non-capitalized'. Essentially, it becomes trust, and a trust that is not based on calculation.

Trust – especially in its fundamental forms as credibility and credit – is where we will now begin the detailed study of how letters are capitalized, or of *Literature and Capital*.

PART ONE

Land and Literature

1

Capital and the Embrace of Letters

1

Decadence is the happy bedfellow of unearned privilege. Our contemporary moment, witnessing the decadence and decay of politics, certainly, is also witnessing a decay of interest in fundamental aspects of culture and of education. It would be a crass simplification to propose here a 'decline of civilization' story. That is certainly not our predicament, notwithstanding some recent very obvious attacks on both culture and education. We can avoid the wholesale chiliastic overstatements made by commentators such as Edward Luce that we are witnessing 'the retreat of western liberalism', with its echoes of Spengler's 1918 *Decline of the West*, while still attending to some historical particulars that offer testimony of a specific decaying of belief in the values of the arts, education and even, in the extreme, the decay of belief in politics itself.[1]

The American Academy of Arts and Sciences, for instance, reported in its most recent analysis that humanities majors in the United States have decreased by 10 per cent between 2012 and 2015. The trend is comparable to those elsewhere; consequently, some departments of literary study are being closed down completely. In 2016, among the highest profile cases was that of Johns Hopkins, which threatened to close its Humanities Center entirely. That threat followed the Japanese government's intervention in 2015, when they proposed the closure of virtually all of the social sciences and humanities faculties in the nation's eighty-six universities. Similar developments are under way in the UK, where the government withdrew all financial interest in supporting teaching in the arts and humanities (and some social sciences) after the Browne Review, *Securing a Sustainable Future for Higher Education*, in 2010. The UK government made it clear that all funding for tuition in humanities disciplines would now come entirely from student loans and the attendant private debt. The State would retain an official interest, financially, only in so-called STEMM subjects: science, technology, engineering, mathematics and medicine.

There is a certain 'new Puritanism' at work in this. Literary study – along with other humanities disciplines – is regarded as a privileged luxury: Toby Belch's 'cakes and ale' in a Malvolio-inspired age of supposed austerity.[2] That Puritanism states that 'we' cannot afford to fund indulgent luxuries, like reading, writing and talking about books. One obvious paradox is that the university is perhaps the single most important site and institution in and through which we have developed the idea of cultural capital. At the same time, the university is bearing witness to the decay in cultural capital associated with literature and with all forms of cultural engagement. Some ISIS religious fundamentalists trash Palmyra and refuse to tolerate music; other fundamentalists – market fundamentalists – trash the arts in general, and, like Michael Gove, encourage us to despise 'experts' and their forms of knowledge.[3] This is the scenario that provides the backdrop against which the argument of this book will emerge.

This collocation of a UK Conservative MP with a far-right terrorist organization may appear a crass comparison; but the two phenomena are indeed related in terms of what they both construe as 'valuable'. Behind both there lies a historically shifting dialectic between values and money, or between values and different forms of capital.

Across modernity, we have seen the emergence of basic conflicts among these different forms of capital. After Marx, capital was conventionally considered primarily in terms of the transformational value of labour and its reflection in the ownership of the means and modes of production – and profits – within a social formation. Labour would permit us to overcome our domination by the crude world of natural and physical forces, as we learned how to manipulate resources and to control or at least find a solid accommodation with our ecology. However, 'ownership' – here meaning ownership of the resources and of the labour – was key to understanding our sociopolitical relations. Within that ownership, there lies a residual sense of a basic form of capital that was inscribed in the ownership not just of machinery but also of land itself and what it contained.

The struggle over control of resources continues, certainly. Modern and contemporary 'petro-fictions' – from Upton Sinclair's *1927 Oil!* via John McGrath's *The Cheviot, the Stag, and the Black, Black Oil* (1973) to Patrick Chamoiseau's *Texaco* in 1992 and many others since – will attest fully to our committed political interest in the struggle for resources, be it oil, water or food.[4] Alongside this – essentially a map of our changing relations to our ecological predicaments – there has grown an interest in different forms of capital. In the face of failed revolutions between 1848 and 1968, critics, thinkers and writers all found a displaced solace, in culture and in 'cultural capital'. Cultural capital has itself become a fundamental resource; and, for the political optimist, cultural capital offers a mode of 'ownership' that transcends the seeming stability of fixed land, 'real' estate. Cultural capital is mobile in ways that the land is not; and those in possession of cultural capital are themselves set free to roam, not tied to any one specific locale for their metaphorical wealth.

Perhaps with a developing sense that Marx's revolution might be endlessly deferred, critics, thinkers and writers have increasingly looked to the possibilities of a revolutionary potential that can be found and exploited within this new form of capital. Land might remain in private hands, but we proponents of cultural capital have something more mobile, agile, not limited by place. The transformative power of our physical labour is displaced onto the transformative power of our knowledge and our intellectual capacities: investment in music, painting, sculpture, dance, architecture, languages and literature. Most importantly, however, the key difference between this and the capital that is vested in material and physical resources is that, while the latter is determined by a logic of economic privatization, cultural capital instead is a site of sharing, and of a proposed possible equalization of resources – knowledge – through the distributional force of education, *Bildung*.

It is through the normalization of such cultural capital that, historically, we established an entity called 'literature'. The development of a particular form of attention that is given to some writings has been shown decisively to be an event that takes place in complete accordance with some important historical changes that occur across the eighteenth and nineteenth centuries. Those changes are not just political, but are also related to fundamental economic conditions, such as the development of the banking system and the increasing strength of the new paper money as a social factor tying individuals together in debts and credits. It is unsurprising that literary figures feature on bank notes: Scott, Shakespeare, Dickens, Austen, for examples. Ownership of material resources – economic wealth itself – is now in interplay with the 'ownership' of something that is less obviously 'material': a specific kind of consciousness and conscience. We find this not in the ownership of material books but in a relation to the ideas invested in those books by the cultural conversations that accrue around them. The economic parallel is the establishment of a kind of faith in the writing on a bank note, that promise of economic return for the writing itself.

In the nineteenth century, religious faith itself was also giving way (across Europe and other so-called advanced economies of the period) to the prevalence of this new kind of social bond. Matthew Arnold and many others saw that religious faith could and would be supplemented – even supplanted – by a new kind of organization of our social beliefs, found in literature more than anywhere else. This attitude persists to the present day in minor ways. In Richard Ford's 2017 memoir of his parents, *Between Them*, Ford comments that 'I do not know about my father's faith – if he had any . . . I know he didn't take pleasure in books – where he could've found what we all find if we don't have faith: testimony that there is an alternate way to think about life, different from the ways we're naturally equipped. Seeking imaginative alternatives would not have been his habit'.[5]

Seeking imaginative alternatives to how the world is currently shaped is of the essence of cultural capital. This helps explain the political changes that began broadly in the 1960s, when people of the political left began to realize that there was a link between culture, labour and the management of our relation to the planet itself. While nineteenth-century radicalism presupposed that the human individual would master the world of nature, we have more recently come to realize the necessity of finding a more sustainable accommodation to nature, one that will allow humanity as such, beyond the individual, to persist. Thus began the political shift 'from red to green' as in the political thought of Rudolf Bahro or Daniel Cohn-Bendit – and as in the title of Naomi Klein's recent study, *This Changes Everything*,[6] whose subtitle gives the clear guiding argument of the book, 'capitalism vs. the climate'.

The issues that such historical shifts raise are not entirely new, however. Oscar Wilde, for the most obvious example – and one in tune with my presiding theme of decadence – concludes the Preface to his *Picture of Dorian Gray* with the oft-repeated observation that 'All art is quite useless'. That proposition has a certain contemporary poignancy for us, and it is especially telling for anyone who has a substantial personal or professional interest in literature today. Who, today, cares much about literature? It is a truth universally acknowledged today that value – and anything that we should care about – can be realized in only one substantive manner. It has to be made visible; and that means that *qualitative* value has to be realized in *quantifiable* form: specifically, money that can be counted.

Nowadays, such visibility is itself ambiguous, for it rests precisely on the immaterial conditions of the promise, the condition of paper money that *represents* wealth even as it constitutes it. Value is given, now and in our advanced economies, to anything that can be monetized; and if something is inimical to easy and straightforward capital monetization, it is inherently 'quite useless' in those societies. Cultural capital, in these terms, becomes 'useful' when it allows its bearer to receive, on demand, certain sums of money, via employment in a position of social or institutional status.

The aphoristic propositions that immediately precede Wilde's celebrated claim are less frequently noted. He wrote that 'we can forgive a man for making a useful thing as long as he does not admire it. The only excuse for making a useless thing is that one admires it intensely'.[7] Today, Edward and Robert Skidelsky give a new rationale to Wilde's ostensibly counter-intuitive statements, when they consider our present-day attitudes to making and admiring today's primary commodity. 'Making money', they write, 'cannot be an end in itself – at least for anyone not suffering from acute mental disorder'.[8] For

David Marquand, extending this kind of insight, we live in *Mammon's Kingdom*, admiring money and the making of money as such. Like the Skidelskys, Marquand thinks of this as a kind of illness, a medical syndrome. To heal us of this illness, the illness that usually goes by the name of 'the post-2008 crisis', Marquand recommends that we will only rediscover health – and thereby sustain ourselves – if we manage to discover a different kind of wealth, which he explicitly calls 'the buried riches of our *culture*'[9] (emphasis added).

Literature and Capital explores the structural relations between these different kinds of 'wealth' or capital; and the major discovery of the book is that the key relation is one that has a history, and a history that is extremely nuanced. It would be a simple matter to make a claim that literature offers us a kind of cultural refuge from the ravages of contemporary savage money-making and barbaric greed: simple, but wrong, in fact. Such a claim is in fact entirely consistent with precisely the kind of populist caricature that envisages literature as essentially a luxurious superfluity and the property of a privileged elite; and this belief, in turn, consolidates the existing understanding of values in which art is useless because it cannot be monetized. The appeal to literature as a site that incipiently or intrinsically resists the ravages of contemporary capital is, in fact, often utterly complicit with the movement of that capital.

Instead of approaching the relationship of capital to literature in this way, as a structured opposition, I will prefer to show the ways in which our understanding of capital itself has shifted; and we will see the role that writing, reading and the institutionalization of the concept of 'literature' as such plays in this. The movement – and the crude shape and trajectory of the argument of this book – can be summarized fairly succinctly.

2

Here is the skeleton of the story.

Capital is associated first with the ownership of land and resources. The attendant form of writing constitutes the double-edged nature of patronage. On one hand, a writer eulogizes a landowner, praising the lord of the manor and describing the estate as a poetic symbol of quasi-eternal perfection. At the same time, the landowner depends on the writer to construct a symbolic legacy that will outlive the physical existence of the landlord himself. Yet this is more than a local issue; and, in a global context appropriate to the emergence of the modern forms of capitalism, it goes hand-in-glove with a specific movement of imperialism, and with the colonial control of lands other than that which is the 'immediate' property of a landlord. In short, it is as relevant to the establishment of Delhi as the capital of India as it is to the stately home of the Sidneys, in the Penshurst that forms the focus of Ben Jonson's praise-poem.

It is, indeed, through these relations that 'writing' becomes initially institutionalized as a site of specific value that we denote as 'literary'; or, to put it another way, it is thanks to what happened in India in 1911, when the British replaced Kolkata with Delhi as the Indian capital, that Ben Jonson's poem of 1616 becomes specifically considered as 'literature' and not just as a non-specific writing. 'English Literature', as a discipline of study that is formulated and consolidated in our universities, for instance, is inaugurated in a specific political economy, and one that is associated with British control of India and other geographical terrains. The inculcation of 'English values' is mobilized, in India, via education in English Literature.

Through this, we start to establish a new form of capital, identified not in the ownership of anything material such as land, but rather in the activation of educational apparatuses. Such apparatuses extend the control of land further, such that people are also now subject to imperial control. The mechanism is a language that 'governs the tongues' of oppressed people. The roots of this are found in the 'management' and control of the Indian people in the mid-1830s. Control of the empire and its people becomes the Petri dish through which education, in England itself, becomes a mechanism for political arrangements.

This assumes a special form through the institution of the university and the ways in which the university institutionalizes certain forms of attention and thinking as knowledge, and certain forms of writing as literary. That institution becomes a central element in the consolidation of a new sense of value – aesthetic value – that is written on the body, certainly (the laughing and sorrowful faces of the theatre's symbolic masks, for instance), but not necessarily in the familiar ways in which physical labour is written on the human body, with its scars, sufferings and fatigue.

The consequence here is a clash between at least two different modes of capital; and this is worked through, broadly, in the development of a form of fiction that takes the shape of the emergent novel genre. As Mary Poovey, among others, has shown, that fictional genre is intimately related to the new structures of finance that shape its contemporary society. The founding of the Bank of England in 1694 helps to inaugurate a sense that values can inhere in the form of paper promises, with their writings that are based fundamentally on the notion of credit and debt.[10] This historical shift in our political and social economy helps to propel the sense that value can be inscribed in the transformational powers not of the labouring body but rather in that of a writing that is predicated on a promise, an airy nothing. It is not only in the novel, of course, that we see the new formulations of cultural capital at work.

A number of other texts attend to the same pressing issues that concerned the emergent novel, perhaps most especially the novel's exploration of space, consistent with the interest in colonial expansion of markets. Swift's *Gulliver's Travels* is a case in point, combining notions of exploration with plays on the science of perspective. Perspective is about the manipulation of space, but also about its transformation. Transformation of nature by labour that played a part in eulogy and in systems of patronage gives way to explorations of a different kind of transformation: the transformations associated with modern and empirical science. This, too, yields cultural capital, as Swift seeks new forms of value-system in his satires.

Transformations of space, in turn, give place in literature to a central interest in time: by the end of the eighteenth century, and turning to the nineteenth, Swift's spatial perspectives yield to the primacy of a temporal perspective that we find, classically, in the paradigmatic example of Wordsworth. There, memory becomes a repository – a depository – of value; and cultural capital itself becomes identified precisely *as* the temporal transformations that, through the workings of memory, make 'the present' different from what it is, because differently remembered or experienced via memory. Writ large, this becomes something like Prussian *Bildung*. It produces texts concerned with the growth and development of the mind of the writer whose text we are currently reading, as in *The Prelude*, a text that, in turn, opens the way for the kinds of modernist self-reflection that we will eventually accept as normative in writers like Joyce, with his *Portrait of the Artist as a Young Man*, or Proust, whose *A la recherche du temps perdu* is, at one level, the story of how it comes itself to be written. In Genette's famous abridgement of the plot, 'Marcel deviant écrivain'.[11]

By this point of high modernism, cultural capital is assuming the values of work that is characterized primarily by self-reflection; and the growth of the mind is aligned with – but in contradistinction to – the growth of the modern economy. Virginia Woolf lamented the materialism of Wells, Bennett and Galsworthy, who attended, she thought, to too many external signs of material wealth and existence. Bennett's characters 'spend their time in some softly padded first-class railway carriage ... and the destiny to which they travel so luxuriously becomes more and more unquestionably an eternity of bliss spent in the very best hotel in Brighton'. Against this, she advised self-reflective introspection: 'Look within', she argued, if you want to find where substantive reality lies.[12] 'Development' becomes the key idea; but this will itself be further stymied in a new modification. Development of the mind becomes the fundamental element in education, especially in its institutionalized forms as in the university and schools. Given the tension between intellectual and economic models of growth and development, the institutions of education themselves become subjected increasingly to political control, in order to be re-inserted into a specific capitalist economy.

That attempt at control leads to several new turns in our story. First, both the university and schooling become expressly politicized. As we know only too well, universities in particular have to earn their own institutional standing not in terms of the production of cultural capital at all, but rather in terms of the production of a workforce that will sit comfortably within the existing economic structures of our time. Those economic structures – at least since the 1980s – have been shaped by neo-liberal market fundamentalism. Thus, the second new turn is that the cultural capital of our students must itself be 'colonized' by the economy, as the student must be instructed to see herself or himself primarily as 'human capital'.

That is the story in a nutshell. The rest of this book explores the nuances, sinuous twists and turns, and instances of struggle and harm that figure and disfigure the details of literature's relation to capital.

3

The stages of this have been laid fully clear within large-scale politics; and the large scale in question here is recapitulated in the local scale of our institutions. Thus, the twentieth century bears witness to a process in which cultural capital is first seen as a threat to land-based and property-owning capital; and the presiding modes of government will try to control the radical power of cultural capital by demanding that it has to be assimilated into political capital and existing power structures. Through this, we see the establishment of a very specific kind of *institutional* capital. Capital here works through institutions in order to circumvent any radical potential that might be found within cultural capital. In the large scale, we find it within Stalinist political models. Julian Barnes explores precisely this in his novel about Shostakovich. When, for example, Stalin listens to *Lady Macbeth of Mtensk*, he proclaims – via *Pravda* – that this is 'muddle instead of music'. For Shostakovich, this is not just a bit of musical criticism; it is a threat to his very existence.

In a similar manner, if in a much more localized scale, literature – and its practice within the university institution – also increasingly finds itself today in a position that is every bit as fraught, ideologically, as Shostakovich's music. On one hand, the duty of literature – especially in its institutionalized forms where specific kinds of literary criticism validate it – is to engage in the extension of the new forms of capital associated with knowledge. Literature, we are told, is essential to the knowledge-economy, an economy that is to be based in cultural capital as such. At the same time, the very act of reducing literature and literary criticism to activities that are designed to boost the financial economy is an act that must ignore the very possibility of critiquing that economy in the first place.

One way of putting this would be to ask the Wildean question invited by the Preface to *Dorian Gray*. Is it useful to know that 'all art is quite useless'? That is to say, does literary criticism itself threaten to undo the power of literature, by accepting that the function of literary criticism is to convert cultural capital to human capital, via the 'instrument' of the student and the medium of the pedagogical processes?

Human capital is our latest version of the capital turn; and the problem for the student of letters is that the very engagement with institutional forms of literature might itself turn out to be complicit with the contemporary authoritarian turn against culture and its power. Instead, the student and teacher are increasingly required – rather like Shostakovich – to become mere agents of the institutional forms of the State; and in the instance of the contemporary advanced economies, that means becoming an agent of finance capital. In our case, this means that we are expected or required to instrumentalize culture in order to produce ourselves purely and simply as human capital, available for exploitation.

As human capital or human resource, we are a formation or material realization of the knowledge economy that puts us in a specific place within the economy as such; and that place is one where we are valued precisely to the extent that we confirm and conform to the dominant modes of operation of capital in our time. If we are looking for a full realization of Wildean decadence, it is to be found here, in the corruption of our institutions of learning – and our cultural institutions and being.[13]

We become, as human capital, returned to the very model with which we began. Structurally, human capital serves – as serfs once did – the patrons of our time. Those patrons are no longer necessarily exactly the same as the landowning classes of the early modern period. In fact, as we can see in any of the major world cities that form centres of contemporary financial capital, they are often entirely absent. These are the new instances of the paradigmatic example of the 'absentee landlords' who scarred Ireland and its history, typified in Maria Edgeworth's *Castle Rackrent* in 1800. As we see in more recent texts such as Jonathan Coe's novel, *Number 11*, or in John Lanchester's novel, *Capital,* the world's hyper-wealthy no longer need to actually live in the property they own in London. On the contrary, it makes more money for them if they exclude the very human capital that built it. These new lords of the land retain control increasingly of geography from Delhi to Dublin, and they also retain control of specific places, and people.

The only available response to this is through a mode of criticism that will attend to what I call, towards the end of this book, 'radical geography'. Radical geography proposes a criticism that attends to the intrinsic difficulty of finding a possibility of establishing the literary as a form of capital – capital letters – that is not subsumed under the rather pessimistic spiral, in which we escape from feudal structures only to find that, through the various vagaries of a developing idea of capitalism itself, we end up back in the same place.

4

Two years after making *Dorian Gray*, Wilde wrote *Lady Windermere's Fan*. It is there that Lord Darlington describes a cynic as 'a man who knows the price of everything and the value of nothing'. In the play, Cecil Graham immediately counters that with an equally acerbic observation that 'a sentimentalist ... is a man who sees absurd value in everything, and doesn't know the market-price of any single thing'.[14] Empirically, art has itself become a quite remarkably valuable commodity, with paintings, for example, trading (like footballers) at extraordinary prices. That simple fact raises the issue of how we might properly understand the relation between 'market price' and 'value'.

It is this constantly shifting relation that this book seeks to understand. It is worth recalling that, in the example of the UK's jurisdiction, copyright becomes effective only really in the early decades of the eighteenth century; and Alexander Pope is among the first writers to make use of it to make some financial capital from his writings. In the present day, arguments over 'intellectual property' – and of who 'owns' its means and mode of production, in a university setting, for example – remain vibrant. Values and money – letters and capital – continue to sit in uneasy relation.

Wilde's aphoristic comments find a ready audience in our own historical moment, which might also be characterized as a period of decay in various ways. Literature and literary study themselves are ostensibly in retreat, and they have at best a kind of moribund existence, challenged by new media. This phenomenon is most pressing – and, indeed, perhaps most evident – in the state of humanities disciplines within the academy. In subsequent chapters, I show how we can and must counter this.

Historically, then, we have a shift from land-based capital to cultural capital. In the middle of these, we face the eruption of financial capital. Financial capital – the rise of money – is a medium between the two forms of land-capital and culture-capital. Paper money is based not on the solidity of an object, but on the immateriality of a promise. It is oriented to a future, and acknowledges, implicitly in this, that time itself is the site of change and of the shifts of power among individuals and classes. Money 'makes the world go round', as in *Cabaret*; but it does so through a kind of 'soft' movement, an immaterialization of capital in which all that is solid land melts into the softness of paper, with its attendant construction of an interpersonal relation between parties to a promise. The promise occurs in a mode of writing, as on the standard UK sterling note: 'I promise to pay the bearer on demand . . . '

Cultural capital takes this softening movement yet further. It acknowledges that literary knowledge is not money, while being potentially the route to forms of power that are different from the power that is vested in land or other forms of material possession. Poets become, via their cultural capital, what Shelley famously described as 'the unacknowledged legislators of the world'.[15] Through the institutionalization of poetry, in the form of the concept of 'literature', the critic starts to assume this place of legislation – the judge who confounds aesthetics with politics – for herself, and seeks to claim an institutional form of capital that will authorize and validate her propositions.

Historically, the instability continues yet further, however. Within our institutions of education – the sites for the production of cultural capital itself – culture and literature find themselves in decay. I will show that the logic that is at work here is one that makes another shift in capital itself inevitable: cultural capital becomes valuable only to the extent that our institutions convert individual subjects into human capital. That human capital works in the service not just of the culture industries, but also in the service of the institutions of literature themselves. The result is a return to a new form of the feudal relation, a neo-feudalism. This final decay is one that can be and must be resisted; and *Literature and Capital* seeks to find a serious way out of our current predicament. It is vital to map this route, for without it the decay of politics, and with that the decay of the social will continue; and unearned privilege will find little or no resistance. The rest of the argument that follows here is a first step outwards in embracing that resistance.

2

On the Credibility of Writing: Material Promises

1

At the opening of *Capital*, his book on Delhi, Rana Dasgupta makes an interesting observation about the early formation of the mercantile culture of the city. Delhi is a city marked by what he calls 'the catastrophe of partition'; but the key thing that he emphasizes right at the start is that it is also historically marked by the formations and deformations of a very specific mercantile past. It only became India's capital city in 1911, when the British essentially sidestepped the unrest in Bengal that was making it awkward to run the country from Kolkata. Yet, for centuries prior to this – and prior to the nation's political position under imperial British rule – Delhi had been a major crossroads of trade in the northern part of the country.

Dasgupta introduces us to Rakesh, a successful Delhi-based businessman whose 'merchant forebears were involved in commercial networks that extended not only across the Indian subcontinent but also along the trade routes leading west to Arabia and Africa, and east to China'.[1] Those merchant forbears dealt in jewellery, doubtless deriving from the locally available natural resources; and, because of the high costs of the goods, 'there was at every link in the jewellery supply chain an issue of credit'. The question for the merchants was how to build such credit. Dasgupta explains that 'Merchants also invested heavily in their own reputations' therefore, and this entailed them not only living in ostentatious wealth, but also being openly philanthropic.[2] In this way, their wealth, their credit-worthiness and their importance, were all endorsed and substantiated. Their credibility, in short, was given a material reality, visible in both material goods and material actions that extended their wealth beyond their own wallets.

Such ostentatiousness deals in material demonstrations, proof of wealth: it reveals, in the buildings or estates that they owned, or their ease in dispensing hard cash, that they are people whose wealth is utterly visible in property, utterly material: they are literally people of substance, people whose wealth is substantial in every sense. Yet there is another means of establishing credit revealed by Dasgupta. It pertains to the fact that the capital wealth that interests us here is made visible also beyond the actual historical domain of the merchants of Delhi.

Alongside material demonstrations of wealth, there is also something immaterial, something less obviously or immediately substantive; and it is something that puts literature at the centre of our relation to material capital, and to those forms of credit that contribute to social and cultural standing. It thereby raises a fundamental question about the value of literature itself and invites a reflection on the nature of literature's relation to capital and to capitalism as such. The merchants, not yet content with the obviously present, visible, physical manifestations of wealth, turned specifically and intently to literature in order to boost their credit-worthiness and their social and cultural value: as Dasgupta writes, 'they employed poets to eulogise their wealth and integrity'.[3] What they need is not just the presence of their wealth and standing, but a material promise that it will be sustained and will survive into a future.

This cultural capital is not just aligned with financial capital, but is also a vehicle through which capital credit-worthiness is established. Cultural capital in the form of poetry thus becomes precisely the motor or engine driving financial capital itself. Poetry, contra Auden, makes things happen; it turns the wheels of capital, enabling a general culture of 'circulation' of words with money.[4] More specifically still, poetry turns the wheels of commerce, with all the corollary effects that follow in commercial capitalism: wealth, property, social class and distinction, business and busy-ness, the proliferation and circulation of goods and money, identified in contemporary economics as Gross Domestic Product, the mechanism that is used for the measurement of national wealth.[5]

Rakesh's forebears knew that while material wealth (such as real estate) might be transitory and therefore precarious, cultural standing is essentially a form of promise. Transcending whatever are the current circumstances – through the ostensible permanence of writing – culture (here, poetry) offers a guarantee of future wealth and standing. Poetic eulogy promises surrogate survival.

Furthermore, because poetry is visible and available beyond the occasion of its writing, it is unlike material wealth that is only visible in 'real' estate. Poetry remains something of which we can 'avail' – it is literally 'available' – even if we do not 'own' it personally. The reality of real estate is fixed and immobile, attached to a specific location; by contrast, poetry, however firmly tied it may be to an originating source, nonetheless has a reach and visibility that is 'unfettered', centrifugal with respect to the occasion of its writing. A new formulation follows from this: poetry – or the aesthetic in general – can here be a driver not just (in the first place) of the current economic condition but also (in the final analysis and instance) of the future political State.

The relations between literature and capital are relations that Dasgupta's account of Delhi as a capital city seems implicitly to demand. The case is not specific to Delhi as such, however useful a paradigm that might be, especially under the sign of globalization. It is interesting to note the coincidence that, around the same time that Dasgupta published *Capital*, 2014, John Lanchester published a novel with the same title (*Capital*, 2012); and Thomas Piketty published a book of economics (*Capital*, 2013 in French; 2014 for English translation). This is an interesting titular phenomenon: three books – a novel, an economic tract, a nonfiction study of a city – all focused on similar issues, and all with an interest in globalization and its discontents, all historically coincident with each other. It is also extremely interesting that the least 'literary' of these – Piketty's study of economics – is itself very heavily indebted to literature.

David Marquand's 2013 lament for the condition of contemporary economics, *Mammon's Kingdom*, opens with a series of literary references, all substantiating his claim that 'There is a dark fascination about money and its power to exalt and destroy'. His opening sentences refer to the narrative myth of King Midas, the biblical Golden Calf, the story of King Croesus, Molière's *The Miser*, Shylock, Malmotte in Trollope's *The Way We Live Now*, and Scrooge. At key points in his argument in *Postcapitalism*, Paul Mason also has significant recourse to fictions, such as those by John Braine, Keith Waterhouse, Alan Sillitoe and, from a recognizable strain in literary history, Shakespeare, Dickens, D. H. Lawrence, Yeats and Orwell.[6] Mason is also profoundly aware of the impetus given to the movement of capital as such by the consolidation of letters in the form of Gutenberg's printing press. In a line that could be taken from W. J. Ong or Marshall McLuhan, Mason points out that 'Printing transformed the way human beings think'. One of the reasons for this is that the print shop itself 'brought together scholars, priests, authors and metalworkers into a business environment that no other social situation within feudalism could have created'.[7] This, as I indicated in the introductory chapter above, was central to the emergence of modern fiction, in the early English novel of Samuel Richardson.

For Piketty, a key text in the understanding of contemporary capital and capitalism is Balzac's 1835 novel, *Le Père Goriot* which, in Piketty's reading, stages a contest between the economics of inheritance and the economics of meritocratic self-advancement, precisely the kind of bourgeois notion of individual progress that sits underneath the English novels of the previous century, in Richardson or Defoe especially. Piketty has a special interest in the advice that Vautrin gives Rastignac regarding wealth. The disreputable Vautrin tries to persuade the earnest young law-student, Rastignac, that there is an easier and more efficient way to establish financial security than through bourgeois merit (the study of law, hard work and the gaining of a respectable legal career). Vautrin tells him he should instead woo Victorine, the woman who stands to inherit great wealth. Only Victorine's brother stands in the way of that inheritance; and, for a fee, Vautrin can arrange for him to be disposed of in a duel. This is an argument about economic efficiency, essentially: inherited substantial property is a surer security than any wealth that might be gained through labour and the merits associated with working.[8]

The fact that this plan also involves subterfuge and crime is itself significant. The contemporary popular crime novelist, Ian Rankin, sums this up well. His detective, John Rebus, finds himself always coming face to face with the arch Edinburgh criminal, Morris Gerald Cafferty. Cafferty is a typical gangster, and, as Rankin describes it, 'Cafferty had long known that the world of the gangster was the world of the capitalist. Markets had to be created, sustained and expanded, competition nullified'.[9] Cafferty is extremely wealthy, but bears all the bling-type characteristics of the *nouveau riche*: his wealth establishes a visible discrepancy between his moral worth and his capital; and, in many ways, this might encapsulate the history of literary fiction from the eighteenth century up to modernism.

The key lesson that Piketty draws from the Balzac example (to which we can now add Rankin as an exemplar of how this operates in popular writing) is not just economic, but political. He points out that 'democratic modernity is founded on the belief that inequalities based on individual talent and effort are more justified than other inequalities'. Indeed, he goes on to say (in an argument showing the relevance of this 1835 text to our contemporary moment), 'During the decades that followed World War II, inherited wealth lost much of its importance, and for the first time in history, perhaps, work and study became the surest routes to the top'.[10] It is perhaps, therefore, no coincidence that this period – post-1945 – also witnesses the rise of that modern version of the *Bildungsroman*, the campus novel (or *Professorroman*, as Elaine Showalter names it).

This interplay between property and merit is also central to Dasgupta's exploration of Delhi. *Capital* is largely made up of the accounts that current inhabitants of Delhi give of their situations and histories, their successes and predicaments; and many such accounts are structurally governed by the shifting grounds of capital in a globalizing city. Those unstable grounds also destabilize the public realm, as globalization encourages individuals to see their lives in terms of business investments, and as if the very function of living was to contribute to the circulation of capital itself.

Dasgupta's opening gambit – recalling those merchants who were praised in poetic eulogy – also corroborates the sense that literature is important, perhaps even central, to our understanding of capital, both in the historical past and in the contemporary moment. It is not only Piketty's Balzac whose work is relevant here. In fact, literature has historically been at the centre of the relations between material and immaterial forms of capital and has thus also been key to our understanding of 'democratic modernity' itself. Piketty turns at many points to a whole series of other novels, including, very substantially and significantly, Jane Austen, Dickens, Hugo, Zola. These writers, from both the English and French tradition, help significantly to advance and substantiate his case in exemplary fashion.[11]

While it is not too surprising that we will have a series of studies of the state of capital at this period, precisely in the wake of the financial crisis and storm of 2007–8, it is nonetheless striking that they make a collocation between financial capital and the idea of the political capital cities of nation States that are in various ways and times emergent centres of globalization. There is, however, a relevant historical predecessor to this, to which we can now turn.

2

The contemporary cultural and political predicaments that provoke those new and varied studies of various 'capitals' as such are in many ways entirely at odds with the earlier moment of financial crisis: the South Sea Bubble of the early eighteenth century. In this earlier moment whose tercentenary is marked by the 2008 crash, we see the emergence of what was for the eighteenth century a new set of economic values, and with it a specific valorization of modes of cultural capital associated with writing. It was in 1694 that the Bank of England was established, essentially on the construction of a National Debt. This was a moment of real economic disruption, usually thought of as a 'financial revolution'. It is a moment when the relationship between individual activity and the State changes fundamentally. The Bank gets the right to print paper money, which can now be used by ordinary people; so, as Lanchester writes, 'It's at this point that banks, money and the modern state become fused together',[12] and in that fusion they embrace a general public who share not only money but the space of all transactions. Indeed, this is also the start of the idea of the State precisely as a transactional space, a 'market' or 'business'.

Colin Nicholson showed that 'By the end of the Nine Years War of 1688–97, no one could deny that England had become a trading nation and at a very rapid pace an entity known as Trade entered the political vocabulary to an extent that all writers engaged with its significance'.[13] This could equally well be the description of Dasgupta's Delhi in 2015. In the earlier historical case, this was part of a more general transformation of the condition of the citizen, deriving from a fundamental shift in the location of wealth itself. Wealth had previously been located in and identified with the fixity and stability of land and its ownership and control: a material, visible and substantial asset. However, when the King needed to raise money (for war), he turned to the merchant class for a loan; and the means of securing this loan was to be the establishment of a bank of funds whose return to the lenders, with enhancement to make it 'interesting' to the merchant class (that is, explicitly by yielding 'interest'), would be realized in the future through the levying of taxes

New excise taxes would allow the State to raise, *in time*, the necessary funds to repay the loan. The incentive for lending was to be financial growth: more would be returned than was lent – at least, that was the promise. The difference that made interest possible was time: the delay in returning the money would be compensated with more money. As Nicholson describes the fundamentals here, 'the bank had established a national debt dependant [sic] upon public credit'. Despite the fact that the initial money was essentially squandered in war, the merchant class had confidence that they would *in time* get their funds back, with interest; and so they continued to lend. Now, 'when shareholders in the public funds realized that they could trade their shares for profit, the state itself could be perceived as a marketable property'.[14] This is a huge political event, but one that occurs without a big bang; instead, it has a steadily growing percussive effect whose vibrations change the tone of world history, and literature.

Time becomes a determinant of social relations, governing those relations in terms of debts owed and to be repaid at some other moment in the future. The deferral of repayment – time itself – produces a financial interest and profit; and a new form of capital arises, one based on debts and credits whose hidden motor is time itself. That new form of capital, predicated on the manipulation of debt and credit through the control of time, also changes the once stable relations between the State and its individuals in the merchant class, relations that had previously been considered in terms of space or the relations of people according to place and rank. From now on, the merchant class, having lent money to the State, gains in power over it – *temporally* – for as long as the State remains indebted.

As a passing but important aside here, we might consider the broad trajectory of English literature through the eighteenth century. At the start, there is an obsession with space and its attendant issues of perspective. The paradigmatic example is Swift's *Gulliver's Travels*, combining ideas of spatial exploration with the ways in which space itself might be available for manipulation by the intervention of the human eye. This yields a visual aestheticization of the polity, in which the primacy of the speculative eye becomes the instrument for colonial control of the spaces of the material world. The control of perspective is coterminous with the control of all forms of speculation, including the financial.

That concern for the control of space is equally apparent in Swift's attitude to gender and to human relations. When he examines the beauty of a woman's breast, say, he becomes increasingly visually forensic in the magnification of the image, until present beauty is replaced by impending death. When Gulliver sees a woman in Brobdingnag nursing a child, he says that 'I must confess no object ever disgusted me so much as the sight of her monstrous breast'. A few pages later, in the street, he sees 'a woman with a cancer in her breast, swelled to a monstrous size, full of holes, in two or three of which I could have easily crept'.[15]

By the end of the century, we find an obsession with time; and, in this case, the paradigmatic example is Wordsworth, say, whose poetry becomes a kind of repository of time past, and of the persistence of the past in the present. When he looks at a landscape, as in his 'Lines' composed overlooking Tintern Abbey, Wordsworth sees time rather than space: 'Five years have past; five summers, with the length / Of five long winters! And again I hear / These waters'. The poem then stresses the temporal aspect of the experience, with all the references to 'again', 'once again', 'and again'. *The Prelude*, whose very title acknowledges the primacy of the temporal, of the beforehand, is a poem describing the 'growth of the poet's mind', a growth whose ground is not spatial but temporal, a *Bildung* and formation of the development of the very poem that we are reading. [16] Where space was money for the proto-colonial speculations of perspective in the earlier part of the century, time has become the source of wealth in the latter years of the eighteenth and then onto the nineteenth century. This literary transition relates fundamentally to the developing shape of capital across those years, as my further explorations here will show.

Debt and credit – both founded in this shift from spatial property to temporal occupation – constitute the new arrangements of relations that constitute society, politics and the State. This is simply another way of saying that printed money inserts itself into previously stable power relations, relations that had essentially been based on the supposed stability of inherited property and privilege. However, the difference here is that printed money – like the poetry that supports those former Delhi merchants – is much less fixed and stable than property and inherited wealth. Consequently, previously stable social relations are now thrown into flux. Famously, 'all that is solid melts into air', and print is related to survival and to the proposed material realization of a promise. This is a monetization of the eulogy.

Credit – and its correlate in 'credibility' – is what allows us to understand the emergence of modern capital as essentially a matter of gaining time and thus of surviving – living on – beyond whatever constitutes the present condition and state of social relations. It offers the solace of pretence that we can control our future, or that we can control events to come, as a means of survival or an insurance policy of self-protection. For Jean-François Lyotard capital was defined as 'time stocked in view of forestalling what comes about'. [17]

Yet credit itself is also intrinsically subject to risk, and may indeed even be described as being constituted entirely by risk, by speculation as to the future outcome of present events and situations: in short, it is constituted by trust as its key and determining element. Dasgupta gives a troubling account of the collapse of trust in one crucial relation: that between doctor and patient in the new India. It is a collapse of trust that goes beyond personal relations and that extends into grave repercussions for the whole of the political sphere. In the fifth chapter of *Capital*, he describes a series of harrowing situations regarding the collapse of public health systems. Doctors used to be trusted not just because they were good and knew their jobs, but also because they had no financial stake in the health or well-being of their patients. Their interest was entirely medical. However, things changed. 'On 24 July 1991, Manmohan Singh, India's new finance minister, announced in his budget speech that his nation would henceforth embrace the principles of open markets and free enterprise. Life changed immediately, even in its most basic elements'[18]; and, among those basic elements, we find a changed relation to health and the public good. Crucially, this shift depends on the growth of distrust in language and communications.

With privatization and corporatization, doctors in India have to earn their keep and they therefore have an interest in increasing their salaries – precisely as an understandable stocking of time, insurance against 'what comes about'. Patients then lose their previously abiding trust, knowing that the diagnoses they are given are tainted by the doctor's now fundamental demand for profit. It gets worse: having lost trust in their doctor, they then compound the problem – quite understandably but catastrophically – by insisting on second, third, even fourth consultations – each involving an inflation of costs. All this takes time, the time that could have been used (or 'spent' – the locution is itself telling) in addressing their ailments. The exponential increase in communications yields further health and wealth inequalities: doctors 'earn' more; patients suffer more.

Each new consultation works like a textual commentary on the previous consultations. This parallels the exponential growth of literary criticism and commentary that we find accruing around literature, as a derivative of the original acts of writing themselves. It produces growth: an economic surplus based on that growth of texts.[19]

The issue of time as capital (and its relations to survival) returns yet more directly in Dasgupta's descriptions of Delhi. We should here recall as our relevant backdrop that time-as-capital is precisely the constituent of those literary eulogies – those capital letters – sought by the historical merchant classes of Delhi. Dasgupta outlines the many movements of people across national borders that shaped the moment of partition; and this leads him to a meditation on the nature of migration in general. 'We tend to think of migration', he writes, 'as movement in space; but in some ways this kind of migration is a sideways step within the far grander, onward exodus that everyone who lives amid the churn of capitalism is part of: the migration across the plains of time'.[20] This shapes globalization and its concurrent economics of international 'outsourcing'.

Outsourcing of US and British services (sometimes explicitly described as the 'free' movement of 'human capital') to India is a major fact of contemporary business culture. It starts, for Delhi, after India's financial crisis of 1991. It works because of the time difference between Delhi and Washington, or between Delhi and London. 'Indian consultants worked alongside their US clients during the American day and then sent a brief to India. Indian software teams work through their day – the US night – and American clients could view the results first thing in the morning. Two working days had been extracted from one'.[21] Once again, however, this is related to the conditions of trade with which we began, those 'trading families' that had, 'for centuries spread their members out to different places on the planet in order to spot the commercial gradients between them'.[22]

Summing this up, Dasgupta suggests that the privatization agenda was essentially forced on India by the financial crisis of 1991 (although he also notes that Manmohan Singh had been aching to advance it for ideological reasons even before then). And so, as he puts it, stressing the double-edged nature of capital, 'India "came into" globalization in the same sense as someone "comes into" an inheritance: with a sense both of new economic possibility, and of crippling bereavement. Money would arrive, but everything exalted and nurturing was passing away, and nothing could replace it except a flood of baseness'.[23]

Where does literature sit in relation to these kinds of change? For the answer, we should not only learn from the moment of the South Sea Bubble and inauguration of banking, but we should also turn to a yet earlier historical moment, a moment before we thought of specific forms of writing as being 'literature' as such. What we have already seen, however, is the emergence of diverse forms of capital – from land that was fought over rather than bought through to a capital that is written into finance and commercial transactions – all the while accompanied by cultural forms that seek to dignify such base capital, as in eulogy or poetry more generally, while constructing human individuals themselves as forms of resource or 'human capital'.

3

After 1694, the establishment of the Bank of England changes the very nature of wealth itself. Suddenly, personal wealth is now increasingly based primarily on the immaterial condition of a promise, a written contract stating that 'I promise to pay the bearer on demand the sum of . . . ' In this, we have a binding tie that links writing directly to capital. This new bond is based on a fundamental shift in the relations between citizens and the State. It also entails a further shift in the social relations among citizens themselves; and this new social arrangement is one that is basically dependent on a cultural moment, in which the immaterialities of a written promise replace the ostensible securities of material economic wealth, vested in land or property. This is also, most pertinently for the present argument, a shift in which writing itself becomes the fundamental signifier of value and even of wealth. It is certainly the marker of capital as such.

This situation signals a more fundamental set of social changes. For Nicholson, this new 'paper-money of credit' leads to a significant modification in how people think about themselves and their relations and, above all, how they 'represent' themselves. He means how they represent themselves in fiction and literature; but this will surely also refer to the changes in their mode of political existence, as parliamentary representation itself is subject to new political understanding and conceptualization. In Nicholson's succinct formulation, 'The emergence of classes whose property consisted not of land or goods or even bullion, but of paper promises to repay in an undefined future, was seen as entailing the emergence of new types of personality, unprecedentedly dangerous and unstable'.[24] This is noted by writers, among them Defoe who had seen, by 1725, 'that writing "is becoming a very considerable Branch of the English Commerce . . . " '.[25]

Defoe is not alone in this, of course. The changes that follow the establishment of the Bank of England in 1694 quickly produce a mentality or set of cultural norms that establish an intimacy in the fundamental relations between economics and morality, as seen in Adam Smith's *Theory of Moral Sentiments* in 1759, where human feeling – sympathy itself – is 'economized', seen in terms of an exchange of interests that seek a common increase in the profit of good (and the good of profit, as in the later *Wealth of Nations*). It is in the earlier Smith text, *The Theory of Moral Sentiments*, that we first encounter the celebrated 'invisible hand', which leads the wealthy 'to make nearly the same distribution of the necessaries of life, which would have been made, had the earth been divided into equal portions among all its inhabitants, and thus … advance the interest of the society, and afford means to the multiplication of the species'.[26] As we saw also in the literary example of Swift, Smith is establishing here, in a scientific modulation of the literary insight, an intimacy between aesthetics (in its most literal sense as the science of perception, the way in which we perceive and engage our sensuous experience of each other, with our hands) with economics (the production and distribution of goods in material and commercial terms); and what brings these together is an understanding of what representation as such actually means, both aesthetically and politically.

Although the development of banking founded on credit and debt may offer a link between *writing* and capital, it does not yet offer any fundamental tie between 'literature' and capital. The writing of the promissory note does not qualify the banknote as literary in any sense that we would currently give that term. However, it is worth stressing that Smith's 'invisible hand' is, above all, a metaphor: a rhetorical trope that might reasonably be considered to be every bit as 'literary' as the appearance of Balzac or Zola in Piketty's much later economics text. Moreover, Smith's key principle, in the *Theory of Moral Sentiments*, is to take human relations – sensibilities – and consider them in relation to reason – sense. In many ways, this text is a direct precursor of Jane Austen's *Sense and Sensibility* some fifty years later; and it is certainly concerned with the same fundamental issues as we see in the emergent novel form through the eighteenth century.

Mary Poovey helpfully describes the situation here as one in which the distinction between truth and falsehood is blurred, through the development of the category of the fictional, especially in its relation to finance. David Hume, for example, opposed the use of paper money, seeing it as a mode of counterfeit; and Patrick Murray (the fifth Lord Elibank) likewise discouraged it, describing paper money explicitly as 'a fiction'. It is in this way that Defoe – who had an explicit interest in credit, as he depended on it so often – addressed financial matters not in abstract philosophical terms, but through his fictions.[27] Capital here is hovering somewhere between the stability of land-value (or material property) and the theatrical airiness of literary value (the rhetorical 'properties' of metaphor). It is the moment when we see the emergence of that specific conundrum that we now identify as 'cultural capital' itself.

An earlier poetic phenomenon will allow us to address the relation of literature to capital more directly. In 1956, G. R. Hibbard identified a series of poems as constitutive of a new genre that he called 'the country-house poem'. Initially, he identified seven poems as constitutive of the genre: Jonson's 'To Penshurst' and 'Sir Robert Wroth; Carew's 'To Saxham' and 'To my friend G. N. from Wrest'; Herrick's 'A Country Life' and 'A Panegyrick to Lewis Pemberton'; and, completing the 'tradition', Marvell's 'Upon Appleton House'. Alastair Fowler went on to group some seventy-seven such poems – extending from Geoffrey Whitney's 1586 'Patria Cuique Cara: to Richard Cotton Esquire' all the way through to Pope's 'Palace of Alcinous' from his translation of Homer's *Odyssey* in 1725.[28] This enlarged tradition is better described, says Fowler, as 'estate poems'. They are concerned with an understanding, literally, of real estate.

One thing that these poems generally have in common is praise: they are characteristic of a patronage model of economics. They can also be aligned with those praise poems commissioned by Dasgupta's historic merchant class in India. The poet – especially in the narrower range of texts given by Hibbard – typically praises not just the house, but also, at least by metonymy, its owner or lord. The house, as in 'To Penshurst' becomes a model of proper living, of good morals, and of sound economic relations between the lord and the country (in a deliberately vague and far-reaching sense of that term: meaning both nation and rural location). The lord of the house presides over a good relation to the environment, in which the house or estate sits properly; and the lord also stands over good social relations. Repeated references to 'the lord' of the house also invite us to think in theological terms: it is not just that the house is heavenly, but also that it transcends its specific historical locality. It is not just for now, but for all time; not secular but unchangeable because sacred. This promise offers eternal survival, with the most extreme forms of validation, credit and credibility: a *credo* of sorts.

The house itself is 'of its place', located and specific; yet the values associated with it reach beyond its locale. In this respect, the structure again is like that described by Dasgupta; and key to both situations here is that literature is at once tied to capital (in its form as material and real estate) yet is simultaneously released from any such fixed stability, reaching beyond the locale to an idea that is not time-limited, not affected by death. The value system that the house models can be attained elsewhere and by others; and it is in this way that the real estate is merely exemplary. In identifying ourselves, as readers, with the model, we too become 'inhabitants' of the estate, occupants representative of its values.

As Hibbard put it, describing Jonson's 'To Penshurst', 'To money values, which he regards as unnatural and perverted, Jonson opposed human values',[29] and he further dignified those values by giving them that theological veneer. The series of contrasts that structure the poem is 'between the house as a place to live in, the centre of an organic whole made up of man and nature, and the house as an expression of individual pride, an imposition on the community and a powerful threat to an established way of life'.[30] Perhaps needless to say here, Jonson favours that earlier established way of life. It is in this that he places his *credo*; yet the very articulation of that faith depends precisely on the material capital of real estate.

The way of life in question – the ecology – is one of a certain stability, given to us as being allegedly unquestionable because it has a claim to be natural. The house is said to embody 'a natural bond between lord and tenant. The building of fine new houses very often meant the arbitrary raising of rents and the disruption of all links between landlord and tenant except that of hard cash'.[31] The ecological stability in question might be threatened by the introduction of hard cash or 'money values'. In fact, however, it is fundamentally dependent on capital, in this form as real estate and land ownership, not to mention the feudal relations that such ownership produces as a social norm, with deference before the lord.

Obviously, then, texts such as these are consistent with a specific view of (spatial, 'permanent') social relations. These relations are presented very positively, usually in terms of how well the house is run under the aegis of a presiding ethics of hospitality. For Fowler, 'When the early estate poem moves indoors ... it is usually to praise the lord's hospitality, on which his reputation depended.'[32] Hospitality is constructed around the great manorial hall, where everyone dines together in shared community: 'In manorial society, communal eating – joint consumption of what all joined to produce – had symbolic as well as real value'.[33] Indeed, as Jonson puts it very straightforwardly in the poem, describing Penshurst as a place 'Where the same beer, and bread, and self-same wine / That is his lordship's, shall be also mine'; and this is precisely the same hospitality as King James himself found when he, too, visited.

The pretence or trope is that there is no social distinction here, in the great hall. An 'appropriateness' governs all here, under the social sign of the house as a place of refuge and welcome; and it welcomes a worker as much as a king. Modest and unostentatious it may be; but the suggestion is that we find here the stability in which people can ostensibly overcome, or ignore, the divisions of labour, privilege and wealth in society – divisions that the very existence of Penshurst as a stately home reveals and otherwise exemplifies. 'Hospitality', Hibbard argued, 'is extended as readily and ungrudgingly to the poet as to the King. The house by providing them with a common meeting ground enables all classes to feel themselves members of the whole'.[34]

Against this, Raymond Williams sets the poetry of Stephen Duck, the thresher-poet, noting how Duck, unlike the other more celebrated poets, makes the connection 'between the feast and the work' that has gone into the possibility of its production.[35] Duck's poetry operates as a kind of cultural or historical corrective, for one thing that is generally missing in all the estate poems in Hibbard or Fowler's traditions, one thing that remains invisible, is the labour that goes into the making of the house and the production of the very resources that allow it to be a centre of hospitality.

In 'The Thresher's Labour', for the key instance here, Duck explicitly points out that the material realities of labour work against an easeful culture of hospitable togetherness, and specifically against the literature of storytelling. As the threshers work, they think to 'tell a merry tale', in order 'the tedious Labour to beguile'; but 'The Voice is lost, drown'd by the louder Flail'. In any case, 'Alas! What pleasing thing, / Here, to the Mind, can the dull Fancy bring? / Our eye beholds no pleasing Object here, / No chearful Sound diverts our list'ning Ear.'[36]

Estate poems through the period of transition that culminates in the financial revolution are governed essentially by nostalgia. They look back somewhat longingly to medieval social structures, even to pre-capitalist feudal structures. This is unsurprising, given that, as Fowler himself indicates, 'Literature sometimes addresses values most directly when they are under threat'.[37] Kari Boyd McBride helpfully delineates some of the threats in question; and they turn out to be threats that derive from shifts in the location of wealth. As she puts it, 'disruptions to order – the agrarian revolution, a rising population, inflation, an active land market, the rise of the middle class, nascent capitalism, exploration and colonization, the woman controversy, the emergence of alternative religious, social, and political perspectives and subjectivities – forced both a renewed articulation of traditional justifications for privilege and, at the same time, an accommodation of newness'.[38]

The texts here are struggling to retain a certain set of values – essentially those pre-capitalist feudal values, given as if eternal, even sacred – against the pressure of texts such as those of Stephen Duck, texts that reveal the fragility and precariousness of the feudal order of things and that won't be satisfied by occasional ritual moments of 'hospitality' that are really just attempts to co-opt the oppressed labourer and to make him complicit in his own systemic oppression under feudalism. The labourer presents a secular threat, as it were, to the supposed or hoped-for eternal stability of feudal relations. And that is to say: poetry here is 'what happens' as the product of tensions about wealth, as the introduction of secular values into supposed transcendent and unchanging economic norms.

4

Feudal society, based on patronage and fundamentally inimical to modern democratic economic arrangements, is, of course, hierarchical. Its strength lies in its alleged alignment with a supposedly natural order of things, an order that is non-historical, non-negotiable, and assured in its fixed stabilities. The financial revolution threatens all of this, precisely because it threatens the 'ownership' of the estate itself. Jonson would have us believe, in 'To Penshurst', that the great dinners in the hall come to the plates without human intervention: 'Each bank doth yield thee conies'; pheasants and partridge fulfill their proper role and gain contentment by allowing themselves to be killed; crazily, 'Thou hast thy ponds, that pay thee tribute fish: / Fat, agèd carps, that run into thy net ... / Bright eels ... leap on land / Before the fisher, or into his hand'.[39] Duck, by contrast, knows that the ritual hospitality of the great hall is a 'Cheat'; and the rising pressures of disenchanted and oppressed labour presents a danger to the feudal order, because that labour is starting to make it known that it is being cheated out of its 'proper' rewards, its merited property.

In short, we might say that the key pressure here is in terms of the shift among different modes of ownership or appropriation. Putting it in rather crude terms, land was once fought for, but now it is subject to being bought. That is an extremely dramatic change: the utterly immaterial power vested in a written promise now outweighs completely the power of physical and material force. Words have become more substantial than sticks-and-stones. Inscribed within the value of land, further, we are witnessing the transformative force of labour, which will become key to Marx's later analyses of the workings of capital. These poems prefigure this, and they are written in the attempt to ward off the future, for they fear that that future is one that will be owned, potentially, by the labourers and threshers such as Stephen Duck, or by a rising bourgeois class identified by their dynamic energy with its intrinsic demand for change, propelled forwards and motivated by money, material promises.

Estate poems are an example of literature whose very existence is determined and shaped by the rise of capital, and most especially by its realization in various modes. This coincides with the population shifts that begin to form our developing cities. Virginia C. Kenny prefigures McBride in arguing that these poems 'reveal the cultural values that are seen to have stood the test of generations of hierarchical society'. However, the very shape and content of the texts are given by the fact that these older values 'are contrasted ... with the parvenu values of the city culture'. One reason for this is that these years 'were ... times of rapid increase in the wealth of England'. Further, 'The discoveries and inflation of the sixteenth century had led inevitably to the commercialization of land, and where enclosure had occurred it had destroyed the customary society about the manor'.[40] Almost all the critics who write about the tensions in these poems cite J. G. A. Pocock's 1975 study of *The Machiavellian Moment*; and the key passage for our purposes is that cited here by Kenny: 'land, which had been valued for the services provide by tenants, was now valued for the rents they paid'.[41] Pocock reveals here what becomes the presiding tension that produces the poems: a tension between material wealth evidenced by real estate on one hand, and the immaterial forms of wealth that arise from wage earning and the precariousness of financial promises on the other.

According to Kenny, by the eighteenth century, 'The power of inherited land to span generations and to transcend individual mortality gave it a special virtue as the foundation of society'. Through inheritance, an individual 'survives' – outlives his own individual death – in the ownership of land; and the stability of the name of the landowner, guaranteed in this way, becomes the ground for our social relations, which remain spatial, hierarchical. (Hence, we might note, the importance of the funereal monument or family tomb). However, she goes on to add that 'competing and more ephemeral forms of property, such as public credit, salaries and patronage, were seen as a threat to this foundation and were condemned as fanciful and potentially corrupting'.[42] What they threaten to 'corrupt' is the acceptance of eternal stability and unchanging order and hierarchy: in short, they turn the promise of an eternal survival into a merely capital exchange and thus a purely secular transaction, one which embraces the possibility of a change in the order of things. The landlord might 'really' die, once and for all.

It looks as if we have come a long way from contemporary Delhi here. However, we have not. Dasgupta reminds us that this version of the world – and the versions of philosophy and literature that follow from it – is not somehow naturally occurring. That is to say: our understanding of the relation between literature and imperialism – and, behind that, between literature and capitalist *trade* – is more complicated and differently centred from the ways in which we have become accustomed to think of it. Among many other things, it depends on the idea of capital as something understood in its form as straightforward finance, of course – with all the instability and commercial exchangeability and mutability (or circulation) that this implies – and, simultaneously, capital as something that is firmly tied to or identified not necessarily with a specific house, but still with a place (a capital city, or capital precisely as 'the city').[43]

Delhi was essentially entirely re-configured when, with a design by Lutyens, the British decided to make it the capital city of India in 1911. The presiding idea for the shape of the new city was European: 'The imperialists would design a city so geometrically European that it would defeat, with its very layout, the benighted orientalism of all its past and set the stage for a new, enlightened future'.[44] What followed were some things that we have associated with European models of democracy: open spaces and boulevards, and, crucially, a large central *agora* on the ancient Greek model. Yet this imposition of Europe onto Delhi had intrinsic and structural problems.[45]

The imperialist planners had not understood why the city was shaped as it was before they imposed their plans. The climate makes it more congenial to have narrow streets, which 'had prevented direct sun from reaching pedestrians'.[46] These tiny lanes, like an Indian version of the Algerian Kasbah, made a certain kind of commercial culture possible; and this was lost. As Dasgupta has it, 'All in all, a reversal' happened when the imperialists decided to invent New Delhi on the space that had been Shahjahanabad: 'where Shahjahanabad's streets were narrow and labyrinthine, New Delhi would have vast, geometrical avenues; where commerce in the old city took place in a profusion of packed bazaars, it would be confined in the new to a pillared circle, eventually named Connaught Circus'.[47] One consequence is that Delhi becomes 'managed' space; and the further corollary is that all gatherings and assembly, including commercial and capital forms of assembly, become bureaucratized.

Pedestrians leave the streets, and move into cars. Delhi becomes a city that lacks democratic spaces, run and organized essentially for automobiles. The result of the crowding is status and performance anxiety: the presiding ethos is governed by the basic demand for survival. This is not the survival into eternity envisaged through feudal hierarchy; rather, it is survival as the simple ability to keep the secular body going for another day, another hour. 'Delhi', writes Dasgupta, 'is a place where people generally assume ... that the world is programmed to deny them everything, and that making a proper life will therefore require constant hustle – and manipulation of the rules. Everyone, myself included, uses bribes and connections to get the things they need'.[48]

The possibility of democracy is thereby threatened, replaced by forms of naturalized and normalized corruption. Now, 'no one wants to be just one of the anonymous mass for whom nothing ever happens'. Yet the demand for democracy does not arise still. As Dasgupta puts it, in words that should now recall those English estate poems, 'One might think that a place of inequalities as entrenched as Delhi's would breed democratic yearnings, but it is not the case: Delhi's fantasies are feudal. Even those who have rather little social power respect the privileges of those who have a lot – perhaps hoping that one day they will enjoy for themselves their same exemption from law and custom'.[49] The daily and hourly struggle for survival of those at the bottom of the social order here becomes something that is endured, while at the same time the lives of the privileged yield the image of a hoped-for but never-achieved change in the condition of the poor.

We often think of globalization as a fundamentally modernizing trend within world economies. However, it is now a moot point as to whether this belief is actually a cover for an entirely different state of affairs: the return of patronage and of feudal social relations, in which privilege (based in inheritance and material wealth such as real estate) re-asserts itself over merit and labour, which are becoming increasingly precarious, and even degraded. We can explore this partly through the historical shifts that we witness in literary culture as it wrestles with the fundamental issues of commerce and value, or as literature enters the terrain of a theory of moral sentiments, and of the ethics of wealth. This wealth, and its corollary of value under the sign of capital, needs also to be considered especially in the context of massive and structural social and financial inequalities, inequalities that are consistent with a social structure that is identifiably feudal, a social structure that pre-dates modernity and that was already visible in English literary texts from the early modern and pre-capitalist period.

5

It is interesting that the eighteenth century in England ostensibly witnesses a shift away from the mode of governance and government that is associated with feudal and inherited values, with a corresponding literary shift. The movement is clearly away from feudal relations that are tacitly endorsed in Jonson's 'To Penshurst', say, towards the more democratic relations that are often characterized as fundamental features of the emergent form of the fictional novel. In economic terms, this maps onto a shift from material conditions and sources of wealth (in property and land) to less material resources, as in credit or promise; and this, classically, is an endorsement of bourgeois mercantilism, such as we see it illustrated in Defoe. This latter, offering a specific (if limited) version of democracy, is also, of course, entirely consistent with the emergence of capitalism as the dominant economic mode that shapes society and social relations. This is *why* literature not only exists, but exists as a marketable entity.

Yet the interesting thing now in our contemporary moment is that, after the 2008 financial crisis, the kinds of shift that we saw in the South Sea Bubble have gone into reverse. Whereas in 1720, we witnessed a shift from material to immaterial wealth (from property to paper promise and writing), now we have this simply turned on its head; and wealth is again being associated with the house, with material and substantive wealth and property. Perhaps the single most obvious literary articulation of this is in Lanchester's novel, *Capital*; but it is also apparent in Jonathan Coe's 2015 novel, *Number 11*. Beyond the realm of the literary, this may also help explain the popularity and fascination with TV series such as *Downton Abbey*.[50] Perhaps the mood that Dasgupta describes in feudal Delhi lives on in the UK in this series, watched by those who are encouraged to imagine that the life of privilege and exclusion might also be theirs, especially given the repeated refrain from the real 'Number 11', the office of the Chancellor of the Exchequer in the UK, that 'we are all in it together'.[51]

There is in popular UK culture an abiding fascination with wealth and privilege. Historically, it has roots precisely in feudalism, and in an evident abiding fascination with royalty and its associated myth of inherited value.[52] The tabloid press, for example, encourages the belief that 'we are all in it together' through its affectionate (highly personalized) references to members of the royal family by their first or even pet names, as if we common readers enjoyed a real intimacy with them. The fascination is continued through so-called high culture in texts/films such as *Brideshead Revisited*, or Merchant-Ivory films, where the lives of the landed and privileged remain a constant, paradoxically even when they are being satirized as ridiculous.

The satire again encourages a belief in our having such an intimacy with this way of life that we not only know it well but we can also see through its vacuities. This simply produces yet further endorsement, not just of the values of the text, but of us as readers who share the privilege of exclusivity and upper-class values: we are *so* of this class that we are actually *above* those represented in the texts.

Finally, in this vein, we have witnessed, precisely in the years leading to the financial crash, a celebration of the values of real estate in countless TV series that focus on the transformation of houses, a transformation whose value is measured in terms of the eternal rise in property prices. That rise, of course, was part of the problem that led to the crash in the first place. The question that we are addressing – the relation of literature to real estate and to different models of wealth (capitalist or feudal) – is an abiding one.

In Lanchester's novel, the only seeming absolute certainty – the only stability, however false or ill-founded it may be – is that the houses on London's Pepys Road will steadily rise in monetary value. This remains the case despite all other forms of financial and value-crashing elsewhere. We meet Roger Yount, the banker in the novel working at the fictional Pinker Lloyd bank, on the day when he expects to receive his usual bonus. He even expects its level to rise, as it has steadily been doing throughout the boom years since the financial 'big bang' of 1986. He 'sat at his office desk at his bank, Pinker Lloyd, doing sums. He was trying to work out if his bonus that year would come to a million pounds'[53]; and he encourages his wife, Arabella, to plan not for the expected £1m, but for more. He goes into the office of the boss, to engage in the ritual bonus conversation; and, as he listens to his German boss, Lothar Billinghoffer outlining the bank's performance, he starts mentally calculating ever-increasing bonuses based on Lothar's language, going well beyond £2m in his imaginings. Yet, when Lothar hands him his letter notifying him of the bonus, it turns out to be the comparatively paltry figure of £30,000. This is a literal 'reality cheque', as it were; and it makes Yount feel suddenly as if the entirety of his life is precarious and as if he himself has no real capital worth or value.

Precarious living – a threat to mere survival – is also the condition of other characters; and, for these characters who are genuinely without substantial capital, the precariousness is a real threat to their biological existence. Quentina Mkfesi, the Zimbabwean refugee who is working illegally, and who has nothing at all in terms of real estate, finds that the precariousness of her position can be resolved, but only in the negative direction: her wage-labour is rejected, and she is deported. Freddie Kamo, the young Senegalese footballer, finds his career and pending wealth rubbed out, after a tackle in his first full match catastrophically breaks his leg, and the insurers find every which way to avoid paying out. The Polish builder, Zbigniew Tomascewski (or 'Bogdan the builder' as Roger's wife, Arabella, calls him) discovers a huge amount of cash in the house of Mrs. Petunia Howe, and hesitates over whether to hold onto it or not. When he returns it to Mary, the daughter of the now-deceased Mrs. Howe, it turns out to be so dated that it is no longer legal tender and thus almost worthless. The only real security turns out to be the reality of real estate, when Roger and Arabella realize their wealth by selling their house after Roger is sacked.

Coe's *Number 11* also plays on the question of property prices, the playing of capital in the capital city. Livia, the Romanian dog-walker in Chelsea, draws frank attention to the absurdity. As she walks the dogs of the residents, she passes countless houses that are empty, even empty of furniture: 'Once I walked back from the park with Jane, through the streets of Chelsea, and she explained to me that people buy these houses now – rich people – and then just let them stand there, watching money attach to them like barnacles to a sunken ship'.[54] In this satire, however, the only way is down: Sir Gilbert and Lady Madiana Gunn have started to dig deeper and deeper under their house, to the point where the basement will have eleven descending levels. Wealth has literally gone underground; and, in the end of the novel, it will collapse in on itself, consumed in a vampire-like metaphor in which the wretched of the earth essentially exact their revenge on unearned privilege.

The contemporary crisis that is realized formally in these texts is one where there is a battle between two forms of wealth: one based on real estate, the other based on what we might call, following the language of our political class, 'aspiration'. In the London examples, we have real estate winning out over wage income: Roger Yount triumphs over Quentina Mkfesi, as it were. In Delhi, we have wages now threatening property, with a precariat beginning to realize that, paradoxically, its very precariousness does indeed give it some limited power.

Delhi's capitalist bosses may not pay well and may not provide any form of security, but what this means is that the workers also have absolutely no loyalty. This situation, described by Dasgupta as 'uncontrolled', is one that was 'inconvenient for employers too, because their workers had no stake in their enterprise, and came and went without warning'. In this state of affairs, 'The only interface they [the bosses] had with the inscrutable worker psyche was money, so this was where they applied their pressure.'[55]

The real point here, though, is that this is not just local to Delhi. It is itself a near-global phenomenon: 'By the early twenty-first century, in fact, it could be said that much of the global economy was running off the desperation of the Asian countryside'. One of Dasgupta's wealthy employer interviewees is candid: 'We live in an age when we all know what we do is disgusting but we still carry on doing it.'[56] This employer has seen the laboring hands of Stephen Duck, as it were; and he is helpless in the face of what he sees as the coming tensions between real estate and wage-labour. It is this that shapes so much of contemporary fiction, so much of our literature and so much of our cultural activity. Numerous economists identify it as the problem of inequality.

Inequality in the contemporary moment is intimately related to the changing location of value and of wealth. Increasingly, there is an opposition between the two: wealth is material, found in land and property; value has had to occupy the terrain instead of the seemingly immaterial world. For Oscar Wilde in 1892, it is a cynic who knows the price of everything and the value of nothing; and we might well characterize the contemporary predicament in which there is such a fundamental clash between wealth (the price of everything) and worth (value) precisely as a period of high cynicism.

Social and economic inequality, it follows from this, is a consequence of the operation of a cynical reason that fetishizes 'modernization' as a cover for of the revival of feudalism.[57]

It is in this context that we can explore the relation of literature – as a realm concerned with immaterial forms of value – to capital, as a realm in which money is the only real substance that the cynic acknowledges as real. To describe literature in terms of 'immaterial value', however, is most certainly not supposed to make us consider it as lacking in effect or reality. On the contrary, one of the major shifts in contemporary economics is precisely the engagement with non-material forms of labour, for example.

To understand this, we also need to understand that 'literature' itself is not some naturally occurring phenomenon. 'Literature' is that mode of writing that becomes institutionalized in very specific ways, and with the consequence that it has a particular force and resonance within a society that sees the transformations of capital as it moves from stable physical property into culture. When the poor or disaffected cannot manage to change material conditions of economic reality, they can turn the struggle for forms of equality elsewhere, and find a new terrain for their battles within cultural forms, such as that in poetry and writing more generally. This is where we must turn next.

3

The Career of English

1

My focus here is not just on 'literature'. We will make more substantial discoveries if we focus more precisely on 'the institutions of literature'. By this, I mean to indicate two things. First, as has been noted many times, 'literature' is a concept of relatively recent historical date, no matter how long we have had forms of textual inscription or writing.[1] Secondly, that concept, as a construct specific to particular historical moments and conditions, gets its meaning from its relationship with specific institutions, primarily those that govern culture, the arts, and education. In other words, as a historical phenomenon, literature is something that 'happens' or that 'takes place': it 'occurs' or has its proper occasion.

Once we construe it in this more precise historical and conceptual fashion, literature takes its place in specific contexts that also allow us meaningfully to consider the related activity of criticism. If there is a link between literature and criticism, such that they essentially partner each other, then it also follows – given that I am arguing the link of literature with capital – that there is equally a link between capital and criticism. The site for these 'collisions' or partnerships is not just a social one – the university or school; it is also a constitutional one, in the State and in the idea of 'English literature'. This is so, given especially the status of English as a world language, the language of world literatures. This status, as we know, is contested, and indeed must be contested.

In previous chapters here, I indicated that literature occurs in a particular way: it is tied to property but it also extends its reach beyond that specific location. In the tension that results, we face the fundamental literary issue of credibility. Can we 'credit' this text? Do we 'owe' any allegiance to its author? In the historical period when 'literature' becomes a dominant social and cultural phenomenon, largely through the nineteenth century in Europe, we learned to call this series of questions by a different name: we asked if the text was 'realistic' as our way of asking if we could credit its contents and assumptions. The 'realistic' acknowledges that there is an ambiguous terrain between truth and falsehood: we know that the writing is not one whose truth is validated by reference to empirical reality or history, yet simultaneously, we acknowledge that it functions precisely as if it were to be thus validated. We can thus 'credit' the story while not 'buying' it, in the slang parlance of our present times.

It is Fredric Jameson who has examined the very idea of realism most thoroughly and rigorously. He proposes a very specific understanding of the term in his 2013 study of *The Antimonies of Realism*. Jameson sets up realism in terms of a tension between narrative and affect, which he describes as a tension of 'destiny versus the eternal present'. Narrative is focused on the preterite tense, and describes something that has happened, incontrovertibly; affect, however, is marked by the present of the reader's body.[2] It is in the tension of these two elements set against each other that we find the mood and mode of 'realism', which Jameson also identifies with a specific moment of capitalism, in the mid-nineteenth century, wherein he locates the emergence of a specific bourgeois manner of experiencing the body as such.

We can re-conceptualize these insights in terms closer to those of my own argument. My claim has been that there is a dialectical tension that emerges at the moment of the 'financial revolution' at the turn of the seventeenth and eighteenth centuries in England. That tension is materialized through the pressures to which the feudal principles of authority, based on land ownership, are being subjected in the wake of the emergence of an economy that is based increasingly on the less material terms of the financial promise. In short, credibility is itself marked by a dialectic between what is (land, say) and what might be (the promise).

This tension results in a writing in which we have a specific problem of authority and authenticity. No longer is authority straightforwardly vested in the ownership of land as such – that is, in wealth, conventionally understood. Rather, authority is now contested: it stands between the stability of wealth on one side, and the unpredictability of the promise on the other– or the authority of writing as such. We might re-cast this in simple terms as a contest between State or political authority on one hand (what 'is' the case) set against authorship (the inauguration of a promissory text, a text describing what 'might be') on the other.

In Jameson's terms, we have a very similar structure. However, instead of finding the stable element here in the ownership of land, Jameson essentially finds it in the 'eternal present' of the reader and her or his affect. It is this that will propose the possibility of a stable authority for the text's meaning, all the while seeing that authority de-stabilized as part of the quite literally 'tensing' processes that establish realism precisely as an antinomy.

Yet what is actually at stake in all this? Fundamentally, we are concerned with what we might properly term the worldliness of literature. We are trying to grasp the ways in which literature is of the world, the ways in which it is located in material and historical terms. What 'matters' – or 'what constitutes material existence as such' – is the key question. For Jameson, what matters is the dialectic between whatever the narrative establishes as 'what has really happened' and 'what is really happening'. That dialectical antinomy produces not the 'effet de réel' once discussed by Barthes; but also, and more importantly, it is the articulation or realization of a specific moment in the history of capitalist socio-political and economic relations.

Such thinking is also at the root of contemporary debates about what we can call the location of literature as such. It lies at the heart of debates around 'world literature' as an institutional advance that addresses the ideological blindness of comparative literature – 'Comp Lit' – say; and it fundamentally addresses the historical relationship between the institutionalization of 'literature' as such and the locations in which it happens, such as the nation-State. It is in these terms that we can explore here 'the career of English', by which I want to signal not just a new telling of the rise of 'English Literature', but also a more accurate consideration of the relation between a literature, a nation, a State and a language. Within this, we will see how capital interests tie up to the politics of land ownership, and how that relation is underpinned by the formation of an institution of literature, and, more specifically, the formation of the institution that we now know as 'English Literature' and its corollary in criticism.

2

In Coetzee's 1999 novel, *Disgrace*, the literature professor, David Lurie, finds himself contemplating how to reveal the reality and the truth of his contemporary South Africa. There are things, he feels, that cannot be said, and this is for two reasons. First, language is now heavily policed, and speakers must always be careful of the words they choose, censoring themselves and censoring their thoughts. In recent times, this is a phenomenon that is experienced daily in universities worldwide: a troubling paradox is that institutions whose very function is to examine, explore and extend the range of meaningful discourses in all spheres are increasingly hampered by the idea that language itself can be taken as being 'offensive'.[3]

Secondly, there are, as in Jameson, things that are more to do with affect than with meaning. There is no language adequate to the specificity of Lurie's bodily response to the horrors that have been visited upon him (exposure of his improper or questionable sexual activities with students; loss of academic position and standing; physical assault, and so on) and upon his daughter, Lucy (physical assault, multiple rape, loss of her farm smallholding and land). Nor can he find words adequate to the situation when he finds himself confronting the parents of Melissa, the student with whom he had sexual relations. The obvious paradox, of course, is that in *saying* that no words are adequate to the affects here, he nonetheless *reveals* precisely those affects. In an odd resolution of the antinomies of which Jameson writes, the affect is dissolved into a kind of second order of narrative: the affect in question here cannot be experienced, but can nonetheless be narrated.

Lurie suspects Petrus of being involved in the attack on him and Lucy, but finds it awkward to address the subject. He acknowledges to himself that 'Doubtless Petrus has been through a lot, doubtless he has a story to tell'; and the presumption must be that this story will pertain to life for a black man under Apartheid. Lurie thinks that 'He would not mind hearing Petrus's story one day', adding, however, 'But preferably not reduced to English'. In this case, the story spoken in English would be a 'reduction' of sorts, and would subtract from its reality and affective value (in Jameson's sense of 'affect' here). 'More and more he is convinced', writes Coetzee, 'that English is an unfit medium for the truth of South Africa'.[4]

This repeats the obvious paradox that is pertinent to Lurie's own experiences; but locates the issue in terms of the question of an appropriate language or tongue: Petrus's story is told precisely in the medium of English, here in the novel. Coetzee – or Lurie, his character – identifies the problematic issue of how to relate to Petrus specifically as a language issue, and one that ties the language to a place, even a nation. In this instance, the issue is not that of a dialectic between narrative and affect; rather it is about the discrepancy between them, the radical disengagement of the narrative from the affect, precisely as a condition of the language in which the narrative may be spoken.

As Coetzee elaborates, ostensibly speaking in the mind of Lurie, 'Stretches of English code whole sentences long have thickened, lost their articulations, their articulateness. Like a dinosaur expiring and settling in the mud, the language has stiffened.' This offers an obvious suggestion that the speaking and writing of English within South Africa has played a part in the historical construction of the nation; and that the construction is one that has now essentially led to a form of paralysis.[5] It is, as it were, not just heading to extinction, but is already deathly. As he goes on, Lurie considers the story of Petrus, the farmhand who had helped his daughter, Lucy, and who now has seized control and ownership of her land, having been party to the gang-rape: 'Pressed into the mould of English, Petrus's story would come out arthritic, bygone'.[6]

The question of the place of the English language in literatures other than those produced within the confines of the geographical space of England is, clearly, a major issue here. *Disgrace*, however, is a fiction, however 'realistic' or not it may be. Yet we find a similar predicament in the real historical case of Delhi, as outlined by Dasgupta; and we will find that this historical example offers a way in to exploring the 'career of English' and the formation of 'English Literature' as a specifically capitalist project.

Dasgupta explains that, after Lutyens and others built the new city of Delhi on the European model, none of the indigenous population wanted to live there. So a plan was needed, and it involved land ownership, rehearsing precisely the same predicament that Coetzee is exploring in *Disgrace* when Petrus acquires Lucy's land. In Delhi, the plan was to offer preferential treatment and conditions to all the contractors who had helped to do the actual physical building of the new city: 'the administrators offered them large plots of land at a greatly reduced rate'. These contractors were people who had already made considerable sums of money in the construction, and now 'they snapped up sites in the centre of the city for their own mansions, and also bought up large areas of city land as investments.' As was the historical case of the merchant class who crossed paths in Delhi centuries before, 'the estates they now owned in the centre of what was to become a major capital city guaranteed their families wealth and prestige for a century to come. These contractors, in fact, became Delhi's new aristocracy'.[7]

As the new aristocracy, they mixed commercially and personally with the administrators who had coordinated the building. They therefore also committed to learning English as their normative medium of communication. The result is disastrous for the existing indigenous languages: 'English took over, and even though they passed on fabulous estates to their descendants they could not pass on their own tongues'. After 1947, Hindi becomes an official language in India; but the power of English remained so strong, even after that date, that plans to abolish its use (by 1965) had to be abandoned. English remains the official language of the Constitution.

The consequence of these language struggles, as Dasgupta points out, is that now, 'most books, books that did not directly further one's career, represented an expense without return'.[8] Books become associated firmly with precisely the social rise of a new bourgeoisie, those contractors who mimic the earlier merchants in basing their position on the combination of material wealth in buildings or real estate and the international prestige of English as a major mode and medium of communication and of community.

The career of English in India has been well charted, and it is no longer the case that scholarship thinks of this in terms of crude models of any straightforward forceful imposition of a language as a raw demonstration of imperial power. Recent serious scholarship has attended more fully to the nuances involved in the interplay between English and the already existing languages of India. Central to our understanding now is a distinction that is to be made between the question of the use of English as a functional and instrumental language in India on one hand, and the deployment of what is an entirely new phenomenon in mid-nineteenth-century India: English literature.

In 'The Burden of English', given as the inaugural V. Krishna Memorial Lecture in Miranda House, Delhi, in February 1987, Gayatri Spivak pointed to the central issue here, locating it specifically in the context of the educational institutions and establishment: 'there is a certain difference in orientation between the language classroom and the literature classroom', she argued. In the language classroom, the pedagogical goal 'is an active and reflexive use of the mechanics of the language.' The language class is utilitarian and instrumentalist, its aim being to permit the student to develop a fluency in the *use* of English as a linguistic medium. Things are different in the literature class. Here, 'the goal is at least to shape the mind of the student so that it can resemble the mind of the so-called implied reader of the literary text, even when that is a historically-distanced cultural fiction'.[9]

This is a hugely significant distinction. The language class keeps the student in the position of mastery and control; and the point of language acquisition is to allow the student to be able to do more than she or he was able to do before attending the class. In the literature class, by contrast, there is much less attention paid to the crude instrumental use of the language itself. Indeed, this is taken 'as read'; and the point instead is to enable the student to so master herself or himself that they can *become* someone other, someone identifying with the 'implied reader' of the text. When that text – being read in Delhi, say – is formulated as part of the construction of Englishness, there is a different issue of mastery and control at stake. It is a question of larger-scale political and civic control that is now at stake.

Paradoxically, then, it follows that the teaching of English literature in this context is a process that instrumentalizes literature – and, specifically in this context, that means 'English literature' – precisely at the moment in which the literature is proposed as the counter to everything that is 'merely' instrumentalist. English literature is used as a means to make the Indian reader identify with Englishness, to the extent that such Englishness and its attendant value systems constitute that implied English reader.

The history of this process dates precisely from the moment that has been interesting us already in previous chapters: 1835. As is well known, it is in that year that Macaulay wrote up his 'Minute' on the proposed educational statutes for India, where he served as a Member of the Council. William Bentinck, at the time Governor-General in India, warmly gave his 'entire concurrence to the sentiments expressed in this Minute', thus giving it full legitimacy and political endorsement.[10]

There are a series of consequences following on from the adoption of the Macaulay Minute; and a series of fundamental ideological positions that inform it. A primary question, however, relates to why it was written at all. Its motivation, in fact, relates directly to finance. More specifically, it relates to the conditions under which the British East India Company exerts its responsibilities for education in India, as a condition of its charter.

The Company had a long history of financial difficulties, exacerbated by economic trading conditions in Europe, under which Britain had been suffering ever since the struggles with Napoleon's Continental System – which had effected an embargo on British trading – between 1806 and 1814. In 1813, the East India Company's charter came up for renewal, which was granted, but with conditions. It was at this time that the Company started to lose effective power in the commercial sphere, while gaining it in administrative importance in India where it essentially became the vehicle for British control. Then, in 1833, the charter was up for renewal again; and, this time, the shift in the Company's status – from having a commercial monopoly to becoming a purely administrative body – was completed.

Part of the Act of 1833 was a determination of how to deal with the Company's debts. India itself would have to cover the debts; but, in a kind of recompense, the specific educational provisions that had been put in place as a condition of the earlier 1813 Act were now considered more systematically. In 1813, a sum of one lakh of rupees (100,000 rupees) was to be given over to the education of the Indian population 'for the revival and promotion of literature, and the encouragement of the learned natives of India, and for the introduction and promotion of a knowledge of the sciences among the inhabitants of the British territories'.[11] A further important modification to the administration was also effected by the 1833 Act: Indians could now themselves become, for the first time, administrators in government, at least in principle. To be thus admitted, however, would be difficult; if it were to happen, an appropriate education would be required.

It is with this in mind that Macaulay turns to examine educational conditions. It is now a question of how to invest that lakh in education, with a view to consolidating the control of the land mass of India. How better to bring this about than to involve the native population in the activity itself: education would require the internalization of the imperialist mindset, the inculcation of the British (more specifically 'English') spirit.

Macaulay starts from an ostensibly sensible utilitarian argument: 'We have a fund to be employed as Government shall direct for the intellectual improvement of the people of this country. The simple question is, what is the most useful way of employing it?' (paragraph 7). Next, he asks about the medium of instruction: 'All parties seem to be agreed on one point', he writes, 'that the dialects commonly spoken among the natives of this part of India contain neither literary nor scientific information', and so it follows that 'the intellectual improvement of those classes of the people who have the means of pursuing higher studies can at present be affected [sic] only by means of some language not vernacular to them' (paragraph 8).

There is a debate about whether this language should be Arabic and Sanskrit or English; and Macaulay, although acknowledging his own ignorance of both Arabic and Sanskrit, is in no doubt. Having asked the question in utilitarian fashion in the ninth paragraph of his Minute – 'which language is the best worth knowing?' – the answer is given, unequivocally, as 'English'. In making the case, Macaulay essentially here elides the distinction to which Spivak drew our attention above, for he immediately swerves from the utilitarian deployment of the English language into a series of positive evaluations of English literature, at the same time demeaning the works of Arabic and Sanskrit writers and thinkers. There is not even a single orientalist, he claims 'who could deny that a single shelf of a good European library was worth the whole native literature of India and Arabia', given the 'intrinsic superiority of the Western literature' (paragraph 10).[12]

Why is English the most appropriate solution to what Macaulay has posed as the predicament, in which 'we have to educate a people who cannot at present be educated by means of their mother-tongue' (paragraph 12)? His response bears little if any relation to the instrumental uses of English; rather, he turns to the metaphysical and moral superiority, as he sees it, of English literature. 'It abounds with works of imagination … with models of every species of eloquence … with historical composition, which, considered merely as narratives, have never been equaled – with just and lively representations of human life and human nature, – with the most profound speculations on metaphysics, morals, government, jurisprudence, trade, – with full and correct information respecting every experimental science which tends to preserve the health, or increase the comfort, or to expand the intellect of man' (paragraph 12). It is only *after* this that Macaulay turns to empirical and instrumental uses of the *language*, arguing that 'In India, English is the language spoken by the ruling class. It is likely to become the language of commerce throughout the seas of the East' (paragraph 12).

Finally, in this regard, the market speaks: 'we are forced to pay our Arabic and Sanscrit [sic] students while those who learn English are willing to pay us' (paragraph 19). The deployment of English is a commercial matter, related to State finances; but Macaulay establishes that the conditions of this 'market-economy' in the language are established fully by the legitimization of English as a *literature* and as a *culture* that is superior, advanced and progressive. 'We owe it to the natives', is the burden of the argument, 'to give them access to these riches'. Remember too that among these native Indians are some – not many, but an elite – who will henceforth be admitted to work in the offices of the administration; and it becomes clear that they need to start thinking as 'we' do; they have to 'become' as-if-English, like fictional English characters.

This is a further step beyond the kind of blurring of truth and falsehood that Mary Poovey delineated in the emergence of fiction. Cultural capital – in the form of the acquisition of 'English literature' – edges into the deployments of 'human capital'. A select few Indian individuals are introduced into Englishness, with all the 'privileges' associated with that, by a process in which they are encouraged to behave like the characters of the very fictions that they are reading. In this case, the internalization of cultural capital is what produces the Indian individual *as* human capital, as a 'human resource' for the safe establishment of an imperialist mentality.

In his Minute, Macaulay forces a coalescence between capital and culture in the logic of this argument. Essentially, in advocating English – more than just the utilitarian language – as the solution to the predicament concerning Indian education, Macaulay is prefiguring the argument of Matthew Arnold in *Culture and Anarchy*. For Macaulay, matter that is written in English and embodying certain values, is matter that is intrinsically cultured, for it 'contains' what Arnold will call 'the best which has been thought and said in the world'.[13] Perhaps most interestingly for the current argument here, Macaulay also prefigures a specific aspect of a mode of thought that has shaped a good deal of modern and contemporary institutionalizations of 'English Literature': the critical ideology of F. R. Leavis.

Macaulay is aware that education is expensive, and that there is a limit to what can be achieved with restricted funding. This literary formation is going to be based in a specific economic configuration. He argues that 'it is impossible for us, with our limited means, to attempt to educate the body of the people.' The literary education paid for by the lakh must be rationed. He then prefigures almost precisely the thinking that shaped Leavis, when Leavis proposed that the 'English Literature' syllabus would be for an elite, and certainly not for all. Here is Macaulay: 'We must at present do our best to form a class who may be interpreters between us and the millions whom we govern, – a class of persons Indian in blood and colour, but English in tastes, in opinions, in morals and in intellect' (paragraph 34). And here is Leavis, on his proposed Part II (the major part) of a proposed new English Literature syllabus in Cambridge, which 'would be essentially designed for an elite ... To be content with modest numbers, but to provide a standard, a centre and a source of stimulus and suggestion – that would be the aim'.[14]

It is interesting to locate Macaulay, then, as a kind of silent and unacknowledged source for one of the twentieth-century's most influential literary critics, a critic whose views on the position of English Literature in the formation of a specific national consciousness and culture, were percolated through an entire secondary-level educational apparatus for decades. As is well known, one of the elements in Leavis's cultural strategy was to place his students – individuals from this elite – in secondary schools, where they could extend the reach and influence of his work, inculcating the values that he took as elemental. Macaulay had also prefigured this, writing 'To that class [of 'interpreters between us and the millions whom we govern'] we may leave it to refine the vernacular dialects of the country, to enrich those dialects with terms of science borrowed from the Western nomenclature, and to render them by degrees fit vehicles for conveying knowledge to the great mass of the population' (Minute, paragraph 34).

One reason for this interesting collocation of two disparate historical figures becomes clear when we see what is at stake in the nineteenth-century Indian context. Gauri Viswanathan has indicated the peculiar paradox that governs the initial formations of the discipline of English Literature. She refers to 'the irony that English literature appeared as a subject in the curriculum of the colonies long before it was institutionalized in the home country'.[15] It is with the 1835 Act (following Macaulay's Minute) that the English language becomes an official medium of instruction in India. Prior to this, there had of course already been a fair amount of instruction carried out in English. However, the significant change that the Macaulay Minute brings about is that, with effect from 1835, the language becomes really rather incidental to the literature as an institution and as an institutionalizing force. And it is here, therefore, that Viswanathan finds the inauguration date of the discipline, some thirty-five years before similar courses start to appear in the curricula of English universities.[16]

One question that might be asked here is the obvious one: why would an imperial power go to all this trouble rather than just imposing a language by force? The answer is itself instructive regarding the function of English Literature in this and subsequent contexts: force would be a manifestation of precisely the crude barbarism that the imperial power ascribes to the natives and never to itself. The Macaulay Minute is entirely consistent with the attitude that the English literary education is concerned to produce the cultivated and civilized spirit that it claims is intrinsic to the very being of 'Englishness' as such.

Yet: how can these English literary texts be read at all by the Indian? The texts are valued in the first place in England precisely because their 'implied reader' is always already English: the texts and the reader exist in a dialectical relation that strengthens both in their position and identity. The reader understands the text because he (it is nearly always coded as 'he') is confirmed in his identity as English by the values that he finds in the text; and, tautologically, the text is valued precisely because it consolidates the reader in that identity and thus values him as the privileged reader who can glean the text's inner senses.

In the context of 1835 India, this means that we have a further paradoxical situation. In order to grasp the meaning and significance of these English literary texts, the reader has always already to be endowed with precisely the values (the 'Englishness') that the texts impart; yet, at the same time, the texts are being prescribed precisely because these are the values that the Indian reader allegedly lacks. Viswanathan is clear on the implications of this, writing that 'The claim that literature can be read meaningfully only when a high degree of morality and understanding is present in the reader implied that certain controlled measures were required to bring the reader up to the desired level.' The reader thus had to be taught, but, 'paradoxically, those measures took the form of instruction in that same literature for which preparation was deemed necessary'.[17]

In England, the fundamental moral structures and values that were to be associated with this 'civilization' derived from multiple sources within the society; but central to them was the moral authority of the church. That same foundation could not be appealed to in the very different religious cultures of India. The consequence of this is that 'fresh pressure [was] applied to a seemingly innocuous and not yet fully formed discipline, English literature, to perform the functions of those social institutions (such as the church) that, in England, served as the chief disseminators of value, tradition, and authority'.[18] There then follows the further corollary, in a reverse percussive effect on the teaching of English literature in England: if English values can be inculcated in India without the substratum of solid foundations in the church and other such social centres of authority, then, now by logical extension, the same can be applied in England. Thus begins the secularization of English literature within England itself, whereby it becomes eventually seen (by Arnold and others who share the legacy) as a kind of substitute for the Bible.

Yet there persists a quasi-religious impulse in criticism, which is also emerging in its modern form at precisely this same moment. As Viswanathan argues, even within England itself, the activity that was emerging as what we now call literary criticism stems from a fundamental religious idea of a cleavage within the self, between what Arnold would call an 'ordinary self' and a 'best self'; and the task of criticism was to find and release the best self that lay hidden and even oppressed by the daily ordinary self. In his analysis of 'Literature and Education', Lionel Grossman indicates an abiding theme in this emergent modern literary education and its fundamental purposes: 'it enacted a distinction between the human and the animal, the urban and the rural, the self-conscious and the unconscious, law and custom, paternal and maternal', and finally here 'the governors and the governed'. It follows that 'Literary taste ... was a way of inculcating a certain manner of conceiving the social and historical order, of acting within it, and of perpetuating it.'[19]

Viswanathan glosses this by pointing out that it presupposes a fundamentally Calvinist formulation 'that assumed a condition of inner depravity' from which the cultivated self had to be set free.[20] The point, however, is that this quasi-religious impulse is transplanted into a literary education that is becoming avowedly secular; and the consequence of this is that, instead of concentrating eschatologically on our final destinations, criticism starts to focus instead on the ways in which, first, we find and consolidate a 'best self', and secondly, how we can improve the world socially, culturally and politically.

The activity we now recognize as 'criticism' is coeval with the emergence of 'English Literature' as an institutional form; and it depends upon this specific historical context in which the British government is concerned by the economic position of the East India Company and wants to find the best way to administer its Indian lands. India is the laboratory in which the British explore the possibility of establishing a fundamental relation between a literary education, focused specifically on English literature, and the capital interests of the State.

India is not the only such laboratory for the British at this time. Similar things are happening closer to the imperial home, in Ireland.

Declan Kiberd reminds us that 'through many centuries, Ireland was pressed into service as a foil to set off English virtues, as a laboratory in which to conduct experiments, and as a fantasy-land in which to meet fairies and monsters'.[21] The Irish people, 'the first modern people to decolonize in the twentieth century' found themselves in the position that Macaulay's Minute implied for the Indian: they were 'both exponents and victims of British imperialism', at once subjected by it yet simultaneously enacting it in various ways.[22] That, of course, was the logic in which Indians were themselves to 'learn English' and thus become suitable administrators over what had been their own land but that had now been appropriated by the British – the whole enterprise here being governed by the institution of English Literature.

3

We can build upon Kiberd's presiding understanding of what constitutes literature here – writing that is specifically 'literary' – in order to open the next section of the argument, which has to be about the place of literature in the world, the now vexed idea of 'world literature' itself. That presiding idea has something of the revolutionary aspect of the traditional within it.

Kiberd's analysis of the inventing of Ireland depends on him seeing 'works of art as products of their age', certainly. He stresses that it is equally important for us to see them intertextually, and, above all 'to celebrate that phase in their existence when they transcend the field of force out of which they came'. He is assiduously historicist in acknowledging that works will have 'a silent reference' to the 'limitations of their time and place'. However, he inserts a very important nuanced modification, saying that notwithstanding these historical constraints, 'it is wise to recognize – despite current critical fashions – that certain masterpieces do float free of their enabling conditions to make their home in the world'.[23] The case of Ireland is particularly interesting to Kiberd not just because of his own personal and professional immersion within and commitments to its culture, but also because 'Ireland, precisely because its writers have been fiercely loyal to their own localities, has produced a large number of these masterpieces, and in an extraordinarily concentrated phase of expression'.[24]

This is a precise reiteration – albeit informed by a very different set of political motivations – of the very impulse that drove Macaulay in India. Macaulay's conviction that English literature transcended its locality, precisely because it is committed to it and to its intrinsic idea of Englishness, is what makes it not only available to India but also a necessary constituent of India's modernization, even of its civilization. The imperialist mentality here, then, needs to be placed into the context of an understanding of world literature, and one that is alert to the necessity of criticizing (or at least identifying) an intrinsic imperialist consciousness. After all, what remains at stake in all this writing is a specific relation of literature to locality, of literature to capital property as vested in the ownership of national identities and nation States.[25]

As Kiberd shows – and this is what makes his work a template for an understanding of our predicaments – colonialism took various forms in the Irish case: 'political rule from London through the medium of Dublin Castle; economic expropriation by planters who came in various waves of settlement; and an accompanying psychology of self-doubt and dependency among the Irish, linked to the loss of economic and political power but also the decline of the native language and culture'. After 1921, when the imperial rule ended, 'many descendants of settler families continued to hold much land and wealth'; but this was also the moment that presaged the gradual decolonization of most of Britain's imperial terrains. The newly emerging world system, according to Kiberd, 'was ... dominated by the Americans who, learning from the mistakes of predecessors, concluded that there was no need to rule vassal states and so were content simply to "own" them'.[26]

It is this 'ownership' – of land, of States, of cultural identities – that the category of 'world literature' exists to scrutinize. Within this, we also start to see a new relationship between literature and capital, in which explicitly material control of land starts to cede place to less immediately material manifestations of power and control, of land and of wealth. Literature is the key to understanding this, and, within that, specifically now 'literature in English', as opposed to the earlier formation of the institution of 'English Literature' as such. This 'literature in English' will include work that has been translated into the English language; and this, paradoxically, raises further the prestige of the English language. In this context, the undertow states that the works have 'failed' because of the imprecisions and inadequacies of their original linguistic formation, their domestic tongue: they need to be formulated in English in order for that language to align itself with 'the best that has been thought and said', even if it was said imperfectly until translated and made available via English.

It is worth noting, in passing, that the most serious critical work on this question, within the British Isles, has been done by those working outside of the norms of the Englishness of 'English Literature': critics and thinkers such as Kiberd himself, Seamus Deane, Robert Crawford, Michael Gardiner and Cairns Craig. There seems to be much less questioning of the 'project of English literature' from within the English critical establishment, even if we do find there many critical histories of the formation of the discipline, as in the work of Stefan Collini and (from a different political perspective) Terry Eagleton and Francis Mulhearn. The difference here is the difference between those who are concerned primarily with social class (the English writers here) and those who see the effect of class upon national identity. Further, as I will be exploring in subsequent chapters here, that 'class' is itself often described precisely in terms of capital, be it actual wealth, land, or 'cultural capital' which, in this case, often comes down to the question of accent. 'Whose English?' is coterminous with 'Who's English?'

4

If it is a World Language, as is obviously the case, then what is the relation between English and World Literature, be it Goethe's *Weltliteratur* or Franco Moretti's world of *Graphs, Maps, Trees* or anything in between these disparate constructions of a world-of-letters, a Casanovan *World Republic of Letters*? In his consideration of how we might attempt to define 'World Literature' in any useful or meaningful sense, David Damrosch proposes to take a line that follows almost directly from Goethe's 1827 conversation with Johann Peter Eckermann. In that conversation, Goethe argued famously that

the era of 'national' literatures was over, and that we must 'hasten
the approach' of a new 'epoch of world literature': Nationalliteratur
will jetzt nicht viel sagen, die Epoche der Weltliteratur ist an der Zeit,
und jeder muß jetzt dazu wirken, diese Epoche zu beschleunigen'
['National literature means not very much nowadays, the age of world
literature is upon us, and we must now all work to speed these times
up'].[27] Essentially, Goethe welcomes the increasingly ready availability
and circulation of literature in translation. He identifies world literature
essentially with a writing that has displaced its intimacy with a specific
location: we enter a new republic, a Republic of Letters. This is an
area that Seamus Heaney favoured, a literature that comes 'From the
Frontier of Writing', and a literature that is therefore defined precisely
by its mobility and centrifugal flight from a single place, leaving the
poet always conditioned by the tension between being 'arraigned yet
freed', and with 'that quiver in the self'.[28]

   This Republic, however, should not be confused with the 'world
republic of letters' described by Pascale Casanova, and nor should the
very term of a 'republic' be understood with the same inflection that
Pascale Casanova gives to the term. Casanova, in her re-coining of this
phenomenon, describes this republic of letters as something that is
distanced from any simple intimacy with the economy, even if figured
in terms of modes of circulation. She is especially interested in a kind
of 'aesthetic inequality', inequalities that construct certain locations
as 'minor' (in some ideological contexts, 'Ireland' is construed as
one such 'minor' location) in a global power structure that we should
understand in terms that are not, in the first instance, economic but
aesthetic. Instead, we might consider it as a republic – and thus as
a fully political entity – conditioned by translation or translatability.[29]
In this sense, the republic in question is not quite 'located' for the
simple reason that it always hovers uncertainly between at least two
languages.

   The languages might be English and Gaelic, or they might be
English and Hindi, or English and Arabic; and the 'quivering' speech
that comes out of such hybridity is what constitutes the possibility of
a 'worldliness' in which, as in Heaney, poetry sits in the same sphere
as the sniper, that 'marksman training down / out of the sun upon you
like a hawk'. That position is precisely where Heaney in fact began his
entire oeuvre, in the celebrated 'Digging' which positions the poet

as the sniper, looking down on the past as he looks down on his father, keeping him 'under cover'. Heaney's first lines catch precisely the condition of this hybrid being, between writing and the material realities of history and violence: 'Between my finger and my thumb / The squat pen rests, snug as a gun', with 'Under my window ... // My father, digging'.[30]

Notwithstanding the cultural importance of other languages (historically, German for Goethe; in the contemporary situation, Spanish or Mandarin) one of the abiding and ever-present, ever-forceful languages in this new republic is English. There is, though, no such thing as 'World English'; rather, there are only multiple versions of 'English', many of them at odds with each other, many of them (as is the case in Scotland, say) sitting uneasily within each other, contesting a locale and an identity. In this sense at least, 'English' is precisely the site of translation and of translatability in our time; and the reasons for this lie in its historical imperial role and in the role that we have seen above, wherein English *language* veers directly and seamlessly into 'English *Literature*' and vice-versa. The question here is, what happens when 'English Literature' mutates further, and becomes instead 'literature in English'?

Damrosch's view, deriving from Goethe but also with the awareness of the relative autonomy of the aesthetic such as we see it in Casanova, finds something of a solution to the problem of definition essentially in the availability of translation. 'I take world literature', he writes, 'to encompass all literary works that circulate beyond their culture of origin, either in translation or in their original language', and the example he gives of the latter is Virgil, whose Latin was an almost equal first language for readers – that literate minority – in Europe right through the early modern period. He goes on to define things yet more clearly, by arguing that 'In its most expansive sense, world literature could include any work that has ever reached beyond its home base'.[31]

These terms, however, describe perfectly what I have looked at in previous chapters here, where literature sits uneasily between the stability of feudal ownership in the land (its 'home base'), and the wider purview that it reaches through its 'promise' or credibility, its aesthetic 'realism'. Damrosch indicates that there is 'a double process' through which some writing becomes 'world literature': 'A work enters world literature by a double process: first, by being read as literature; second, by circulating out into a broader world beyond its linguistic and cultural point of origin'.[32]

The conditions for this must be historically contingent on several factors, however. First, there must be the ready availability of the texts in the first place: that is, there must be a relatively high level of production. Second, that production must be something that is happening more or less simultaneously in several locations, those locations being identified either as nations or as emergent nation-States. Third, the works must be transportable, by which I mean there must also be a set of conditions that makes translation not only possible but relatively commonplace. All of these factors depend on specific economic preconditions, related to modes of production of texts *and also* to modes of reception of texts. In this sense, the kind of dialectic envisaged by both Damrosch and Jameson depends, in different ways, on the reality of the body of the reader, and especially that of the quasi-professional reader, or critic.

Goethe's formulation was made in conversation in 1827, yet it was not published or circulated until 1835. The date is significant, for the reasons outlined in the argument up to this point. This broad period seems to have been significant in the formulation of the *institutions* that we now identify as those governed by 'English Literature' and by 'criticism' as such. We might understand the stakes of the question here, then, by answering Damrosch's first condition for how a work becomes 'world literature': that is, it must be read as being 'literary'. One way of opening this question up is by a fairly crude distinction. Chaucer, we know, wrote poetry; but Heaney, who also wrote poetry, made something that was identifiable, even as he wrote, as 'literature'. Chaucer – and, I will now argue – most writers prior to our crucial and pivotal moment, in the period from the 1820s to the 1850s – had no idea what 'literature' is, if we construe the word in its contemporary sense; and they did not think they were making such literature, but rather quite simply that they were writing poetry, say.

It is instructive here to recall the literary base on which Thomas Piketty rested some of his arguments. The key example is Balzac's *Le Père Goriot*, a text that also dates precisely from 1835. We should also recall the key lesson that Piketty draws from this, for it is a lesson precisely about the relation of real estate and inherited wealth on one hand (that is to say: questions regarding the ownership of land or location, and thus by extension ownership of 'the world' in its material sense), and bourgeois graft on the other. This yields Piketty's fundamental insights. 'Democratic modernity', he argues, as a phenomenon emerging in nascent form around 1835, legitimizes inequality, provided that such economic inequality is grounded not in inheritance or the unearned privileges of real estate and property but rather on graft and the effortful work of the individual. An emergent modern literature – in this instance French literature – registers precisely the inauguration of this intimacy between modernity and economic inequality; and my contention is that this is indeed 'literature' precisely because it engages the real world (real estate) and labour, especially in this instance intellectual labour.

Further, the economic conditions of the period up to and including the 1840s – during which we see the emergence of this contest between real estate and individual effort, between privilege and labour – prepare the ground for the prospering of the capitalist system. As Piketty puts it, 'capital prospered in the 1840s and industrial profits grew, while labor incomes stagnated'. Perhaps unsurprisingly, 'It was in this context that the first communist and socialist movements developed.'[33]

It is also at roughly this moment, indeed, that Marx and Engels also 'discover' the importance of 'world literature', writing about it in the 1847–8 *Communist Manifesto*. There, Marx and Engels explain that the bourgeoisie has created what we would now call a series of global markets; and such markets, rising to preeminence within each nation State, do two things. They start to undermine and wear away the tie of a product to a place: they start to destroy the idea of local tradition or 'patrimoine'. 'The bourgeoisie', they write, 'has through its exploitation of the world market given a cosmopolitan character to production and consumption in every country'. There is a further consequence of this in that 'it has drawn from under the feet of industry the *national* ground on which it stood' (stress added).[34] Furthermore, they propose a mode of commerce that explicitly depends upon the transience of commodities, their essential contingency and vacuity: commodities are emptied of their specific national identity (they are, as it were, taken out of the conditions of feudalism that would locate them in real estate), and they float free, dependent now upon how the consumer will engage with them for whatever value or identity they will have.

In this regard, these commodities are exactly like the texts that circulate as in Damrosch's description, getting whatever stability they have from the engagement with actual readers. In this sense, the text is a form of 'immaterial labour', set up in a dialectical relation with the material conditions of a wealth that is grounded in property and real estate. It follows from this that, for Marx and Engels, 'National one-sidedness and narrow-mindedness become more and more impossible, and from the numerous national and local literatures there arises a world literature'.[35] As Damrosch puts it, it is now the case that for Marx, Engels – and Goethe – 'world literature is the quintessential literature of modern times'.[36]

This world literature is the site in which the stability of a concrete historical world – whose values are underpinned by the fixity and solidity of real estate and the privileges of property – begins to become uprooted and destabilized. Value starts to move into the immaterial conditions not just of a text that now is the property of the world as a whole and of no individual; but also, and even beyond that, value is found in the act of reading itself. Thus, as Marx and Engels put it, 'the feudal relations of property became no longer compatible with the already developed productive forces' of society.[37]

It is interesting that these texts all date from the 1840s; for it is also precisely this period that Raymond Williams sees as the moment when our modern and contemporary sense of 'literature' as an institutional and cultural form and phenomenon emerges. This brings us to a fuller explanation of what constitutes 'literature', of how a text becomes, as Damrosch has it 'literary'. It helps explain the difference that I indicate between Chaucer and Heaney. Both are poets, but one writes poetry, the other makes literature *by* writing poetry. The explanation for such a distinction might lie in the emergence also of the modern quasi- or proto-professional reader, the critic; for it is here, in the figure of the critic – or simply that of the reader – that we find the new source of post-feudal value; and it is such value that we distinguish as 'literary'.

The emergence of the category of 'the literary' as such is coeval not just with the inauguration of 'literary criticism' within the institutions of education, but also with the emergence of this new form of capital. We have learned to call this 'cultural capital', to indicate its divergence from the feudal ownership of property, and thus to indicate its 'portability'. It can become completely unfettered and un-rooted, like the intellectual who practices the literary criticism that de-stabilizes any sense of located selfhood. Cultural capital, as acquired through the engagement with 'English literature', may indeed be marked by possession; but this is less the possession of land, and more the possession of what we will eventually identify as 'human capital'.

This also affects that particular combination of literature and criticism that gives body to the modern figure of the intellectual. Stefan Collini traces the emergence of this figure to the nineteenth century; and, specifically, he construes it in terms of an English reaction to the French Revolution. As also in the Burkean account of modern history, the English 'national character' is one that is not shaped by the priority of ideas, but rather one that acts entirely pragmatically.[38] Such pragmatism allows for the English to be somewhat whimsical about matters of aesthetic taste, or criticism; but it is the pressures exerted by England's relation to other nation States – its international position especially as a trading and imperial power – that forces England into establishing a national character in the first place. Culture – and a culture of literariness and mysterious taste that is associated with class – becomes the means through which such a national character and identity can be formulated. For this, however, the English needed to consolidate a specific idea of what was literature in the first place; and it is therefore in this period that we see an institutionalization of 'English Literature' in its emergent state.

5

A brief survey of some historical literary and poetic motifs – and particularly of those moments when we can track the disappearance of 'poesy' and the appearance instead of literature and its attendant partner, criticism – is appropriate here.

When Sidney explained the importance of the 'literary' in 1595 he wrote 'An Apology for *Poetry*' (emphasis added), not for 'literature'; George Puttenham had already explained 'The Art of English Poesy' in

1588; Dryden wrote the 'Essay of Dramatic *Poetry*' (stress added) in 1668; Johnson wrote *Lives of the Poets* and not of the literati. When Shelley did the same kind of thing as late as 1821, his defense was 'A Defense of Poetry' and not of 'literature'. Yet, after this date, we start to see the emergence of criticism that explicitly does address literature and criticism as such. By the 1860s, Arnold was writing *Essays in Criticism* and *Culture and Anarchy*; Taine writes his *Histoire de la littérature anglaise* in 1864. Philosophy had, as it were, straddled these two periods, with Kant's *Critique of Judgment* – a criticism of criticism itself, in many ways – a key text from 1790.

Although there are exceptions to this kind of crude history (Pope's 'Essay on Criticism' dates from around 1709–1710), nonetheless the general trajectory remains clear and fairly unambiguous: 'literature' starts to become a key term in the first half of the nineteenth century, replacing that of 'poetry' and poetics, such that we are no longer just in the realm of 'making' (*poiesis*) but of a new and differently specifically valued currency, that of 'literature', with its attendant 'criticism'.

Raymond Williams's analysis is much more subtle and nuanced than my crude statement here. In *Keywords*, he traced the modifications of meaning in some of the historical usages of the term 'literature'. During precisely this eighteenth- and nineteenth-century period, the word's meanings and usage change quite fundamentally, and they change in ways that start to denote a different kind of *value* for literature as such.

In earlier usage, the word was associated with literacy; and it indicated that someone was 'in possession of' what Williams called 'polite learning'. An individual versed in literature was one who was basically able to read and write, one who was 'literate', able to engage with print culture and books. This individual was literate precisely to the extent that she or he could 'handle' books, as we might put it, stressing the materiality of the engagement between hand and artifact. This arrangement coincides, obviously, with the growing importance of print, which also means that we are establishing a material entity – the book as such – as a location of value and worth or wealth.

It is salutary to remember, of course, that prior to Allen Lane and Penguin Books in the UK, books have always been prohibitively expensive: until very recent times, only the wealthy could have access to the extended print culture of the book as such. The wealthy in question would be those who were associated with religious foundations or those who owned land and houses within which it was expected practice to house books and libraries, essentially as a visible adornment of the owner. In monasteries, individual monks did not own books, but the institution held the books in common; and it was thus in the library that the central labour and work of the monastery was registered, with the power and authority being vested not in individuals as such but rather in the institution of the church. This was every bit as feudal as in the more material conditions of land ownership and its attendant authority and power.

Yet, through the eighteenth and nineteenth centuries, while books remained expensive, print culture was also spreading more democratically, and making some texts that we now identify as literature more available and accessible. Newspapers and magazines, sometimes including prose fiction, gradually brought the writing of some key and canonical figures to a wider audience, an audience that was not necessarily vested and invested in the kinds of 'polite learning' previously associated with material wealth or property.[39]

In 'The Writer: Commitment and Alignment', Williams offers a further precise historical focus for the changes in question. It is really since the 1830s that writers can start to make a profession and to live by their writing. That is due to several factors: 'the extraordinary expansion of magazine publications, the cheapening of books and the huge growth of the newspaper and periodical press'.[40] Effective copyright begins in the UK, properly, only in around 1710. It becomes consolidated further through the Copyright Act of 1842; and it is this that provides a *temporal* dimension to the ownership of a work, with copyright lasting for a prescribed number of years.

It is worth noting the coincidence between this and the dates in which Piketty also finds a significant economic change, arguing that 'capital prospered in the 1840s and industrial profits grew, while labor incomes stagnated'. It is then understandable that 'it was in this context that the first communist and socialist movements developed'.[41] In these conditions, then, we start to see the challenge to land-based wealth, and we see also that such a challenge lies in the hands of the growing and more democratic mass of individual readers and acts of reading. It is now, in these different readers that we start to find a 'democracy' based on the different values to be ascribed to individual books, arguments and persons. Those different values promulgate other modes of difference – social and economic inequality – that form the inaugural moment of modernity.

So, we know that the word 'literature' starts to undergo, during the eighteenth century, the semantic shift that it will consolidate during the nineteenth, when it starts to mean writing to which we ascribe a specific kind of value, by various means. The value in question hovers uncertainly during this period (and this continues even up to today) between material and financial value on one side (and this is political, related to the price and marketing of books) and a less immediately substantive, and more immaterial kind of value on the other (related to aesthetics as such). From now on, not all writing is literary; and literature pertains to only those instances of writing to which we ascribe particular (if vague) values.

That this all depends on the formation of a *national* debt, or upon the marketization of the State, is important. It sits comfortably alongside the observation made by Williams, that when we establish the modern and contemporary idea of 'literature', we do so partly through the construction of a series of precise *national* literatures. In this sense, the semantic shift – like the economic shift with which it is contemporaneous – is also a civic and political matter. As Williams points out, 'literature' starts to be associated with the equally emergent idea of the nation and its corollary, national identity.

There may well be a specific historical source of the emergence of such a thing as 'national character'; and, if so, it can be found in the political turmoil of the French Revolution, a political upheaval that changed the landscape – and the principles of land- and nation-ownership – across Europe and beyond. Seamus Deane argued that the original construction of 'national character' is to be found in Edmund Burke, nervously warning the English against the possibility of following and extending the French Revolution closer to home. The French – or so goes Burke's argument – are given to fissiparous tendencies to division; by contrast, the English are shaped by a commonsensical alignment with a supposed fixed natural order of things. That order would be described as a condition of liberty that had already been achieved. In France, however, the nature of the people was such that they were liable to the kind of derangement that he viewed as the condition of revolution.[42] For Burke, there exists a fundamental relation between England and the condition of liberty itself; and that relation yields a dialectic in which one need not decide 'whether the English tradition of liberty had formed the national character or whether the national character had formed the tradition of liberty', because what remains of importance is the interrelation of the two.[43] That is to say: first, a phenomenon identifiable as a 'national character' exists; and, second, it is manifest in the actual bodily conditions of the English.

6

We began this chapter from the antinomy noted by Jameson between narrative and affect as the condition of realism. At this stage, we might claim a substantial modification of this position, and suggest instead that the antinomy in question is that between the literary formation of a national characterological stereotype and an actual material individual body. This, I contend, is the constitution of the English. It is a position that underlies Bagehot when he argues, in the conclusion of *The English Constitution*, that the English 'have ... inherited the traditions of conflict' such that 'we look on State action, not as our own action, but as alien action; as an imposed tyranny from without'. In exemplifying this, he posits, literally, the body of an old lady against this national character as embodied in the State. He recalls a conversation with 'a very sensible old lady' on the occasion of her having to respond to the questions in the 1851 census, in which she said that the 'liberties of England were at an end'. Bagehot explains her position: 'if Government might be thus inquisitorial, if they might ask who slept in your house, or what your age was, what, she argued, might they not ask and what might they not do?'.[44]

Prior to the French Revolution, ideas of national character were already in the air; and they were slowly being given form and identity precisely by the emergence of 'literature' as a conceptual phenomenon. That phenomenon depended precisely upon the kind of dialectic that Deane reveals in Burke's conception of the English and that I am tracing here via the unlikely combination of Bagehot and Jameson. It depends fundamentally on the emergence of the individualized reader and act of reading – criticism – as the cornerstone of all values. Williams points to the historical coincidence, in the mid-eighteenth century, by which Germany establishes a *Nationalliteratur* as in Herder's 1767 *Ober die neuere deutsche Litteratur*, France constructs *Les Siècles de la littérature française* in 1772, and, in that same year, Italy produces its *Storia della letteratura italiana*. National character is now being defined by national literature; and the relation of the two yields a disposition in which criticism 'locates' and gives an identity to individual readers. The identity, however, is no longer one that is given by land, estate or place. From now on, in this growing modernity, it is a *cultural* identity, founded in a specific mode of writing and reading.

It is at this time that we find a more explicit determination of what had been implicit in Samuel Johnson, the category of 'English Literature' which will, in time, develop as a specific educational and cultural discipline of thought. 'The sense of "a nation" having "a literature" ', Williams writes, 'is a crucial social and cultural, probably also political, development'.[45] It is also, I argue, a significant *economic* development, tied to debts and its correlate in 'duties' (including civic duty, martial duty, and taxation and customs as duty).

Terry Eagleton, the heir of Williams, also argues that the category of literature is of very recent date. He suggests that it arises during a period of great historical turmoil – which remains nonetheless somewhat indeterminate in his formulation. For Eagleton, that period includes things like the French Revolution, the Industrial Revolution and the great series of failed revolutions all across Europe in 1848, so it may encompass as much as a half-century. The argument remains clear, however. During this time, regular property can no longer be seen as a secure location for one's wealth. Revolutionaries can un-house the wealthy elites; the poor can 'occupy' the estates of the wealthy as the growing importance of wage wealth starts to supplant inherited wealth; they can contest 'enclosures'; and they can start to stake a personal claim upon a proper share in the distribution of wealth that is inscribed in material substance, be it estates, land, or just houses. So, it follows, the rich have to find other ways of protecting their wealth (and its corollary in distinction and privilege), which means finding another home or another location for it, so to speak; and one such home is art, and, within that, literature.

Eagleton develops this thought further when he tries to identify literature as a kind of activity that is intrinsically resistant to the emerging forms and modes of capital: 'One of the most vital functions of the work of art since Romanticism,' he writes, 'has been to exemplify that which is gloriously, almost uniquely free of a function, and thus, by virtue of what it shows rather than what it says, act as an implicit rebuke to a civilization in thrall to utility, exchange-value and calculative reason. The function of art on this viewpoint is not to have a function.'[46]

Essentially, and by his own acknowledgement, this derives in fact more or less directly from Williams who had already argued that 'the idea of "creative" or "imaginative" literature emerges for the first time in the late eighteenth century as a form of resistance to an increasingly prosaic, utilitarian social order.' For Eagleton, who at this period has already made a quasi-religious turn in his own criticism, the logic is clear. This 'literature' now 'represents one of the last besieged outposts of transcendent truth in a harshly pragmatic environment. The transcendent imagination and early industrial capitalism are born at a stroke. Literature and the arts become forms of displaced religion, protected enclaves within which values now seen as socially dysfunctional can take shelter'.[47]

In this sense, however, literature is not so much an active mode of resistance; rather, it is a passive shelter from the storm of capitalism; and equally, a shelter from the impending storm of the French Revolution and its upsetting of social hierarchy, especially of hierarchies based on property ownership. This is what Burke knew. This explains why someone like Burke, who had been a vociferous critic of the British in India, can try to call the English back to their 'best self', as Arnold characterizes it, by eschewing the possibility of mimicking the French. It is important here to recall where this idea of a 'best self' came from: its roots lie in the residually religious impulse in criticism at the time of Macaulay's Minute. It is an 1835 construct, one corollary of which is the division of the reading-self into two: Arnold's ordinary anarchic self and his civilized best self. Furthermore, as Viswanathan showed us, the very idea of such a best self is integral to the construction of English Literature as a formal institutional discipline in India.

The consequence of this is that the modern reader is herself or himself precisely a construct of reading and, by extension, she or he is constituted at least partly by aesthetics.

7

Yet what this further shows is the intimate link between aesthetics and politics, which is also, at this time, being broken – or, much more precisely, *analyzed* and divided into constituent elements – so that we can have a separate category of 'the aesthetic' and of 'the political' or 'the economic', each divested of the interests of the others. John Guillory has an interesting take on this, when he points out that 'The problem of "aesthetic value" is not in fact a perennial problem, but can be posed as such only after the divergence of aesthetics and political economy, and as a consequence of the repression of their convergent origin'.[48]

This problem – the problem of theory that we know as the question concerning aesthetic value – is conditioned by the occluded origins of our literary studies. Those studies, however, are not and never have been simply studies in 'English literature'. The history shows instead that the origins of this, as a national and characterological construct, lie instead in specific attitudes to the world and to the economics of imperialism. The category of 'literature in English' – which is itself a specific version or account of 'world literature' – is central to this formation.

What if we avoid what Guillory calls the repression of the convergent origin of aesthetics and political economy? There is no denying that the history of both aesthetics and of political economy is driven by moments of crisis in various ways. It is instructive to consider the coincidence between, on one hand, the crisis in 'Comp Lit' studies that has led to a re-invigoration of the concept of 'world literature' and, on the other hand, the recent financial crisis originating in the housing market in 2007. Both are associated with the forms and practices of globalization.

Martin Wolf points out that, in 2001, even before the most recent major crash in world financial sectors, the World Bank 'estimated that there had been 112 systemic banking crises in 93 countries between the late 1970s and the end of the twentieth century'.[49] The 2008 crisis, in this sense, is nothing new, but rather the culmination of one major historical phase of crisis. Just as interesting as this fact is Wolf's gloss on this troubled financial history: 'To have had one crisis may have been a misfortune; to have had 112 was surely the result of extreme carelessness'.[50] It is literature that provides the appropriate mood and tone for his response to the economic issue: specifically, of course, Wilde's famous lines from his 1898 play, The Importance of Being Earnest. Lady Bracknell, the forerunner of the Countess Dowager of Downton Abbey says that 'To lose one parent ... may be regarded as a misfortune; to lose both looks like carelessness'.

To what extent is financial loss also 'carelessness' as opposed to misfortune? Wolf points out that the function of crisis seems to have been endemic to the banking industry worldwide from 1973 onwards. As he puts it, 'The age of financial liberalization was, in short, an age of crises'. Those economies that managed to weather the storms did also have crises, but were able to 'manage' them 'because of the credit-worthiness of their governments'.[51] In other words, credit and credibility became the primary source of value and valuation.

Arjun Appadurai has also analyzed what went wrong economically in this period, and, for him, the crisis was a crisis of language. In Banking on Words, he shows how trading in derivatives does several things that we have seen emerging here as themes in the relation between language, literature, and capital. Derivatives trading modifies Marx's well-worn formula describing the growth of an economy. Marx gave the formula as M-C-M, where we can track a movement from money to commodity to money again. Derivatives, however, remove the materiality of the commodity itself; and now, money breeds money, without the intervention of commodities at all. In short, commodities are replaced by promises. The process begins, argues Appadurai, in the middle of the nineteenth century 'when it became possible to make wagers on future commodity prices without ever acquiring or using the commodities in which trade was occurring'.[52] This is the logic of the futures market, which depends upon the language and literature of future promises. The logic begins precisely at the moment when we are developing English Literature as a discipline; and, as that discipline mutates into 'world literature in English', so we also have an accompanying process in which we have a new transvaluation of all values.

The more recent shift in the economy relates to finance capital itself. Trades are now increasingly independent of the actual values of any commodity or service in any meaningful material sense; and trade becomes a purely linguistic exercise. We know and identify that exercise in our parallel literary fields as the process of translation. It is translation that allows 'world literature' to extend beyond its immediate historical and material locality; and it is translation that turns literature into a capital exercise.

It is a capital exercise because translation expands the market. It quite literally monetizes the literary work precisely by making it 'transportable' in the terms I used above. It is also subject to the logic of the derivative, 'an instrument that has allowed financial technicians and managers to make virtually every part of our lives susceptible to monetization', as Appadurai puts it.[53] In the logic of world literary studies, we have a similar construction. Where, in finance, 'the derivative is a market in promises, each of which leverages a prior promise'[54] in a kind of Ponzi-scheme without original material investment and substance, in literature we have now a structure of intertextuality, each text being derivative of others, and all building to a world literature that grows increasingly in value the wider we draw its margins.

Appadurai's analysis, however, has a dark consequence. With the increasing removal of material commodities and their replacement with promises, we also have an economic structure that is necessarily built upon the amassing of debts, since debts are the underside of a promise. A debt is, as it were, the 'duty' owed to a promise; and as we build promise upon promise so also we amass and spread debt. As is well known, and as Wolf makes clear, 'the liabilities of the banking system are in fact contingent public debt: the banking industry privatizes its gains and socializes its losses'.[55] This means that 'the major form of labor today is not labor for wages but rather labor for the production of debt'.[56]

8

We can reach a provisional conclusion to this part of the argument by bringing together these two phenomena at their moment of change.

Two things – banking with its construction of a nation grounded in debt, and revolutionary change such as we see it struggling to emerge in the mid-nineteenth century – are more or less commensurate with each other. It is not simply the case that wealth is shifting from material to immaterial; it is also the case that such a shift entails a different set of social and political relations. It also marks a major cultural shift, and one in which the term 'cultural capital' starts to make sense, precisely because the cultural or aesthetic has been artificially disentangled from the political and economic.

Once such a disengagement or 'divergence', to borrow Guillory's term, can happen, it follows that we can start to recognize, in the category of literature, a specific kind of value. What this means, then, is that the shift in the semantic content of 'literature' goes along with the search for a location of value at precisely the moment when land and property as the material condition or realization of wealth is under threat.

The consequence of all this is a direct and intimate relation between literature – precisely *as literature* in our contemporary understanding of the term – and capital; and, within this, a marketization of something that we start now to identify precisely as cultural value, and as literary value; and it yields a classic bourgeois definition of freedom, as one grounded in marketization, or the 'freedom' simply of markets.

We can dramatize this – and see its material and bodily consequences – by returning to the opening scene of Delhi once again. Rana Dasgupta focuses on what he calls 'Partition refugees', individuals who had been deprived of their material assets as a more or less direct result of the manner in which de-colonization – with its attendant partition – occurred. They were, as he puts it, 'magnetically drawn to the consolations of property, and they acquired as much of it as they could'.[57] The consolation turns out to be better than they had ever imagined, because 'with the recent boom in property prices, they have seen their fortunes turn fabulous.' They become members of that new class of individuals who have emerged worldwide after 1989: the wandering, rootless, tax-avoiding oligarch, flaunting property once again as a sign of their standing. This new class, however, buys property: houses, not homes – for they have no intention of inhabiting the property, which might entail the commitment to a locale and a *patrimoine* that means they would be liable to taxation. The property is itself as rootless and empty as the oligarch class itself. In the Indian case, these ostensibly lucky individuals assume an extreme of self-assurance, as they 'find themselves rich on a global scale, and without doing very much'.[58]

A new relation between individual and State now emerges; and it follows the model of this rootless class, such that the new and more generalized middle-class of people adopt a new position with regard to the State and its public existence and visibility. 'For most middle-class families,' writes Dasgupta, 'government has retreated drastically from social and economic life over the last two decades, to the point that they hardly see it anymore.' This is not, of course, just specific to Delhi or even India as a whole. It is indeed a new worldwide phenomenon, often seen in terms of a willed disengagement of peoples from their governments, the members and representatives of which are now seen as out-of-touch elites. Furthermore, the generality of people in Delhi 'like it like this: they idealise government withdrawal and "deregulation"'. That, of course, is the key term used to advance neo-liberal economic policies worldwide. But many people 'do not realize how much work the city government does to protect their class from the enormous mass of poverty that surrounds them, which is firmly prevented from having any claim on city space or resources'.[59]

So much, we might say, for the elite and the middle class; but what of the rest? Dasgupta is clear; 'It is the poor who understand how the city is truly managed. They have a far greater intimacy with government and, indeed, a far greater bureaucratic burden'.[60] The effect of this becomes apparent, and shocking. Land is increasingly appropriated by the elites, but even more so by large multinational corporate industries and businesses. They are encouraged in this by governments, especially when those governments are themselves beholden to multinationals in that too-close relation between business and government that George Soros once defined as the essence of fascist politics.[61] This is all done in the interests of what neo-liberalism glorifies as 'free trade'. Free trade, however, it is not free at all; it comes at a price.

The price is not just financial. Pablo Mukherjee cites the horrifying evidence of the consequences of all this. He points out that, 'in the ten years between 1997 and 2007, 182,936 Indian farmers killed themselves', and, from 2002 to 2007, the rate of such suicides was a horrifying two every hour. Most of these farmers died by the same means, 'after drinking the very pesticide that was supposed to make the "high-yield" seeds manufactured by giant agro-business transnational corporations like Monsanto bloom into profit-producing cash crops'.[62]

This is where culture touches the material earth and becomes agriculture; and vice-versa. It is where narrative touches the body; it is where corporate business and its associated globalized financial structures impact directly upon the body. These call into question not just the workings of capital but also those of culture in its most fundamental form. The 'free trade' that underpins this structure – and that is certainly neither 'free' nor liberating – is one that calls our ideas of cultural value into serious question. This is the question that we know most clearly as that of 'cultural capital', to which we can now turn yet more directly.

PART TWO

Culture and Capital

4

Governing the Tongue

1

In 1941, George Orwell published his essay on 'England Your England'. He is exploring the idea of a national character, the ways in which an individual might identify with a nation or might 'embody' the national identity. The term most readily available for him to describe this at the period – in the midst of the Second War – is 'patriotism'. As he points out in opening the essay, 'As I write, highly civilized human beings are flying overhead, trying to kill me'.[1] The nation is at war, and he is writing under life-threatening constraints that might throw not just the material conditions of civilization into doubt, but also even the very idea of civilization itself.[2]

Although skeptical about the possibility of defining a national character in any theoretical sense, he takes the empirical view that there is indeed something very specific about 'England'.[3] He comes up with a 'minor English trait' that is notable but not often noted, 'and that is a love of flowers' and what he calls 'the addiction to hobbies and spare-time occupations'. We are, he states, 'a nation of flower-lovers, but also a nation of stamp-collectors, pigeon-fanciers, amateur carpenters, coupon-snippers, darts-players, crossword-puzzle fans'. He then does indeed theorize or conceptualize what underpins this, and discovers what he calls 'the *privateness* of English life'.[4] It is here – in the particular characteristic of a specific privacy – that he finds the fundamental version of liberty that he says is a basic facet of the English national character.

A part of this privacy is manifest in a more or less explicit cultural turn 'inwards'. Stefan Collini has pointed out that 'In literary and cultural terms, the period after1945 … saw a self-conscious return to values and forms of expression identified as essentially English', and this, he adds, is an explicit turn away from modernist 'internationalism'. Larkin and Kingsley Amis stand as paradigmatic literary examples of such a set of priorities, typical of a suspicion of 'high-flown or overly abstract ideas', which were often 'stigmatized as "foreign" '.[5]

There is a distinction between the kind of values associated with these private concerns and an entirely different kind of liberty, the 'economic liberty' associated with nineteenth-century capitalism and, behind that, eighteenth-century *laissez-faire*. Orwell's concern is that this private liberty (and thus Englishness itself) is in danger of being steadily eradicated in the emergent bureaucratic and administered society of 1941 in England. The war above his head might be won in martial terms, but it might ultimately be lost – if this version of 'your England' is defeated in cultural terms.

A part of this privacy is 'Literature'. Having argued that the English are not much good at the arts in general, Orwell then makes an exception for English Literature, the one area in which the English are indeed extremely distinguished. However, in saying this, he characterizes literature as a deeply internalized affair, as something that is deeply particular, private. As he puts it, in flagrant contradiction of the later emergence of our new categories of 'world literature', this is 'the one art that cannot cross frontiers. Literature, especially poetry, and lyric poetry most of all, is a kind of family joke, with little or no value outside its own language-group'.[6]

Orwell was much concerned with the relation of literature to the material world and to historical fact. He notes, early in the 'England' essay, something close to his own personal history: the 'world-famed hypocrisy' of the English, as seen in 'their double-faced attitude towards the empire'.[7] In some ways, the entire 'career of English' – and the institutionalization of English Literature – owes its origins precisely to this hypocritical attitude. It is basic to the formation of Eric Blair as he becomes George Orwell, in which guise he can safely address the whole relation of his literary work to politics as such. In this first move, however, he is making a distinction that we will see time and again, in which literature is seen as a kind of refuge from and even at times a refusal of the primacy of the economic as a determinant of both personal and national identities. In Orwell's case, the consequence is the production of a very fraught relation between literature and the world beyond the private self. The structure of this thinking – in which Orwell elides the economic while still trying to attend to the fact that literature has a profound relation to politics – opens up an interesting issue. If it is the case that 'a bought mind is a spoiled mind' – as Orwell writes in 'The Prevention of Literature' at the end of the war – then how exactly might the institutions of literature relate to the institutions of politics, and, above all, to the institution of government[8]? Are there constraints on literature – 'preventions' of literature – that are hidden when we elide the issue of capital and of the economy, and that ought properly to be exposed and examined?

It is obviously not at all the case that Orwell completely ignores issues of the economy. On the contrary, he is at some pains to stress the fact that 'There is no question about the inequality of wealth in England ... Economically, England is certainly two nations [rich and poor], if not three or four'.[9] Yet his case is that, in England at least, this fact is transcended by a more fundamental appeal to an intrinsic sense of national unity, governed by forms of patriotism. After all, he argues, inequality, though worse in England than anywhere else in Europe, is not something that is entirely particular to England, but is rather a worldwide problem. 'In all countries', he writes, 'the poor are more national than the rich, but the English working class are outstanding in their abhorrence of foreign habits'. Poverty in England does not turn the working-class poor against the aristocratic wealthy; rather, it turns the working-class towards a kind of xenophobia, a fear and even a dislike of the foreign in all its guises; and in this prejudice working-class people are aided and abetted, and fully endorsed and encouraged, by the landed aristocracy.[10]

This peculiar fact can be explained partly by parochial English insularity, and by the legacy of a Macaulay-style belief that there is an intrinsic superiority to England (and the English), as seen in its literature which, with the possible exceptions of Shakespeare, Byron and Wilde, are not 'available' to other national cultures, because those national cultures are simply not up to it in the eyes of the native Englishman. This is symptomatic not just of the nineteenth-century imperialist attitude that we saw in Macaulay's Minute, but also symptomatic of 'typically' English no-nonsense empiricism, which equates philosophy and theory or even consistent political thinking precisely as 'nonsense'. Linked to the intrinsic intimacy between the English and their literature 'is the lack of philosophical faculty, the absence in nearly all Englishmen of any need for an ordered system of thought or even for the use of logic'.[11] In Orwell's explications here, pragmatism trumps ideology, in three words.

Yet what this means is that England becomes somehow identified as precisely everything that is lacking in ideology, and is instead a stable centre (as in empire) around which peripheral nations find their value, worth and identity – or their own 'ideology'. Ideologies are what other and foreign nations have, and ideology remains foreign in its totality to the Englishman, who stands as a natural centre of all propriety and of a fundamental state of nature.

The more usual characteristic of this pragmatism, at least as it manifests itself in daily social behaviour, is a form of restraint (that 'privacy' again), a kind of refusal to commit enthusiastically to any specific philosophy or even, indeed, to the issues of politics and economics that afflict English society. There is no doubt, for Orwell, that 'England is the most class-ridden country under the sun. It is a land of snobbery and privilege, ruled largely by the old and silly'.[12] In considering the implications of all this for our case, we can consider the rules, modes and norms of government in relation to the institution of literature, and especially of 'English Literature'; and it is to this that I now turn.

2

One good way of thinking about the relation of literature to capital is through asking a logically prior question about the relation of literature to the material conditions of existence itself. In previous chapters, I indicated how literature is conditioned by the very immaterial status of a 'promise': it is built on credit and credibility. Such things do not have a material existence, yet they are themselves the preconditions of bringing something into material existence: a promise fulfilled is a promise that is 'realized'; 'credibility' is validated when what it foretells – its proposition – becomes a material reality. This suggests that literature is, first and foremost, of the nature of an idea. We might now ask a logically fundamental question. How might literature – ostensibly an immaterial mere idea – be conditioned by its relation to material realities? How 'worldly' must literature be – or how 'mundane' must literature become – in order to find its own substantive reality or to 'realize' itself in a world that is thought of as 'everything that is the purely material case'? This question is further complicated by the fact that the emergence of the very category of literature is itself shaped to some extent by the emergence also of the nation State. Our question becomes a question concerning the realities – or otherwise – of a new 'world literature'. This is what we can now turn to, and we will start our exploration from a condition of Englishness in the formation of English Literature.

Restraint – although not yet constraint – is often associated with the characteristically or stereotypically empirical English. The English – unlike the Americans, say – lack 'enthusiasm'.[13] This is how the English self maintains itself as 'private', in Orwell's sense of that term: not giving oneself away, and having therefore a sense of propriety. Decorous propriety is, as it were, a fundamental 'property' of the English; and it is related to the first determination of the authentic English subject as 'a man of property', to borrow the title of John Galsworthy's 1906 opening novel in his great Edwardian sequence, The Forsyte Saga. The man of property is archetypically English in this text: asserting that he is 'self-made' in an essentially bourgeois or commercial transition from the feudal societies of his ancestry, and living through the tensions associated with that.

'The positions of their houses', we are told early in the novel, 'was of vital importance to the Forsytes ... since the whole spirit of their success was embodied therein', earlier generations having been of 'farming stock'.[14] Old Jolyon, in whose house we start with an 'at home' in Stanhope Gate, had made his money from colonial exploitation of tea, with its aroma and air 'of enterprise and mystery, of special dealings in special ships, at special ports, with special Orientals'.[15] The implicit national self-definition that we see here continues further, and becomes explicit, through Old Jolyon's dislike of 'that fellow Wagner', who had 'ruined everything' on the grounds that his operas are 'new-fangled German pantomimes'.[16]

Old Jolyon, of course, maintains a certain restraint, dealing with the weariness that comes from negotiating his difference from Orientals and Germans; and it is this that distinguishes him from Soames, say, who fails to deal adequately with the threat to 'propriety' as in the perceived threat to his 'property', Irene, whom he rapes.

Orwellian English restraint manifests itself as a form of civilized dignity, in which the possibility of conflict – if not war itself – between different parties is foreseen and defused, or 'prevented'. It is not that peace follows, nor even reconciliation; rather, we have here the establishment and tacit acceptance of a specific normative economy in which truth is reduced to contested opinions, each of which is to be respected. Ideally, in ideological terms, this can lead to political impasse, with a resultant endless deferral of resolution; and such a deferral passes for 'peace' or at least avoidance of direct conflict (including personal conflicts, such as that which is materialized in the physical and sexual violence against Irene in Galsworthy's fiction). In some instances, however, such a structural model of debate or dialogue can result in the validation of falsehood. Falsehood was, for Orwell, a problem that arises thanks not so much to direct political bias in the public media and press, but more because of what is fundamentally a matter of both financial and cultural economics.

One helpful way to explain and illustrate the importance and relevance of this for our contemporary moment will be through a brief consideration of public sector government policy in the age of an emergent neoliberalism. It was politically important during the period when the primacy of 'market fundamentalist' economics was being made normative – broadly the early 1980s – to ensure that any opposition to the supposed economic consensus would be, indeed, 'prevented', forestalled. The key element of neoliberal fundamentalist marketization was a general economic trajectory to diminish the State and to privatize its assets; and the logical (if, perhaps, unintentional) corollary of this, culturally, was an initial move towards what we can call the 'privatization of truth'.[17]

In the 1980s, rejecting proper and intensive scrutiny by journalists, Margaret Thatcher and the Conservative Party called into question the scruples and political positioning of the BBC, especially its news output. They assumed the right to do this, on the grounds that the BBC is a quasi-publicly funded organization, with a remit to be 'independent'. Oddly, paradoxically, senior government politicians believed that the best way to assure themselves of this independence was precisely for the government to interfere. The interference took the form of a demand for 'balance' in all reporting. In media terms, this balance is a precise reiteration of English 'restraint' or 'moderation'.

Balance, ideologically, rests on the unstated philosophical presumption that truth is entirely relative, and that each individual has her or his own and owned truth regarding any proposition. This is exactly what Orwell foresaw, as the truth of what happens materially and historically cedes place to the assumed priority of the *interpretation* of those events. Those interpretations are, fundamentally, private and privatized opinions. The consequence is that, for every statement that claims an application to the material conditions of reality, an equal and opposite statement must be found, on the assumption that we need 'balanced' reporting. There is a specific economics behind this.

Orwell argued that 'the right to report contemporary events truthfully' was under attack in 1945. This is consistent with the fact that 'the independence of the writer and the artist is eaten away by vague economic forces'.[18] In our time and in the paradigmatic cultural example of the BBC, what happens through the economic determinations of neoliberalism is that all that is historically solid must be melted into vague and airy representational and linguistic nothings. Thus it is that we find – for one simple but clear example – that notwithstanding the scientifically determined fact that global warming is happening, that fact must be 'balanced' against an opposing view, an 'alternative fact'. Truth, in short, is to be 'equaled' by falsehood, even falsehood with vested financial interest (as with the oil lobby, say); and balance means that falsehood gets equality of airtime and treatment with truth. 'A bought mind is a spoiled mind' indeed; and this is a spoiling of the collective mind of the public, a spoiling that is conditioned by the fact that government essentially held the purse strings over the financing of the BBC.

The significant consequence is that, in this implementation of governmental policy, the very idea of 'the public' with its shared, equal and communal access to the truth of history, starts to lose its status as 'public' and now becomes privatized. Thus we have a state of affairs in which for each private individual, there is an ownership of her or his own truth, her or his own world. Moreover, descriptions of the public world themselves start to lose any claim upon truth. All reports of 'what happened' are thrown into profound and intrinsic doubt. Any text, then, that makes a claim on 'the world' is immediately rendered somehow inauthentic, non-genuine.[19]

In a world where material realities (what happened) become atomized in this way, a nation needs some 'independent' source of authority and legitimacy; and, in this case, that source must be the source that underpins all others: the government and its authorized institutions. Government is the one entity that *determines* the 'fact' that all truths have become privatized and thus reduced to mere opinion or point of view. The reason that government underpins all this is because of the primacy of financial economics: money predetermines what can be allowed to pass as the truth. As Orwell might have put it, 'all opinions are equal, but some are more equal than others' – and in this case, the overarching opinion – the 'truth' of what happened – is that account that is stated to be the case by government, because government determines the funding of the representation of historical and material realities.[20]

This is a recipe not just for political paralysis, but also for a state of neo-totalitarian governance, in which, as Orwell puts it, 'history is something to be created rather than learned'; or, as Peter Mandelson, the UK Labour politician, once said, the task of a spin-doctor is 'to create the truth'. Orwell described the fundamental problem with this kind of thinking: 'A totalitarian state is in effect a theocracy, and its ruling caste, in order to keep its position, has to be thought of as infallible'[21]. In the 1980s, the task of government was to assume precisely this position, standing above the fray of debate and argument, which would now become the province of the BBC and other journalism or literature all squabbling and vying for attention, while the government simply got on with imposing its own 'truth' onto history. Debate – and with it, both literature and criticism as such – is thus debased and degraded, becoming merely 'academic' and a matter for seminar rooms and not for life on the streets.[22]

In this way, truth is lost; and in its place, we have a 'liberal' economy of equal and opposite propositions. 'Balance' is a key term in this, for it sounds neutral and positive, whereas 'imbalance' sounds rather like something irrational, mad or even controversially extremist. That is to say, we established a kind of competitive market in allegedly freely expressed opinions, none of which need invoke any claims on epistemological truth or historical fact.

Most people would recognize this from their own modern and liberal humanist education, in literature especially. In literary study, as we know, the well-worn dogma is that there is no dogma: there can be no right answers to any literary argument or debate and, instead, everyone is entitled to their own opinion, all supposedly of equal value. This has been a standard cliché in literary education, in schools and universities, ever since the inception of the institutionalization of the discipline as a subject of serious study. It is a position satirized by Howard Jacobson in *Pussy*, his fabular story of the life of Donald Trump, or 'Fracassus'. Fracassus has a private tutor, Professor Kolskeggur Probrius, a man who 'had earned the esteem of students on account of his dedication to their improvement.' Probrius, however, has been fired from his institution during 'the Great Purge of the Illuminati', when he 'found himself accused or cognitive condescension, that is to say of making a virtue of possessing expert knowledge'.

In an age that validates privatized knowledge, it is essentially a crime to claim that one individual has more authority than another, for it leaves students 'distressed by the perceived distance between his attainments and their own'.[23] Neoliberal economics has destroyed the possibility of teaching and learning – above all of teaching and learning about literature – because it claims that everyone is always already in equal possession of the truth, their 'own' and 'owned' truth. This is their capital.

Yet, when this is established as the ground-rule for politics, the situation is one that slips democracy into oligarchy: while the people squabble over what is really happening, the government stands unmoved and untouched, above the domain of mere argument, and in full possession and control of the conditions of material history and actuality. Likewise, in the institutions of literary education, we establish a mode of quiet authoritarianism: all opinions are equal, but the literature teacher grades one opinion at an A, and another as a D or fail; and they do so in a mysterious fashion. However, and as I am arguing here, what is really at stake is the measure of the student's intrinsic 'Englishness', as seen through her or his engagement with

'English Literature'. In the political sphere, absolute power replaces legitimate authority here, as government ensures that there can be no rival institution with the authority to counter or even to challenge its power and claims.

This 'equality of opinion' or 'balance' – ostensibly harmlessly neutral and positively rational in the field of literary education – is also applied in the field of economics, where it assumes the guise of 'equality of opportunity'. It is here that the politics of this fundamentally cultural and literary position – how one's national identity as English has been efficiently internalized through the reading of English Literature – starts to become clear. The liberality of opinion (in literature) is matched by the liberality of opportunity (in economics). Both are set against the assumed fixity of the so-called hard sciences, and above all, the science of number in mathematics.

While all opinions can be equal in literature, where there is supposed to be no legislating for taste, nonetheless it remains the case, always and everywhere, that there is one correct and even dogmatic answer to the question of what 2 + 2 equals. However, in *Nineteen Eighty-Four*, Orwell showed that this, too, is or can become a political question: it, too, can become a matter of 'opinion', when the totalitarian authority of the day holds the only acceptable answer, even if the citizens of the authoritarian state can never know what that answer is.[24] We also now know it not just as the imposition of a totalitarian political rule, but also as the imposition of a totalitarian economic rule, in which the tyranny of mathematical economics triumphed over the idea of economics as being related in any way to the social realities of 'the good life'. This, of course, is but a shorthand description of the great financial crisis of 2007–8.[25]

How has this bad consequence come about from what might have started out as good intention? In *How Much is Enough?* Edward Skidelsky and Robert Skidelsky point to the ways in which the making of money for its own sake has become a new orthodoxy, and come to the fairly obvious (but hardly ever acknowledged) conclusion that 'Making money cannot be an end in itself – at least for anyone not suffering from acute mental disorder'.[26] Making money as precisely such an end in itself, however, has become a central feature of the major institution that encourages the growth of 'Literature' as such: the university institution. Universities, it is increasingly clear, are driven, by the sector's leadership – perhaps for reasons beyond the control of that leadership – by an obsession with money. This becomes an obsession with turnover, for its own sake – or, in many cases, in order to raise the profile of the 'university-as-a-business'.[27] The paradox is that this economics, driven by 'acute mental disorder', should now be governing our institutions of intellectual life, including that of literature itself.

The belief that there is this one field of certainty and truth cedes the entire field of truth to the realm of mathematics. That mathematical realm, however, is not at all neutral, but has instead been silently politicized and mobilized for expressly ideological purposes. As we know, it is the peculiar combination of mathematics and the liberality of economics that leads to, produces, and endorses the 'free-market' logic of the 2008 financial crash and subsequent economic crisis. Geoffrey M. Hodgson has detailed how the institution of economics, especially in the academy, became blind to the upcoming global crisis precisely because of its adherence to the 'truth' of mathematical models. 'Most economists' in our institutions, he writes, 'are taught tools of analysis rather than the intellectual, historical and institutional contexts in which analytical questions arise'. This is a direct consequence of modes of teaching and of institutional orthodoxy: 'As mathematics has swamped the curricula in leading universities and graduate schools, student economists have become neither equipped nor encouraged to prioritize real world economies and institutions'.[28]

Mathematics yields the truth, governed by the logic of mathematical equalities and the rigours of algebraic algorithms; economics yields the flexibility and the corresponding equality of opportunity that says that anyone and everyone can be wealthy. In this structure, wealth is a rational choice; and the poor are responsible for their own poverty, for they have squandered their equality of opportunity. The counterpart in the institution of literary criticism is that 'we are all equal before the text', a clearly ludicrous idea since we clearly do not all begin from the same lexical potential or vocabulary. Some of us might even speak 'foreign' languages. The task of criticism might more properly be described as the attempt to *make* us more equal before the world of textuality and of language. This is the sphere into which the language of 'world literature' enters.

The remainder of the argument in the pages that follow will be organized around the proposition that the 'restraint' of English becomes more or less directly a 'constraint' on the activities and practices of literature as such. The institutionalization of 'English Literature' prevents the possibility of literature engaging directly with the historical realities of the world; and thus the institutionalization of English Literature forestalls and hampers the possibility of establishing a genuinely 'worldly literature'.

3

Yet the political dimension of this prevention of literature is nowhere near as overtly harsh as was the fallout from the 2008 crisis. We can discover the entire structure governing our contemporary predicaments within the institution of government itself; and a good example of it, as I will show, is to be found at precisely the moment when Orwell was writing 'The Prevention of Literature'. It is at the moment when Orwell is worrying about this prevention of literature that we see, institutionally, the formation of a new kind of discipline, that of 'Comparative Literary Studies' or 'Comp. Lit.'

It is largely historical circumstance that led to the development of the field of 'Comp Lit', a field that would eventually in turn be superseded by an equally contentious institutionalization of a yet newer formulation, our new accounts of 'World Literature'.[29] By 1945, a great number of European intellectuals – among them many philologists – had fled Nazi-dominated Europe, and had relocated to the United States. One principle governing the institution of 'Comp. Lit.' is a presumed equality of languages: it is anathema to most institutionalized versions of 'Eng. Lit', for the simple reason that, as we have seen, Eng. Lit depends on an imperialist idea of the intrinsic supremacy of all things English, including the English language. However, for the philologists who found themselves working in second, third and fourth languages – and usually Romance languages at that – 'Comp. Lit.' requires that we embrace not the translatability of cultures, but the *equality of languages* within those cultures.

Erich Auerbach moved to the United States in 1947, after about a decade in Turkey, where he worked after being removed from his academic post in Marburg in 1935 in the early days of Nazi governmental power. His case illustrates clearly the politics of 'Comp. Lit'. In his discussion of Virginia Woolf, he draws attention to what he sees as her ability to find a simple and straightforward equality. In her writing, he says, 'we cannot but see to what an extent – below the surface conflicts – the differences between men's ways of life and forms of thought have already lessened'.[30] These 'surface conflicts' – of a world war that is grounded in racial difference and the claims of an Aryan racial superiority – are, astonishingly, being ostensibly, rhetorically, evacuated here of their actual and material worldly power. The shift here from actual *political* discussion to *cultural* discussion is an attempt to circumvent the horrible realities of the world's condition at this moment. Clearly, however, the politics of the time are not predicated on any such lessening of surface conflicts among peoples. Impotent in the face of the political realities, Auerbach displaces his argument onto the domain of culture, in the form of literature. There, at least, the world he wants to be the case – a world of equality – can at least be imagined to be the case.

This political 'equality' rests on exactly the same structure as that which governs the idea of 'balance' in any literary or journalistic proposition, and which I explored above as a fundamentally economic structure. It operates, as in mathematics, at a purely formal and abstract level in Auerbach's analysis. It presupposes here a kind of 'ur-text' in Woolf's writings that circumvents the vagaries of individualized national and nationalist readings, done according to different language-regimes.

Literature becomes the site not only for the idea of an equality among languages, but also that of a wished-for and fantasized equality among people. It provides a utopian idea of equality in the face of the most profound inequalities that are at work in material history and economics. In this respect, 'Comp. Lit.' begins precisely as the site of a false hope – even, and more pertinently here, of an unrealizable promise, a promise that cannot be fulfilled – and its spread becomes, consequentially and also paradoxically, a part of the economic and political problem that we are now having to revisit under the revised rubric of a new conception of World Literature. The politics of this – in which cultural activity actually replaces the necessity of historical activities whose realization would be too radical – is played out in the UK in 1945.

The post-war UK provides an appropriate example of the political and cultural structure that determines the 'prevention of literature'. Colonel Douglas Clifton-Brown, the Speaker of the House of Commons in 1945, gives us the relevant example, bringing together three things: politics in its most appropriate setting; literature in the form of traditional song; and an idea of national identity.

When the UK Parliament of 1945 convened for the first time, with the key purpose of electing its new Speaker (identified during the session as Clifton-Brown), Winston Churchill arrived to take his seat in front of his heavily depleted Tory benches. The election had seen a complete rout of the Tory party, and a massive mandate for a radical Attlee Labour programme. Labour secured a parliamentary majority of 146 seats, with 48 per cent of the electorate voting for Attlee's party and administration. In the by now fairly standard analysis of this result, a key factor explaining the landslide derived from Churchill's attack on Attlee's Labour during the campaign, in which Churchill suggested that if Labour won, they would 'have to fall back on some kind of Gestapo'.[31] This was a brazen and somewhat desperately partisan attempt to identify Labour with the Nazis; and it was a standard – if scandalously outrageous – rhetorical gesture of identifying any socialist as a kind of 'enemy within', a fifth column determined to restrict freedoms. The implication was that Labour was not genuinely 'English', and that it was fundamentally at odds with an English identity and English national character.

Upon Churchill's arrival (he, at least, had kept his seat), the depleted Tory benches started to sing 'For he's a jolly good fellow'. This was unconventional, improper and unorthodox in the protocols of the House of Commons. The rampantly victorious Labour Party responded with a rousing chorus of the Red Flag. This – especially the Red Flag – was not just unconventional; it was more than dangerously scandalous, reaching the dizzy heights of impropriety – and, worse, it was potentially 'un-English', unlike the Tory 'jolly good fellow' song.[32] But when dragged to the Speaker's Chair in the usual ceremonial fashion, Clifton-Brown remarked 'with the wry humour that Speakers are always meant to show – that he hoped he had been elected

Speaker of the House of Commons and not director of some musical chorus'[33].

Clifton-Brown neutralizes a situation that could become polarized; and he does so by effectuating a mode of restraint in the proceedings. He 'translates' real historical conflict into 'merely' cultural values (as did Auerbach, in his very different context), the value in question here being that of propriety and of properly regulated behaviour in an English-landed house, the House of Commons. This successfully brings a 'proper' mood of sobriety and propriety to the House of Commons; but it also brings about silence, the silencing of the singing, in a House whose very function is supposed to be that of adversarial debate and criticism. Clifford-Brown's jocular remark forestalls the possibility of such debate and such critique. It is, as we will see, a prime example of the 'prevention of literature'.

This is the context in which Orwell was also puzzling over the ways in which certain types of language could be effectively silenced. Indeed, when he wrote a piece for a relatively new journal, *Polemic*, his choice of title – 'The Prevention of Literature' – explicitly invites the idea that a specific type of language or writing is being silenced, its power foreseen and forestalled. Orwell describes attending a PEN club meeting in 1945, on the occasion of the tercentenary of Milton's great tract on press freedom, *Areopagitica*. He laments that no one at the meeting seemed seriously to attend to the issue of the freedom of the press, which, 'if it means anything at all, means the freedom to criticize and oppose'.[34] This is a very important aspect of that specific idea of literary criticism as a mode of speaking out, of (in the cliché) speaking truth to power.

Orwell's observation has a persisting relevance. It has a broad equivalent, for example, in the more recent Leveson Inquiry in the UK. Leveson pointed out – citing the authority of Thomas Jefferson in this regard – that freedom of the press is tied firmly to the operations of democracy. In this regard, Leveson writes that 'I know how vital the press is – all of it – as the guardian of the interests of the public, as a critical witness to events, as the standard bearer for those who have no one else to speak up for them'.[35] He goes further, and uses a terminology that some would find disreputable, as it permits of undignified conduct: 'Some of its most important functions are to inform, educate and entertain and, when doing so, to be irreverent, unruly and opinionated. It adds a diversity of perspective. It explains complex concepts that matter in today's world in language that can be understood by everyone'.[36] Leveson essentially calls into question not only the failed economic structure of the alleged 'balance' of truths and opinions, but also the 'English' characteristic of restraint, a restraint that would lead to censorship and to the silencing of languages that are other than the immediately familiar, the language that one tends to call one's 'own'.

The question becomes whether 'capital letters' – a particular intimacy between nationalist capitalism and English Literature – have conspired to reduce foreign voices, or voices that question English norms, to silence. Is the institution of 'English Literature' intrinsically inimical to 'world literature' as such; and does 'Eng. Lit.' exist therefore primarily in order to bolster – culturally – a national identity and position of privilege that is under threat economically?

4

Orwell, in 1946, situates this question in a wider context, not just recalling the spirit of Milton, but also addressing his contemporary moment. He widens his interest to intellectual liberty in general, which he says is under a two-pronged attack: on one side, from 'apologists of totalitarianism', and on the other, from 'its immediate practical enemies, monopoly and bureaucracy'.[37] Working against genuine intellectual liberty, he argues, we have in 1945 a press oligarchy, a public that does not buy books, official bodies like the British Council whose bureaucratic demands narrow what can be done and which 'dictate [the writer's] opinions'; and all of this is governed by the 'continuous war atmosphere of the last ten years'.[38] We might consider whether similar issues pertain in our own moment, given our own continuous war atmosphere of the last few decades[39].

This cultural condition might be better described not as restraint, but rather as 'constraint'; and, for Orwell, it is most certainly a preventative measure, a mode of censorship or constraint on specific freedoms that he associates directly with literature. Such censorship or constraint is conditioned by the smothering powers that follow from monopolization of the language, in which a specific party or class makes a claim that they speak 'proper' English, say, or that they alone speak it 'properly'. In this regard, they claim authority that is unearned, and thereby claim the language as 'theirs', as if a language and all that is contained in it can be a commodity, or a landmass.

The primary critical example that exposes what is at stake in this is Joyce; and the key scene is the celebrated argument, in *A Portrait of the Artist as a Young Man*, about the word 'tundish'. The young Stephen Dedalus is engaged in a conversation about beauty with the dean of his college. The conversation turns to what Stephen calls a specific difficulty in aesthetic discussion, which he identifies as 'whether words are being used according to the literary tradition or according to the tradition of the market-place'[40]. It is this that leads directly onto not just contested meanings, but contestations over 'proper' English and over the condition of language in 'a market-place'. The dean refers to a funnel that allows oil to be poured into a lamp; and Stephen is puzzled at the word, calling it instead a tundish. 'Is that called a tundish in Ireland?' asks the dean, to which Stephen replies that 'It is called a tundish in Lower Drumcondra ... where they speak the best English'.[41]

The standard critical engagement with this rests on the following paragraphs, in which Stephen 'felt with a smart of dejection that the man to whom he was speaking was a countryman of Ben Jonson', following which he thinks that 'The language in which we are speaking is his before it is mine. How different are the words *home, Christ, ale, master*, on his lips and on mine! I cannot write or speak these words without unrest of spirit. His language, so familiar and so foreign, will always be for me an acquired speech. I have not made or accepted its words. My soul frets in the shadow of his language'.[42]

Most critique follows this through in terms of the logic of colonialism. However, running beneath this is that phrase that opens the entire discussions, in which Stephen suggests that linguistic meaning is shaped by the different traditions of literature on one hand and commerce or capital market-place on the other hand. In the conversation among fellow students after class, Stephen is asked to sign an anti-war testimonial, to which his reply is 'Will you pay me anything if I sign?' Joyce brings together an act of writing and a mercenary impulse. It is as if he finds here a means of reconciling the claims of the literary tradition and the mercantile: in a signature on a political document. It is significant that Stephen refuses to make the conjunction: he refuses to sign. McCann taunts him: 'Minor poets, I suppose, are above such trivial questions as the question of universal peace'.[43] That may be so; but they are certainly not above questions of financial and economic survival, and a survival that is conditioned by writing itself.

The key issues then in this 'tundish' episode, alongside the more commonly discussed colonialism, relate to matters of what we can call the capital of authority, especially in a war-time context. In this I mean to indicate that the dean enjoys greater authority over the English language, not because of anything he has done to earn that authority, but simply because he asserts it.

Stephen, rankling under this realization, essentially wrestles linguistically with McCann; and in that linguistic tussle, both parties try to maintain their dignity. Yet money and capital intervene. Stephen jocularly tries to monetize his writing, seeking payment for his signature; but behind that joke lies the failed attempt to reconcile literature (or writing) and money. Perhaps needless to say, this episode is also one that marks varying degrees of dignity; and the dean's dignity, like the cultural capital that he has in 'owning' the language, is entirely unearned. The relation is not based on financial clout; rather, it is more closely related to the feudal structures that are underpinned through the ownership and control of land. In this case, alongside the question of who owns the land of Ireland, it is also a question of who owns the language. We have here a revisiting of the issue that we saw in the Indian context; and perhaps the proper context for the Joyce passage is given also by Macaulay's Minute. That Minute, it is increasingly clear, is concerned with the establishment of the 'capital of authority' that perplexes Stephen Dedalus. Joyce knows that financial capital is tied intimately to cultural capital; and that both are associated intimately with the authority that underpins the very existence of the literary as such.

The dean rules by virtue of his office: this is Orwellian bureaucracy – rule by the offices – in straightforward operation. It deploys the assertion of a control of language to smother alternative world-views; and it fails to recognize anything that is not expressed in the language of the office itself. The dean's English – unlike that of Lower Drumcondra – is not just 'official', but also 'proper'. It is the property of the dean before it is that of Stephen. Stephen, therefore, is intrinsically 'in debt' to the dean for 'permitting' the use of English; but he must conform to the dean's mindset if he is to be heard at all. Dignified propriety here is aligned with the ownership of a language, as if a language itself were a capitalizable commodity: dignity does not counter capitalism, but rather is the mechanism through which we can confound cultural capital with cultural capitalism.[44]

Joyce's response, finally, is what we can identify as perhaps the first genuine work of world literature, *Finnegans Wake*, a text that so destabilizes the centrality of its English language roots that it becomes genuinely the work of the foreigner, a work of *xenophilia*. *Finnegans Wake* completely ungoverns the tongue; and this is largely the political – and economic – point. It resists easy consumption; it eschews easy comprehension. Most significantly of all, it *delays* the reader, and inaugurates an 'act of literature' in which the reader is systematically displaced, constantly, from a linguistic 'homeland'. The 'base-language' of *Finnegans Wake* is and remains a form of English, to be sure; yet, at the same time, the English-language vocabulary is visited constantly by foreign terms that migrate very visibly and audibly into it; and the lexicon becomes one that is, by definition, indefinable, and neither governed nor circumscribed by place or nation.

The questions that concern Joyce here are, fundamentally, also the very questions that are at the core of 'Orwell's The Prevention of Literature'. Orwell fears that his post-war period is one where 'the liberal culture that we have lived in since the Renaissance' might be coming to an end, to be replaced by the menace of totalitarian modes of government.[45] He fears the increased intrusion of mechanical modes of production into the arts, and the uncritical acceptance of the new and narrowed range of thought and imagination that this will engender. He is deeply concerned about the mechanical commodification of culture, and especially of literature; and he is trying to hang on to the idea that literature is what resists such capital commodification. Disney films, he writes 'are produced by what is essentially a factory process', and the same mode of quasi-industrial production afflicts radio programmes and dramas, as well as 'books and pamphlets commissioned by government departments'.[46]

As he extends this argument, its purchase reaches much wider and his remit extends to embrace a much broader series of cultural phenomena. He laments the rise of 'literary schools', all of them 'offering you ready-made plots at a few shillings a time'; and as he explores further the practice of such schools, he argues that 'It is probably in such a way that the literature of a totalitarian society would be produced'.[47]

Structurally, the kind of quasi-industrial mode of production in writing that Orwell castigates is also dangerously and tantalizingly close to our own contemporary institutions of literature, and to some of our vastly expanding University Creative Writing Programmes.[48] Orwell's view is that, in the situation where literature can be 'prescribed', it is also being necessarily simultaneously 'proscribed'. As he puts it, 'Imagination – even consciousness, so far as possible – would be eliminated from the process of writing. Books would be planned in their broad lines by bureaucrats,' he writes.[49] The impulse to literature, as it were, is being radically constrained by bureaucracy, for it is bureaucracy and its linguistic code that determines the limits of acceptable speech, and thus bureaucracy that determines the proprieties of writing. The literary writer has lost her or his language, and now her or his soul must fret in the shadows of the bureaucrats who determine values.

5

Orwell sees clearly the totalitarian aspect of this. He relates it to religion and its associated fundamentalist claims on truth, and thus on the linguistic meanings that shape our discourse. The dean in Joyce is, of course, Catholic; and Orwell relates such Catholicism directly to the inhibition of literature. 'The Catholic and the Communist are alike', he writes, 'in assuming that an opponent cannot be both honest and intelligent';[50] and this is due to the totalizing tendency of the religion and the politics. Furthermore, '[a] totalitarian state is in effect a theocracy, and its ruling caste, in order to keep its position, has to be thought of as infallible'.[51]

There is a recent fictional discussion of this, in *Conclave*, a 2016 novel by Robert Harris. *Conclave* is structured around the election of a new Pope for the Roman Catholic Church; and one of the key dramatizations in the text is between liberal and 'traditionalist' factions within the church. The traditionalist faction laments the fact that the recently dead Pope had continued in the vein of liberalization that had been started in Vatican II; but the argument between tradition and liberality is hinted at right near the start of the text as an argument about language.

English as a world language has a precedent. In the Europe of the Renaissance, a Europe that was setting out on its imperialist expansion, the world around the western Mediterranean had its own world language in Latin. Cardinal Tedesco in *Conclave* is the traditionalist, arguing that the church should return to saying mass and conducting its official business in Latin. He looks around the conclave as the cardinals sit at dinner, and says 'Observe how unconsciously, how instinctively, we have arranged ourselves according to our native language. We Italians are here – closest to the kitchens, very sensibly. The Spanish-speakers are sitting there. The English-speakers are over towards the reception.' His claim is that, before 1962, the Cardinals would have been able to converse more widely, because they all used Latin, 'But then in 1962, the liberals insisted we should get rid of a dead language in order to make communication easier, and now what do we see? They have only succeeded in making communication harder!'[52]

How, asks Tedesco, can there be a Universal Church – a Catholic Church – when it speaks so many different languages. 'Language', he says, 'is vital. Because from language, over time, arises thought, and from thought arises philosophy and culture … We have become a confederation, at best'.[53] His fear is that, with the distribution of languages comes also the distribution of power; and, most significantly of all, the dispersal of place. He concludes his diatribe with the statement that 'The abandonment of Latin … will lead eventually to the abandonment of Rome'.[54]

Rome, of course, had been 'abandoned' before, most particularly in sixteenth-century England, when Henry VIII established the English church and dissolved the monasteries. That dissolution served many purposes, of course; but one of the key elements in this, important to my argument here, is that it is related to the ownership and control of the land itself that the monasteries (and Rome) occupied both materially and symbolically. One of the things in Henry's mind was the question of the material wealth of the

Roman church; and, in dissolving the monasteries, he began also the process of disengaging the land itself from wealth as such. In a very fundamental, if somewhat cursory, manner, the establishment of a protestant religion coincides with – and perhaps also encourages and accelerates – the emergence of a capitalist ethos, significantly associated explicitly and nominally with the shifting of a capital city. Rome is replaced by Canterbury.

This is also tied to the emergence of a specific version of the institution of literature. Weber's famous 1904–5 thesis regarding *The Protestant Ethic and the Spirit of Capitalism* tied religion firmly to economics. Central to that thesis, controversially, is the 'calling' (*der Ruf*), deriving from Luther but being more firmly established by various puritanisms, including especially that of Calvinism. According to this, *der Ruf* calls us to the fulfilling of our secular duties; and in this regard, it is explicitly opposed to a Catholicism in which the monastery is a space that divorces itself from the material conditions of life. In fact, of course, many of the English monasteries dissolved by Henry were quasi-feudal institutions, in which the local peasant population worked the land for the monks, who gained in wealth thereby while offering spiritual but not financial rewards as a mode of recompense for labour. In this respect, they operated precisely akin to those country houses that I explored when considering 'estate poems' and their relation to feudal literary structures. Yet the monastery is also one of the original 'ivory tower' institutions, diverting attention from mundane everyday existence and towards a spiritual realm. In doing so, it gives a veneer to the church's own capitalization of wealth while ostensibly castigating the very idea of material venality.

Weber ties the calling to another fundamental aspect of Protestantism: Calvinist predestination. If one subscribes to the belief in predestination, then, psychologically, a certain attitude follows, and one that is important for my argument. One can never know for sure that one is predestined for salvation. As a result, one looks at the world constantly (and, paradoxically, superstitiously) for 'signs' that one is of the elect – our contemporary 'elites' – and will be saved. If we are constantly looking for signs of our salvation in the world round about us, then two things follow. First, there is a new attention to be focused specifically on the private individual as such, and we get the establishment of 'character' as a focal point for fiction. Secondly, that individual becomes conditioned by what we might call low-level paranoia, in which he or she starts to see everything in the world as an enigmatic and covert address specifically to them, to be interpreted by them as a secret sign privately and personally indicating salvation. After all, if one is to be damned, one hardly wants advance notice of the fact; and so our interpretation of these mysterious signs is one in which we are already predisposed to find ourselves as being of the elect or the elite (the words are cognate).

Cartesian philosophy – itself a precursor and harbinger of cultural modernity – is a prime example of such thinking.[55] The world becomes a noisy place, as it were; and everything in it that is solid melts into the airy nothing of a sign. Fiction is the exploration of precisely the doubts – the fundamental *dubio* that informs Cartesian philosophy – that exist now as a constituent factor in the everyday life of the individual; and money is likewise not just a *sign* of wealth but also a sign that registers the value, standing and *election* of the private individual. The two go together, and will eventually coalesce in Samuel Johnson's famous statement that 'no one but a blockhead ever wrote for anything except money', or, worse, in the identification of moral value with wealth itself.

Our contemporary version of this lies firmly within the institution of literary studies, but it has migrated into the field of the theory of criticism. More specifically, the rise of contemporary institutionalized versions of cultural studies, focusing largely (though not exclusively) on hermeneutics and semiotics, is shaped by precisely the same mentality. In this modern counterpart, however, we also have a slightly different stage of economic relations. Now, the airy and immaterial sign of things supplants the materiality of the things of the world themselves; and, correspondingly, the sign of money – in our increasingly 'virtual' economies the credit card and e-banking – replaces even the already flimsy reality of the promissory note. We have returned to a credit economy, akin to that which I explored under the heading of 'credibility' in my opening chapter.

Orwell thought less in terms of credibility and more in terms of integrity. Intellectual integrity, Orwell argued, was always marked by a spirit of Protestant rebellion or protest at 'the state of things'. Such a spirit is inimical to deference. It is especially resistant to any notion of deference to unearned authority: the intrinsic deference that structures feudalism, or the blind trust in a lord, master, pope, king, or, indeed, in any unearned authority. The worst of it, for Orwell in 1946, is that the very people who should be defending the writer's freedom and integrity are the people who are most dangerous and threatening towards it. This position is, in fact, still extant in our institutions.

If press freedom is characterized by critique and opposition to orthodoxy, as Orwell suggests, it follows that we have a very specific (and under-explored) paradox in his writing. We must put alongside this view – the view that freedom is marked by the unorthodox – Orwell's further view that 'What is really at issue' in the attacks on press freedom 'is the right to report contemporary events truthfully'.[56] This latter position depends on us seeing what is actually the historical case; and Orwell's view is that this is what the press is actively occluding. Worse, the readership colludes in this; and we get the 'establishment' view of what constitutes historical truth, a view that becomes orthodox and which garners uncritical acceptance among a general readership.

If we have these two positions in mind at the same time – freedom being marked by unorthodox views; and the necessity of truthful and accurate reporting of what has happened – it follows that, for Orwell, the report of the 'truth' of *what has happened* historically is axiomatically different from *what we believe has happened* (this latter being represented as 'the orthodox view'). It further follows that 'reality' is marked by some internal fissure or disintegration; and that 'realism' in writing would have to be itself somehow structurally deconstructive, or marked by a kind of internal dissenting voice.[57] This, in short, is what Fredric Jameson – as we have seen – will eventually attempt to describe as the key factor in what he calls 'the antinomies of realism'.

Jameson argues that, to grasp realism properly, we have to understand that it is not to be understood simply as being in opposition to other, non-realist, modes (romance, modernism, and so on.). Rather, we must see that it is intrinsically linked to dialectical modes of thought, and thus we must work 'by grasping realism as a historical and even evolutionary process in which the negative and the positive are inextricably combined'. In other words, we need to grasp realism 'as a paradox and an anomaly, and the thinking of it as a contradiction or an aporia'.[58] Jameson is putting in quite difficult philosophical terms what Orwell expresses in ostensibly simpler but actually more complex form. Both arrive at a similar position, however, which I will summarize thus: 'literature' is 'what happens' when we discover that there is an inevitable gap between ontological historical matter and epistemological formulations describing or inscribing that matter in the form of language. Put yet more simply: 'literature' (as opposed to more general 'writing') produces dissonance: literature is indeed literary to the extent that it yields unruly and even irreverent attitudes towards history and, yet more importantly, towards the reading or writing subject who believes that she or he can come to 'know' the truth of history. Literature is not only fundamentally critical in this regard (in one formulation of Jameson's, marked by demystification), but it is also inherently conditioned by 'impropriety', by an implicit critique of everything that is marked by 'property' and ownership. Above all, it calls into question the ownership of place: land, estate, nation.

The question of how this plays out within our contemporary institutions of literature – and especially those of education – is the subject of my next chapter.

5

Inequality, Management and the Hatred of Literature

1

The relationship between literature and capital has always been treated with some awkwardness. It is seen as an embarrassing question, largely because it is very controversial. Responses hover uncertainly between two extremes, with many critics sitting uncomfortably somewhere on a spectrum between those extremes, and usually circumventing some fundamental issues. We can loosely identify those fundamental issues as issues related to 'the monetization of the aesthetic function'. Both extremes of the current prevailing positions appear to find the directness of that formulation a kind of embarrassment; and so, they manage to avoid confronting the most fundamental aspect of 'capitalized letters', or of how literature can both be capitalized on and can resist capitalization and the entire economic norms of capitalism.

On one side of the existing critical positions, the argument is that literature transcends economic issues, operating in a metaphysical realm, an immaterial realm of 'spirit' or 'emotional truth' or 'feeling'. These realms are where we circumvent economic and sociopolitical issues; and literature is seen as a protected space that provides an escape from the everyday. This is literature as *Stimmung*, as the production of a mood in which harmonious community is idealized.[1]

At the other extreme, we have an argument that suggests that the relation is one where the economic conditions that organize a social formation determine and condition the stories that it tells to itself. Consequently, literature in this latter view is seen and read as something 'symptomatic' of those conditions: we can read, in these symptoms, the actual condition of the real object of inquiry: the social formation itself. Paradoxically, this second position also dissolves the materiality of literature itself, seeing it as a reflection in some way of an entity that is yet 'more' material: the economic and social conditions that shape everyday life, and that shape 'real individuals, their activity and the material conditions under which they live, both those which they find already existing and those produced by their activity'. This position gives us, as a starting-point, the real and empirical conditions of men and women, what Marx and Engels called the 'existence of living human individuals'.[2]

The first position outlined above tends to a specific kind of 'premature utopianism' in which it is proposed that all readers are somehow always already harmoniously equal, in that we are all supposedly 'equal before the text'. This yields that specific critical ideology that became normative throughout the latter half of the twentieth century, and that went by the name of the New Criticism. The New Criticism strove to disengage the text from its explicit conditions of production, isolating it and bracketing it off from material everyday realities as a 'verbal icon' or 'well-wrought urn'.[3] It invited the reader to focus neither on the production nor on the reception nor even on the relation of the work to the material conditions of history, Instead, we should focus – as in the famous aphorism – on 'the words on the page', and examine how those words are structured internally and intrinsically, with a reference primarily to themselves, and according to a specific kind of physics, as if texts were organized around internal linguistic forces.

The text was to be seen as structured around what is essentially a single characteristic trope, however variously described it may have been: as an internal tension (in Allen Tate); as irony (in Wayne Booth); as a type of ambiguity (in William Empson); or paradox (in Cleanth Brooks); and so on. This had the effect of removing from our primary consideration class-tensions and material struggles or conflicts such as we see it when literature is related to land or nation-State or proprietorial ownership. Yet more historically pertinent, it also removes or distances literature from the very specific historical conflict that was the 1939–45 War. The essence or 'content' of these material conflicts are displaced onto 'culture' itself, where they are safely played out as *formal* tensions within a circumscribed literary criticism. Such conflicts, now relocated as mere tensions, *Spannung*, are 'contained' by literature, exercised only within the non-material or metaphysical space of an ideal reader, even if the ideal is only ever an 'implied' – but unreal – reader.[4]

This implicit evasion of issues of capital was not limited to work in obviously pro-capitalist nations like the United States. It is found also within revolutionary Russia and the USSR. The roots of what we know as 'Russian Formalism' lie within the late nineteenth century, when the Russian 'plebeian intelligentsia' began to organize in opposition to the quasi-feudal aristocracy. That aristocracy controlled not only the land, but also the cultural values around which Russia was organized. As a leisured class, they regarded poetry and the other arts as 'decorative' and 'ornamental', and thus as objects of value that indicated their wealth and aristocratic taste. For these, art was always already at a remove from direct material conditions, while simultaneously advertising the material (and cultural, personal) wealth of its owners. The 'criticism' that this yielded was, for the plebeian intelligentsia, essentially mystifying, because it was always unsystematic and therefore not amenable to rational debate. A mystifying and oblique aestheticist criticism essentially divorced the lower classes from the possibility of sharing in the wealth that was constituted in art. The plebeian intelligentsia therefore rejected this kind of work, and in the rejection there lay a fundamental rejection of aestheticism as such.[5]

At stake, then, as Russia moved into the early twentieth century, was the question of how people – a much wider and more general constituency than just the aristocracy – could regulate and debate questions of cultural value. Given the intrinsic conflict of interests between the aristocracy and the people, these questions would now become the centre of cultural struggles, essentially as a cover for more fundamental struggles over the structure of the economy and the society. No longer was it to be easily tolerated that the aristocracy would 'own' such values, in the ways in which they owned the land; rather, the inherent subjectivism of this was now in contestation with a preferred quasi-scientific and 'objective' set of criteria for the evaluation of works of art. The result of this was a high seriousness that is paid to art; and a seriousness that eventually articulates itself through the texts of Russian Formalist theory, as a phenomenon that emerges from the debate between subjective priority and objective debate. That high seriousness will become yet more pointed and urgent in a time of warfare. Later, its practitioners found themselves in awkward positions with regard to Stalinism.

At the other extreme, we developed, especially in the wake of these Formalist exercises, a more properly Marxist engagement with the relation of literature and capital. This, however, has also had some difficulties in finding its proper articulation. At its weakest, it sees categories and figures that are central to Marxist philosophy being more or less crudely 'imported' into readings of literary texts: Heathcliff in *Wuthering Heights* becomes a representative of the working-class, say, or of the expropriated Irish. Much stronger than this are those engagements – such as in the much more serious and sophisticated work of Fredric Jameson, for example – that delineate structural parallels between what is happening in the economic sphere and what is happening as normative in the realm of values within the field of literary and cultural production more generally. These find their source in debates around the relative worth of Modernist experimentation set against accounts of Realism.[6]

In this latter case, however, while the critic typically seeks to find clearly 'causal' relations between the conditions of capital and the determinations of cultural production, the issue of the specific value of the aesthetic as such can become lost. At its best, as in the work of critics who essentially follow the austerities of Adorno (such as Jameson himself, or Neil Lazarus within world-literary studies), the socio-economic conditions of a social formation are seen as impacting directly not on the *content* of literary works but rather on the constraints of their *form*. This, too, therefore focuses our attention on form as such, even if this time form is itself construed (as with *Stimmung* in Gumbrecht) as a material and essentially historical phenomenon and not just as an aesthetic preference.

The work in the pages that follow will cleave more closely to the path of the second position described here; but I also want to try to continue to drive home the fundamental questions about the real state of the economy. My claim is that we have never quite fully escaped from feudalism as our foundational structure, or – and this may amount to the same thing in practice – that we have entered a new phase of capital that is essentially neo-feudal and a rehabilitation of the value of 'real estate'.[7] At the heart of this is the monetization of the aesthetic, and our ability to capitalize on letters and literature. The exploration of this basic question relies on our being able to map the ways in which 'literature' has been established institutionally; and this means that we need to understand literature as a phenomenon that does not occur just 'innocently' and in isolation from its realization as a material force. Literature is something that is made or 'occasioned' by criticism and by theory, and it is a phenomenon that takes its primary and determining shape from the institutions of education: school and university. It is criticism and theory – as they are enacted in our institutions of education – that transform 'writing' into 'Literature'. In summary, the key to explaining the contemporary relation of literature to capital lies in the question of the institutional framing of some texts precisely as capital-letter L of Literature.

2

Why should there be such a concern about the relation of capital to literature? Above all, why is it the case that, within an explicitly capitalist culture such as that of the United States, there would develop a criticism – American New Criticism – that would claim an already achieved or at least hypothesized 'equality'? And why would that critical ideology gain such ground when it did, in the mid-twentieth century? Why also does it persist in ideas of harmony or Gumbrechtian *Stimmung*? Historically, it is clear that the 1939–45 War had revealed – and even in fact had generated – all sorts of economic inequalities, in terms of the material conditions of the lives of people. The post-1945 period in Europe – but perhaps above all and most characteristically in England – was characterized as what we must now call our *first* 'age of austerity'. It is the 'first' such age because, post-2008, post-9/11, post-Iraq and post-Arab Spring, we live in an alleged new such age of austerity – an age again conditioned by the prevalence of war across the world – as the logic of economic austerity is peddled worldwide as a social necessity by our political class.

Interestingly, our current period of allegedly necessary economic austerity, post-2008 financial crisis, had this serious historical forebear, precisely at the time when Orwell was worried about the prevention of literature in the period between 1945 and 1951. Yet the ideologies of those two periods (1945–51; post-2008) are also remarkably different in at least one significant instance. The difference lies in the attitudes of the polity to its economic predicaments. Our contemporary period is marked by a serious disengagement between, on one hand, a political elite driven by the demands of the 1 per cent hyper-wealthy and, on the other, a remarkably sustained series of moves designed to weaken and disenfranchise the 99 per cent, and to render their needs invisible. Things were different in the earlier period, described by Michael Sissons and Philip French as one where 'The great social experiment that was being conducted gave rise to a sense of crusading idealism, and to virtually all a feeling of involvement in national affairs which was to become muffled in the following decade'.[8]

That 'feeling of involvement' – a feeling that would be gradually but insistently muffled through time – constituted the drive towards a greater degree of social and economic equality; but 'austerity', in our own time, is driven, as we know, by the demand for ever-greater and structural inequality. That 'demand' may be unstated (unsurprisingly), but it is nonetheless entirely undeniable. As Piketty has recently argued, a certain new logic also exists, for, in our time 'the key issue is the *justification of inequalities* rather than their magnitude as such'[9]; and I shall argue here that among the key instruments for establishing that justification is the way in which we have institutionalized literature in the decades around the 2008 crisis. That institutionalization is shaped by a hierarchical structure, not just among texts but also among the institutions in which those texts are read; and the hierarchy in question is itself shaped by differences in wealth. We have the modes of capital that are invested in letters – and thus the very institutionalization of literary study itself – as the very fundamental basis of social inequality.

In political terms, 'harmony' is replaced by a much cruder rhetoric, through which the 'austerity Chancellor' in the UK, George Osborne, repeatedly claimed that 'we are all in this [economic predicament] together'. We might have been 'in it together', but some were drowning while others were surfing serenely, safe, over the bodies of the drowned. In 1986, Primo Levi gathered together a number of his memories related to his time in Auschwitz, *I Sommersi e I Salvati*; and as he opens his meditation on the condition in the camps, he points out that there is 'a paradoxical analogy between the victim and oppressor'. They are 'in it together', certainly, but even though 'both are in the same trap … it is the oppressor, and he alone, who has prepared it and activated it'. The injustice that is governed by such massive inequality before the facts of the case arises from this, because 'if he [the oppressor] suffers from it, it is right that he should suffer; and it is iniquitous that the victim should suffer from it'.[10]

In economic terms – and without the trauma of such memories (though these, too, are shaped by capital) – we can start from a further short engagement with Piketty's analysis of our contemporary legitimizations of gross inequalities in the sphere of capital and the regulations of its distribution; and this will also allow us to explain the contribution to capital inequality that our contemporary institutions of literature are making and endorsing.

Piketty takes France during the twentieth century as a paradigmatic example of his thesis. He finds that wars play a central role in the understanding of how equality and inequality are calibrated. 'In the twentieth century,' he writes, 'it was war, and not harmonious democratic or economic rationality' that changed things in French society and elsewhere. Between 1914 and 1945, inequality was steadily – and greatly – reduced, despite it being also factually the case that 'there was no gradual, consensual, conflict-free evolution toward greater equality'.[11]

That general trajectory held up broadly in France right through the period of the May Events of 1968, themselves partly driven by an ideology that had sharpened its social critique in and through opposition to the Vietnam War. After 1968, a new dispensation and settlement had to be reached in France; and it was done through the Grenelle Accords.[12] These accords had a central economic plank that led to what Piketty describes as a massive compression of wage inequality. For a start, the minimum wage was increased by a factor of some 20 per cent. As a result, viewed historically in the following years, 'The purchasing power of the minimum wage … increased by more than 130 per cent between 1968 and 1983'. Simultaneously, 'the mean wage increased by only about 50 per cent', and these two facts combine to give the resulting effect of 'a very significant compression of wage inequalities'.[13]

In the early 1980s that trend is reversed, not just in France but also worldwide, driven by a new economics of austerity, starting in the first instance in France with a socialist government. Mitterand's government (with Pierre Mauroy as Prime Minister and Jacques Delors as Minister of Economy) had begun by making huge investment in public services, and by addressing the issue of wage inequality and – especially – the inequality of access to elite higher education. This was especially the case in relation to the entry requirements for access to the prestigious ENA (Ecole Nationale d'Administration), where regulations that essentially favoured the already socially and culturally privileged were changed to favour a wider social constituency. However, in terms of economics, the general thrust here – towards reflation that would be grounded in the growth on consumption – led to a significant budgetary deficit; and Delors and Mauroy then instituted an 'austerity budget' in 1983 to try to deal with that deficit.

1983 is also a year in which Reaganomics and Thatcherism are getting properly under way. Both are shaped by supply-side macroeconomic theory, with lower taxation and deregulation as key elements, both of which lead to a systematic transfer of commonly shared wealth into the hands of a smaller number of individuals. The name given to this – especially in the UK under Thatcher – was privatization. It found a generous reception among the English, perhaps revealing once again that trait of English-nationalist privacy that had been noted by Orwell – and discussed in my preceding chapter – as a key determinant of English identity.

This thrust to privatization long pre-dates Thatcher, however. Perhaps paradoxically, it can be traced back to the immediate post-war period – paradoxically precisely because this is the period most usually associated with the radical public service ethos of the 1945 Attlee administration. One of the issues that Attlee faced, however – as had been made clear by the Beveridge Report in 1942 – was a serious housing crisis, exacerbated by the fact that much of the existing housing stock had actually been destroyed by bombing.

A prime location for this social problem was Coventry, which was in desperate need in the late 1940s.

Yet here, as David Kynaston reveals, public spirit was not much in evidence. He cites a survey undertaken in Coventry in 1948, which 'revealed how tenants on one of Coventry's newly built suburban estates (Canley) had at most only a very limited sense of community'. What was of utmost importance to them, it turned out, 'was their privacy'; and 'It was a desire for privacy that extended to their most precious possession'. That most precious possession was not their home; but the cars or motorbikes that they were making during the heyday of car-production in Coventry itself and across the English midlands. Yet, what they really needed was an *extension* of their privacy, in the sense that they needed a private space 'added' to the house, requiring further land: a garage in which they could protect their vehicles.[14]

In the immediate post-war period, economic growth across western Europe and the United States was extraordinarily high. Government investment, following a Keynesian strategy, ensured high levels of employment, and thus high economic general activity. As Jerry Z. Muller points out, 'automobile construction grew from half a million in 1947 to over nine million annually in 1967' in western Europe alone.[15] With the rise of Galbraith's 'new affluence', new levels of comfort were achieved for the many; and this provokes a new cultural development: 'for the first time in history', writes Muller, '"leisure" became a problem'.[16]

If 'leisure' is a problem, it is so only because it intrinsically resists simple commodification: leisure is not a product, like a car or a fridge. This means that leisure is 'a problem' only for capitalism itself: it is clearly not a problem for individual human beings, at least not in principle. As Adorno and others argued, capital quickly found ways of neutralizing leisure's radical potential, by converting cultural activity into an industry that 'produces' culture and leisure as a series of consumable items: culture-for-sale and the monetization of leisure.[17] Reading, of course, is one classic expression of leisure. Literature – which had occasionally been seen in idealized terms as a shelter from the regular modes of capital – finds itself increasingly subsumed into capitalist modes of production and consumption, in the leisure and culture industries, and also, crucially, in educational apparatuses and institutions.

Leisure – when viewed from the perspective of a capitalism that recognizes only production and profit – is a threat to social and political power and control, because leisure is something that – in principle and prior to its industrial commodification – is something that is essentially open to forms of collectivization and public commonality. Capital fears such collective thinking and action as something beyond its control, and therefore as something that menaces the straightforward individualist work-ethic that shapes the capitalist project. Capital is incapable of seeing the human as anything other than as a labouring productive force; and leisure, intrinsically, is not 'productive' – at least not productive of commodities for sale.

Leisure thus has to be captured, controlled and 'domesticated' for capital. Its commodification brings it into line with the atomization of the social space, with a view to ensuring that individualism becomes normative while all forms of collective thought or action become suspect. This, in turn, becomes the core aspect of the Thatcherite privatization agenda, which was centrally concerned with the destruction of trade unions and with the public and community spirit that informed such collectives. By extension, reading is now something that is to be conducted for private purposes, in a room of one's own.

The extension of private property, primarily in the arena of privatized housing, was the cornerstone of Thatcherism. In 1956, the American folk- and protest-singer, Woody Guthrie, had composed his anthemic 'This land', singing that 'This land is our land'. Its key stanza for the argument here is direct: 'There was a big high wall there that tried to stop me; / Sign was painted, it said private property / But on the back side it didn't say nothing / That side was made for you and me'.[18] Between the mid-1950s and the early 1980s, the contestation of land-ownership was central to political culture. The UK's 1913 Census revealed that private home ownership stood then at a mere 23 per cent. It was the period between 1953 and 1971 that saw a huge sudden upsurge in the numbers of privately owned households, such that by 1971, around 50 per cent of homes were in private hands.

Thatcher's 'right to buy' housing project explicitly rejected the claims of egalitarians such as Woody Guthrie, and extended this 50 per cent quite radically, such that by the end of the twentieth century, we had almost the reverse of the position in 1913. In 1913, 23 per cent owned and 77 per cent rented; by 2001, some 69 per cent owned and only 31 per cent rented.[19] In this change – a change that was accelerated ideologically through the 1980s with government-directed support, using government funds raised from general taxation – publicly owned property (council housing) was steadily converted into a series of private goods that amounted to a privatized ownership of land itself: Guthrie's big high walls with no trespassing signs. Private property such as this, however, is a kind of 'stored wealth'. It becomes a form of investment that entails a fall in economic activity, as it takes spending out of the general economy and places it in the acquisition of land by private (and now indebted) individuals. Once again, credit and credibility become axiomatic to survival; but in our contemporary moment, such credibility is directed only towards capital itself; and if literature is to play any part in this, then literature too can survive only by being capitalized in the monetization of aesthetics.[20]

The appropriate measure of this relates to how much actual wealth is embodied in private housing. Danny Dorling has shown that 'between 1971 and 2002 the value of homes held by the population of the United Kingdom rose 50 fold in contemporary prices'; and what this means is that the wealth vested in private housing has gone, in that period, from £44 billion to £2.4 trillion. Furthermore, 'the share of national wealth held in the form of housing has almost doubled from 22.1 per cent to 42 per cent' over this same period.[21] The result of this is the production of 'Generation Rent', an entire generation who are unable to own housing, but who are dependent on a small number of landlords who own the property and own the land. Rentier capitalism is the result; and it has a direct corollary in the field of literary study, to which it is intimately linked, if only at a deep structural level.

That which was once common – space and land itself – becomes subject to the laws of atomized and privatized ownership. In economic terms, both within and beyond the UK, global wealth starts to be distributed extremely unequally, and it is once again dependent on a rentier society with its quasi-feudal structures.

Cultural wealth follows the same pattern. As culture, including literature, becomes mediated first as a leisure activity and then commodified in a series of industrial processes – well tracked by Adorno, Benjamin and others – it, too, is transferred systematically into the hands of an elite or chosen few. This is the key to the institutionalization of literature. It depends on the way in which our society regards it as normative to capitalize on letters, on literature and on all forms of leisure and culture: it depends on literature becoming capital and aesthetics being monetized and evaluated only in the form of money.

3

It is in the wake of this 1980s privatization project that Piketty notes the significant reversal of the earlier positive trend towards greater social equalities. The reversal takes a very specific and significant form. It is marked first of all by the return of a rentier society, rehabilitating the importance of capital wealth as such, especially insofar as that is vested in the ownership of property and land. As we see this reflected in recent English fiction, it produces the new account of the city of London, where foreign citizens buy houses not for the purpose of living there but simply as capital investments. This explains some of the logic that underlines Lanchester's *Capital* and Coe's *Number 11*: houses are not even rented out here, because the capital return on them no longer needs the actual materialization of rent. We have gone even beyond a stage of rentier capitalism; and the consequence, in literature, is a fiction that highlights not just the increasingly immaterial conditions of wealth (in money that has no actual existence, in Lanchester's case), but also the driving of capital further and further underground, into the very substructures of our societies (as in Coe's eleven-story basement).

A new factor also emerges, however; and it is this that is of most significance in relation to the extended institutions of literature. This new element is the rise of the managerial class, with the 'astonishing heights' of salary inflation that are reached by top executives and managers, especially in financial services, but also, increasingly, right across the managerial class as such.[22] We will find that the institutionalization of literature, when related explicitly to capital, requires that literature be subject to management. Furthermore, this management extends to those engaged in the study of literature, such that readers and writers themselves become re-configured in terms of 'human capital'.

The consequence is that as history has continued the trend towards re-establishing large economic inequalities essentially as the normative condition of social life, we have reached a new social construct today. 'To a large extent', argues Piketty, 'we have gone from a society of rentiers to a society of managers'. The distinguishing characteristic of the manager, in terms of labour conditions, is that the manager essentially lives off the labour of others. In feudalism, the lord lived off the fat of the land, a land that was worked by labourers who were dependent on the lord for their survival and livelihood. Now, the manager lives parasitically off the material labour of the office-worker, as it were; and, correspondingly, the office-worker's livelihood is increasingly in the hands of her or his manager. We have moved, therefore from a society of rentiers or 'people who own enough capital to live on the annual income from their wealth', to a new society 'in which the top of the income hierarchy ... consists mainly of highly paid individuals who live on income from labour'.[23]

This meets with little resistance, partly because it seems to be an advance on the servility of feudalism; and the labourer or office worker is encouraged to feel that she or he is earning precisely through their labour itself – which seems fair and equitable in principle. However, what this occludes is the fact that the manager is now essentially a member of an entirely different class; and the structure of the relation between worker and official/manager is extremely close to that of feudalism. There is, as it were, an absolute barrier between the lives and interests of the managerial class and the lives and interests of the 'human resources' whose labour makes the wealth of the managerial class possible. In Piketty's terms, it is as if we have gone from a society of 'superrentiers' to 'a less extreme form of rentier society, with a better balance between success through work and success through capital'.[24] In this, the inequalities and potential injustices involved in the relation are hidden from view, and, being virtually invisible in this way, it is difficult to resist them. Yet, these inequalities and injustices are no less real and substantial for that. The key for us is to understand how it is that the institutions around literature contribute both directly and indirectly – if often invisibly or only in covert fashion – to this extension of economic and associated inequalities.

Historically, a very specific 'invisibility' has dominated a good deal of economic theory, especially around the operations of capital: Adam Smith's famous 'invisible hand'. Put very simply, the invisible hand is a mechanism that is supposed to help to establish equilibrium within a free market. It supposedly translates self-interest into public benefit; and it does this essentially by regulating and calibrating self-interest and benevolence in such a way as to identify the workings of a market with the general workings of all human and natural interactions or communications. Essentially, the exercising of *private capital* by private individuals will engender a more equitable and 'proper' distribution of goods and wealth (and also, of course, the human interactions and communications that constitute literature) than would any public force, such as that of a centralized or *dirigiste* government agency.

How do these two invisibilities relate to each other? And how might they relate to the institution of literature? The answer lies partly in Piketty's alertness to the rise of the managerial class, especially (for the present argument) within our educational institutions, such as schools and universities. The rise of the managerial class has itself produced a specific kind of invisibility: the invisibility – and irresponsibility – of the individual manager.[25] Within our institutions, management *systems* have increasingly replaced *individuals* who will assume responsibility for their acts and judgements. Thus it is that, if we discover some wrong-doing, all the individuals within the system blame the system as such: as individuals, they are nothing more than mere 'operatives' of the system, even when it is a system for whose operation they should be responsible. This is crazy, especially when it reduces students and teachers to being mere 'operatives' of 'the function of criticism'.

As Arendt has told us, 'In every bureaucratic system the shifting of responsibilities is a matter of daily routine'. The resulting 'delegation of blame' leaves individual managers intact, despite the fact that they are themselves in charge of a corrupt system. It follows, for Arendt, that 'if one wishes to define bureaucracy in terms of political science, that is, as a form of government – the rule of offices, as contrasted to the rule of men, of one man, or of the few, or of the many – bureaucracy unhappily is the rule of nobody and for this very reason perhaps the least human and most cruel form of rulership'.[26] We can add to this that, just as this is bad for government of any polity, so also it is bad for governance within any institution. Literature, criticism and literary study all constitute just such an institution and are afflicted by this mode of governance, a mode that is intimately related to the operations of business, capital, and the increased acquisition of private profits that, being private, must also be unequally distributed.

Institutionally, literature and literary criticism have been formed in their basic and fundamental aspects by the bureaucratic condition that shapes our actual experience of them. We can explore this in the 1980s debates around 'the canon' and canon-formations. Those debates were often associated with the so-called 'theory wars'; but, in fact, they were shaped much more by the vested interests of capital.[27] The 'theory wars' were often registered as arguments over the 'canon' of literature. Figures like Allan Bloom, in *The Closing of the American Mind* (1987), Roger Kimball, in *Tenured Radicals* (1990), and Dinesh D'Souza in *Illiberal Education* (1991) all attacked vigorously the movements that had been proposed by colleagues who were interested in the philosophical, cultural and political dimensions of 'continental theory'. Moira Weigel has recently pointed out that the three individuals whom I have named here, like many others involved in the attack on theory, were funded to make their attacks. The funders were explicitly neo-liberal capitalist individuals and organizations, including the Koch Brothers, the Olin Foundation and the Scaife Foundation.[28] These were all concerned to advance the corporatist agenda, an agenda that led to the massive increase in economic inequalities. Those inequalities, in turn, form the solid backdrop to the financial crisis of 2007–8.

When John Guillory decided to explore what he called the crisis in literary study – a crisis that is visible in the continual degradation of the intrinsic value of arts and humanities in our societies – he began from an analysis of how canon formation happens. It is the school, he argues, that 'regulates and thus distributes cultural capital *unequally*'.[29] The canon of literary work, he argues, is not adequately explained by the idea of a 'list' of 'great works', but is instead the product of a dynamic process. This process involves not just a discrete elite subject making a list of what he likes; rather, it involves the whole set of social relations – economic and political – that produced that subject as an elite individual in the first place. That is to say: social relations reproduce themselves and their values through a social process of 'schooling' that confirms, in a self-reflexive manner, those social relations, essentially in a free-floating exercise of self-affirmation.

The literary canon, thus, is not just a body of texts, or a list based on principles of inclusion and exclusion. It is, instead, the very mechanism whereby social relations are themselves 'transmitted' not just to pupils and students but also across generations. The key social question that arises here is not about 'access'. Our focus should instead be on how the canon lends *credibility* – in the form of credentials – to the individuals who engage with it. This is entirely akin to the mode of credibility with which this present argument started. As Guillory says, 'The school functions as a system of credentialization by which it produces a specific *relation* to culture. That relation is different for different people, which is to say that it reproduces social relations'.[30]

Within the school, we establish a syllabus that institutionalizes an already constituted set of social relations. In doing so, the literary syllabus that we engage with in the schools gives a special standing to the work within that syllabus – and more importantly, it organizes those texts in a set of evaluative relations. Where the social relations that pre-exist the school are fundamentally grounded in economic inequality, that inequality is precisely what the syllabus – and our modes of critical evaluation of the works within it – will validate.

As Guillory indicates at one exemplary point, we can have as many black writers on our syllabi as we like; but this will change nothing socially unless and until we have many more black individuals attending university and doing so with social success. The predominant theoretical arguments in our time are predicated on ideas of identity politics; and, in accordance with this, we change the 'lists' of writers that we study: more women, more people of colour, more working-class individuals, people of more diverse sexualities, more writers with various disabilities, and so on through all groups of persons with legally 'protected characteristics'.

Surely, if this *alone* could effect social change, then it might have begun to do so by now. It hasn't. Racism, sexism, homophobia and so on are as rife socially as ever; and they are so because of the existing condition of capital itself and the social relations that it engenders. The institution of literature – and also that of criticism, which we can now identify precisely as this reproduction of social relations – works first and foremost to keep itself credible through its institutions of education: school and university. It is in this way that literature and criticism are both 'prevented' from having any radical function.

Yet it remains true that, once they are validated in the literary programmes of schools and universities, the texts that we study do endorse certain normative modes of evaluation. It follows from this that what is actually at stake in the so-called canon wars was actually the *distribution* of knowledge and of the 'cultural capital' that such knowledge bodies forth. As far as literature is concerned, this is, first of all, '*linguistic* capital, the means by which one attains to a socially credentialed and therefore valued speech'. Then, it is also a form of '*symbolic* capital, a kind of knowledge-capital whose possession can be displayed on request and which thereby entitles its possessor to the cultural and material rewards of the well-educated person'.[31]

All this being true, why is there a contemporary crisis afflicting the study of literature? Given the argument thus far, the answer should be fairly clear. Our contemporary social relations are such that we have given a new and superior value to a newly emergent class: the new 'professional-managerial class' as Guillory calls them, in language very close to that of Piketty. The rise to dominance of this class – and, more importantly their assumption of the fundamental language of our institutions of value, like the university – has produced a massive decline in the standing of literature and other arts. In their place, we have the rise of technical forms of language and study, and, above all, technical forms of knowledge that can be more immediately monetized.

In the UK university sector, for example, the study of foreign literatures has long since ceded place to the study of foreign languages. The structural relation between language and literature that we saw in India at the opening of this book – in which literary study was more highly validated than language study – is here reversed. It is the fact that the study of a foreign language can be immediately instrumentalized for commercial purposes – that is to say, the fact that it can be immediately monetized – that makes it now more highly regarded institutionally than studying the novels of Balzac, the poetry of Dante, the writings of Goethe, the poetry of Pessoa and so on.

That technocratic language is the bureaucracy of management itself; and it is this language that now dominates our institutions, with the corollary that those who speak what we can now identify as a new language, 'Managerian', are in full control not just of the regulatory mechanisms of our institutions, but also of the content of the work that is done there. This new language replaces an understanding of metaphor (the literal 'transfer' from one discursive domain to another), say, with a claim for 'transferable skills'; it replaces the history of literature with a demand for present-day economic 'relevance' and 'utility' (the language of 'innovation'); it replaces aesthetic sensibility or cultural knowledge with 'skills' that 'instrumentalize' transferable abilities; and so on. This is all in the service of economic capital – capitalism in its now later stages – itself.

The resulting monetization is also subject to the prevailing social and economic conditions and relations; and this means that the monetization of knowledge is again not to be distributed evenly among a population. Rather, it is to be distributed in such a way as to extend the existing structure of social and economic inequality; and the best way to do this is to continue the project of the privatization of commonly held capital – in this case knowledge-capital – and to transfer it into a small number of private hands.

In short, through the privatization economic project, we end up with what is essentially our own 'prevention of literature' strategy, which is at work in our own time and in our own institutions. Literature works and exists at all only because of a commonly shared language, in and through which a community can debate meanings and values. If institutionally, this is devalued in favour of the validation instead of a series of 'private' and privatized values, then literature as such enters into an existential crisis. The monetization of the aesthetic function has led to the decline in value ascribed to literature and criticism in our social relations.

In straightforward terms, then, 'English Literature' – which, as we saw, is intimately tied to the power of the English language worldwide – faces the problems posed by the arrival of a new class of people, with their own prevailing and now dominant language: the managerial class speaking their bureaucratic Managerian. This new language infects teaching and research with an anti-intellectual bacterium. To teach and research properly in the field of literature now is actually to be in explicit opposition to the dominant language and linguistic capital of our university and school institutions, because these have contaminated our educational institutions with a hatred of literature as such. The hatred is underpinned by the belief that there remains something within 'the literary' that resists or might potentially resist capitalist appropriation; and it is this that the bacterium must attack.

Without necessarily directly stating or acknowledging it, the new dominant language of business-oriented Managerian, and its associated set of meanings and values, require that we do not 'teach', but instead we 'manage the flow of information'; we do not 'research', but instead we 'capture grants' and 'manage budgets' in order to 'produce output' that demonstrates its financial 'impact' in terms of Gross Domestic Product (GDP) growth or capitalist spin-out business and commercial activity and so on. Managerian encompasses both government and institutional governance; and it goes, supplicant cultural hand in embracing capitalist glove, with the economic social structures that extend inequalities.[32]

In the UK, such a contemporary 'prevention of literature' strategy actually has a name that reveals entirely its more general and far-reaching purpose. It is called *Prevent*, and is a governmental political strategy for ensuring that terrorism will not gain any ground in UK universities or other educational establishments. *Prevent* will 'work with sectors and institutions where there are risks of radicalization', according to the official documentation of the UK government; and the first such sector or institution is 'education ... providers'.[33] Let's examine that.

4

The entire impetus for every revision of the *Prevent* strategy derives from the speech given in Munich on 5 February 2011 by the then UK Prime Minister, David Cameron. That speech suggests that the focus of the strategy is not terrorism as such, but rather something that David Cameron identifies as 'extremism', seen as 'the foundation, the driver for terrorism'.[34] Alex Carlile (Lord Carlile of Berriew QC, who writes the Preface to the published strategy document, and who chaired its review) prioritizes university institutions when he says that the new strategy will 'provide interested organisations, from the student arena to the worlds of business and politics, with an opportunity they should welcome to declare unequivocally that they oppose extremism and all its consequences'.[35]

Paragraph 4.2 of the Prevent Strategy Review document suggests that government will 'examine the role of institutions – such as prisons, higher and further education institutions, schools and mosques – in the delivery of *Prevent*.[36] The collocation of education with prison and mosque is, indeed, striking. Equally striking is the clear echo, in this contemporary counter-terrorism strategy, of Orwell's anxieties about that other 'prevention', the prevention of literature and its links to a religious fundamentalism (as in Orwell's linking of literature to Protestantism, and his dismissing of Catholicism as a mental structure inimical to independent thought).

The *Prevent* document insists (paragraph 10.57) that 'We are completely committed to protecting freedom of speech in this country'. One knows right away that, when the next word is 'But' – as indeed it is – this initial statement will be essentially so qualified that it will become effectively fully denied; and so it is. The document follows a set of rhetorical manoeuvres that Orwell would have recognized in 1945. First, the theme of freedom of speech is bureaucratized; and second, the Newspeak of Managerian is deployed to change the focus of attention.

In order to allow the government to get round the actual and material politics and ethics of the real freedom of speech issue, and to begin the limitation and circumscription of it, we are reminded that universities are charities 'and must comply with charity law' (paragraph 10.58). This reduces our engagement with a very specific and fundamentally political issue to one focused instead on the general codes of institutional governance and law. As charities under this law 'must act to avoid damage to the charity's reputation' (paragraph 10.59), we can shift attention entirely from freedom of speech to something entirely different: the capital value associated with institutional reputations, themselves governed by the capitalist and marketing agenda of brands and branding. Now, higher education institutions and student unions 'can be challenged on whether they have given due consideration to the public benefit and associated risks notably when they, or one of their affiliated societies, invite controversial or extremist speakers to address students' (paragraph 10.59).

This rhetorical posture invokes threat and menace. The government is not directly telling universities to ban speakers, of course. Why would they, given their overblown statement of concern for protecting freedom of speech (being 'completely committed' to it)? Indeed, that would look precisely like the authoritarianism that they ostensibly deplore. Yet, universities – with their implied tendency to be the seat for extremism – are told here to 'ensure compliance with charities legislation, which includes provisions relating to human rights, equalities and political neutrality' (paragraph 10.59).[37]

Even more significant, however, is that neat linguistic slippage that the text effects between 'extremist' and 'controversial', proposed as if they are semantic equivalents: institutions will be challenged if or when they invite 'controversial or extremist' speakers. At this point, we should again recall Orwell, for whom 'Above quite a low level, literature is an attempt to influence the viewpoint of one's contemporaries by recording experience'.[38] There can be no shying away from controversial topics in bringing about such influence either, since 'even a single taboo can have an all-round crippling effect upon the mind, because there is always the danger that any thought which is freely followed up may lead to the forbidden thought'.[39]

It follows further – from our recollection and insertion of Orwell's argument here – not only that there is a complete disjunction between literature and totalitarian societies, but also that we can identify totalitarianism precisely when it drives its writers and thinkers to conformity with an overarching ideology and to a fundamental resistance to any kind of controversy. In Orwell's case, that ideology was the ideology of 'Englishness'. In our case – as *Prevent* inadvertently makes clear – it is a peculiar combination of Englishness with Christianity. And it finds its legitimizing locale – for the political position that endorses such a limitation of free speech – in the institution of education that houses literature itself: the university.

For Orwell, the logic was clear: 'To write in plain, vigorous language one has to think fearlessly, and if one thinks fearlessly one cannot be politically orthodox'.[40] It also follows, just as surely, that one cannot be linguistically orthodox either. *Prevent* is not just about the prevention of terrorism; it is also about the prevention of anything that could be described as 'unorthodox' or 'critical', terms that slip easily into an equivalence, in the strategy, with 'extremism' and with 'controversy'. It proposes a supposedly 'neutral' mindset as normative, and detects any speech that deviates from that as a mode of speech or writing that is intrinsically and by definition veering towards an unbalanced 'extreme'. This is precisely the prevention of literature in exactly the sense that Orwell understood that phrase.

Today, literature itself is tacitly feared, the suspicion being that it is the site for a latent or incipient terror, given that it inevitably proposes the possibility of establishing the legitimacy of a 'point of view' that deviates from any or all existing norms; accordingly, it must be prevented. The 'neutral' way of preventing literature is to prevent discussion and debate; and, behind that, to present the university institution as a 'safe space' where there can be no room for controversy.[41] Controversy itself – once the lifeblood of thought – is now 'controversial' and 'extremist', and must therefore be curtailed. It follows that thinking as such – the product of controversy – is to be policed, via the structures of institutional management. How better to do this than to insist on the university itself as a safe space, a space that will be deprived of controversy, once it can be policed by rules of civility in behaviour? Essentially, this entails the circumscription of the power of ideas through the managing of our language and modes of expression. In short, it curtails the power of literature (and its engendering of ideas) through the establishment of linguistic decorum (by a management that will police our English language).

The theory or unstated proposition underlying this suggests that students and faculty need to be protected from the very act of thinking itself. Furthermore, the best way to ensure such safety is by attacking the validity of our linguistic engagements, invalidating our semantically substantive dialogue and replacing our language with the blandness of Managerian. Managerian is the new dominant language through which senior managers – acting in concert with a government that fears free speech and freethinking – can control all forms of knowledge capital. They now 'own' that capital, and 'own' us as their human resource deployed to operate its mechanisms.

Dealing purely with generalized abstractions, Managerian also lays a claim to total ideological neutrality; and, given its level of abstraction, it is difficult to engage with it on matters of specific substance. It is anathema to the languages of literature. The contemporary 'prevention of literature', however, is focused therefore on much more than just English Literature. The real quarry is the very idea of a community of speakers, an assembly of any kind, even such a hypothetical 'assemblage' of different voices that shapes a text like Joyce's *Finnegans Wake*. The government believes that 'Radicalisation is about "who you know", not just what you know'. 'Who you know' is the quarry here, for it is the phrase that legitimizes the government's identification of specific communities as the real – if unstated – quarry. It is also, of course, the first question posed by any torturer to her or his victim: 'Give me names', 'Who are your associates?' According to the government strategy, group bonding, peer pressure and indoctrination are necessary to encourage the view that violence is 'a legitimate response to perceived injustice' (paragraph 5.23). Furthermore, the government also propounds the view that 'identity and community are essential factors in radicalisation' (paragraph 5.22), because some groups of people 'can find in terrorism a "value system", a community and an apparently just cause' (paragraph 5.22).

At this point, we should note that literature is nothing if it is not the site of a sharing and a site for the making of what has been called a 'community of interpreters', a group of readers as an audience that can 'listen', or 'attend' to a series of linguistic formulations, and who then make a shared meaning for values that constitutes their communal or group identity: an assembly, like a nation, for example.[42] Furthermore, interpretation by its very nature must invite controversy, because hermeneutic can never be finalized. Hermes invites disagreement, in that he invites either corroborative endorsement of his message or, instead, doubt and misunderstandings about what the message might mean.

The impetus behind *Prevent* is interesting because it forms part of an increasingly recognizable social, cultural and political trend towards thinking of 'society' as an atomized agglomeration of discrete – and private or privatized – individuals, rather than as a community with shared and collective interests of any kind. Any discussion among such individuals must, *ipso facto*, become an act of translation between different and discrete identities or 'places' or languages.

Behind this, there lies what Walter J. Ong once called the fallacy of 'place logic', such as we find it in the late medieval or early modern thinking of Rudolph Agricola. 'Place logic' sees communication as a transfer of meanings from one discrete and private space (that of my head, as it were) into another such space (in this case, your head); and Ong reveals the utter ridiculousness of such thinking, for it leads to a condition in which 'the whole mental world has gone hollow'.[43] Importantly, however, it relates also directly to the advent of print culture and to the specific interplay between the development of capitalism as a form of 'stored wealth' and the book as a form of 'stored meanings', as if meanings were now themselves capitalizable, available like commodities for sale. Essentially, such a model of communication, predicated on this 'place logic', leads to a belief in the normativity of the 'privatization' of the self and of identity as such.

In short, the entire *Prevent* strategy rests on the foundation of an extreme privatization of all human interests; and it encourages such privatization as a norm. If communication is to take place at all under this, then it must become purely transactional; and, further, the transaction's value is to be determined not just by a market of equals, but rather by those who control the overarching language and who determine its evaluative norms – prices, as it were.[44] In this case, that language is the language of conservative ideology governing Englishness, governing the 'right' identity: 'us'. After all, the government is clear that 'there should be no "ungoverned spaces" in which extremism is allowed to flourish without firm challenge and, where appropriate, by legal intervention' (paragraph 3.39).

The government of space (of nation, of land) thus becomes also the government of the tongue. The tongue to which we must defer, moreover, is that of the manager: Managerian has replaced English as our real new 'world language', in the global political context. It dislikes and essentially censors the literature that it hates; and it hates that literature precisely because literature retains the possibility of resistance to institutional control, and of resistance to the flow of economic capital. The university, as the site of the institutionalization of literature, has become complicit with the extension of economic inequalities through its assumption of the norms of capitalist market competition. It has further subscribed to the very idea that knowledge as such is private, and that its task thus is to continue that privatization. This is, indeed, complicit with the corruption of a writing that can be bought. Its erstwhile interest in the formulation of cultural capital – as a mode of resistance to economic capital and as a critique of that capital – has shriveled into an interest in the production of human capital, designed to extend the economic inequalities that were there, in essence, within recognizably feudal structures.

The English tongue is the tongue of government, and it governs by the residue of a class-based society that has its roots in the landed gentry of feudalism. The legacy persists, as I have shown in earlier chapters of this study; but it has taken a specific turn in the post-1945 period. Now, to govern our tongue is also to ensure that we do not speak as a member of an engaged community, for there is to be no such community. Any idea of speaking on behalf of others is precluded, 'prevented' by the sense that any community that does not simply rehearse governmental ideology and norms is incipiently terrorist, or at least 'extremist' and therefore suspect.

In short, we might conclude here by noting that Managerian, as a new world language, discredits literature. This – surely based in a fear of the power that literature might have to disrupt the workings of capital – reveals, behind the fear, a profound hatred of literature as such. In this contemporary moment, letters must be minimized, unless governments that are determined to find money as the source and origin of all private value can capitalize on them. The question that this invites is the one that governs my next chapter: is there no shame at this state of affairs? What has happened to the idea of human dignity and worth in the face of the monetization of aesthetics and the tacit hatred of the arts, humanities, and – above all – literature in our times?

6

Cultural Capital and the Shameful University

1

In 1989, at the end of a decade of great political turbulence, Kazuo Ishiguro published his novel, *The Remains of the Day*. The novel's Prologue is dated 1956, a year of crises, including Khrushchev's 'secret speech' at the Twentieth Congress of the Communist Party attacking Stalinism, the Suez Crisis, and the Hungarian Uprising. 1956 is a pivotal year, exactly halfway between the year of the novel's publication, and the period in which the narrative is largely set, the 1930s, another period of huge political turbulence. What have these two periods in common, and why might the historical culture of the 1930s be available and important to a novelist at the end of the 1980s?

The 1930s saw the rise of Fascism and Nazism across Europe; the 1980s saw the ostensible fall of Communism in the face of what was, ostensibly at least, an emergent neoliberal economic consensus, culminating in the fall of the Berlin Wall.[1] For those with a historical eye, the later 1980s were dominated by a series of high-profile prosecutions of elderly Nazis from the 1930s, including John Demjanjuk and Klaus Barbie. These men, like Rudolph Hess who committed suicide on 17 August 1987, straddle this historical period from the thirties to the eighties. The spectre of Nazism – and the fear that it had persisted and secretly triumphed – also haunted a major international institution: it was alleged in 1985 that Kurt Waldheim,

UN Secretary General in the decade between 1972 and 1981, might have been deeply implicated in Nazi atrocities. The Waldheim affair provides the political unconscious that shapes *Remains*. In his 'Ein letztses Wort', a 'final word' written at the remains of Waldheim's days, Waldheim alluded to those allegations, acknowledging that 'Ja, ich habe auch Fehler gemacht' – 'Yes, I also made mistakes'.[2] It is this idea of Nazism as a 'mistake' that forges the specific cultural link here. In *Remains*, the central character, Stevens, served Lord Darlington of Darlington Hall as butler in the 1930s. Darlington had been a Nazi sympathizer who, at one point, requires the dismissal – by a compliant Stevens – of any Jewish staff. Even when the extent of his Nazism has become clear, Stevens exculpates him, reducing Darlington's Nazi allegiance to 'mistakes'. 'Lord Darlington', he says, 'wasn't a bad man. He wasn't a bad man at all. And at least he had the privilege of being able to say at the end of his life that he had made his own mistakes'.[3]

'Mistakes' constitute the core of the narrative. Stevens is on his 1956 tour, revisiting Miss Kenton, because he needs a rest, as he had been 'responsible for a series of small errors in carrying out my duties'.[4] These errors cause him embarrassment or shame; and it is the link between such shame and the political 'error' of Nazism that will ground my argument here.

Political 'errors' of totalitarian government and of authoritarian governance are 'mistakes' that are grounded in the cult of personality. This was the backdrop to Khrushchev's secret speech. In addition, however, this construing of totalitarianism, authoritarianism – and even Nazism – as a mere 'error' is based on the idea that we can align the cult of the personality of an individual (such as Stalin) with the myth of the personality or 'character' of a nation State. 'Mistakes', in this way, can and do become matters that shape not just the political economy of a nation but also its cultural economy. If such errors are a cause of shame, then we see also the emergence of a new form of capital, one that is based not on culture (or literature) as such, but on morality. Shame will yield us a new way of considering the relation of literature to capital, precisely in terms of a 'moral capital' that is associated with shame and its counterpart in 'dignity'.

Towards the end of *Remains*, Stevens and Dr. Carlisle, the doctor in the village of Moscombe, discuss politics. They are especially interested in the politics of Harry Smith, the local working-class man who strives to engage 'ordinary' people with the political process. The sequence is driven by issues of social class. Smith has stressed the 'dignity' of the ordinary working individual, identifying dignity with democracy itself: 'Dignity's not just something for gentlemen'.[5] Stevens regards this view, emanating as it does from the working-class Smith, as not worthy of 'serious consideration'.[6] Suddenly, Carlisle asks Stevens very directly, 'What do *you* think dignity's all about?' Dignity obsesses Stevens, as it does Harry Smith; but Stevens equates dignity with value or worthiness generally, and he identifies such value with class and social standing. Surprised by the directness of the question, he replies, with equally uncharacteristic directness, that 'I suspect it comes down to not removing one's clothes in public'.[7]

This basic statement relates value – capital as 'dignity' – to broader questions of the relations between the private and the public. Furthermore, it relates these issues to corporeal matters of the materiality of the body, of flesh, even of sex, hinting at the frailty of the physical body. For Stevens, the opposite of dignity – and what therefore gives it its full meaning – is shame; and such shame relates to the fact that, as physical human beings, we are subject to the frailty whose realization is death itself. Shame becomes characterized in terms of a relation between *la vita nuda*, Agamben's 'bare life', and its public manifestation in politics: it is conditioned by privacy, by a logic of privatization, in which that which is intrinsically public (politics) can be sequestered away, a private matter.[8]

Shame is a predetermining condition of what we understand as a form of human dignity, or human capital; and such shame relates directly to moral and cultural capital. Intrinsic to this is an argument about our contemporary institutions of value, and above all the institution that prides itself on the advancing of cultural capital, the 'public' university, an institution menaced by the logic of privatization.

I will structure the argument through some exemplary texts. Ishiguro's *Remains of the Day* examines moral capital; *The Noise of Time* by Julian Barnes extends the argument into the conditions of institutional capital where criticism itself is coloured by the shame of cowardice; and J. M. Coetzee's *Disgrace* explores the relations of cultural capital (and the university as its privileged site) to a new feudalism, where real estate and the ownership of private land become the determinants of all forms of value.

Two texts are earlier precursors that will guide us. Tolstoy, in 'Shame' (1896), inserts ethics into politics, individualizing a political situation, thereby raising issues of individual and liberal value (humaneness) against systemic constructions of value (or bureaucracy); and, closer to our own predicaments, Kafka's *Zur Frage der Gesetze* (*On the Question of our Laws*, probably 1920) puts the issue of shame at the heart of politics itself.

2

'Shame' is a short allegorical tract. Its subject is what Tolstoy called 'legalized crime', the constitutional standing of corporal punishment, specifically punishment by flogging or the imposition of political law directly onto the *vita nuda*. For Tolstoy, this issue is marked by politics, class and education. In 1890s Russia, even in the military, corporal punishment has been seen as regressive, repugnant, and barbaric and has therefore long been abandoned. In civic life, it persists as something that is visited upon individuals from the peasant classes. However, it is not applied to all the peasants, 'but only those who have not finished a course in a popular school'. Flogging becomes emblematic of a crime structured around class, administered by the upper classes to less-educated members of the peasant or working classes. Education and class combine to determine the legalization of this barbaric crime. The logical structure here implies that education is itself an insurance against domination by class.

This – education as protection against an intrinsic class domination based on prejudice and unauthorized illegitimate ideas of innate superiority of one class of people over others – is nowadays a standard cliché. It says that knowledge is power, that education offers social mobility (upwards) between classes, and that while an education may not yield money, it nonetheless offers the rewards of 'soft power' in cultural or intellectual capital. The rarely noted downside of this is that to be less well educated – and, even worse, to be under-educated working or peasant class (like Ishiguro's Harry Smith) – is itself somehow intrinsically shameful. The tacit ideology supporting 'social mobility' – a 'progressive' movement, effected through education, from a lower to a higher social class – is that it is a shaming moral failing for a working-class person not to want to escape her or his class position and condition. The class prejudice that stands thus revealed at the core of 'cultural capital' is something that is morally or ethically dubious (even repellent), based as it is on unwarranted claims to innate class superiority – disparagement of the working class – as a structural principle for the organization of society.[9]

For Tolstoy, corporal punishment is intrinsically shameful. Consequently, he argues, 'such things must be arraigned, because these things, when the aspect of legality is given to them, only disgrace all of us who live in the state where such acts are committed'.[10] 'Shame' is one such shaming arraignment of the practice: a shaming story intended to deploy shame itself as a means of changing conduct.

This structures the text's internal logic: shame is a positive factor in changing shameful activities. The narrative concerns a thieving, frequently drunk soldier, caught repeatedly in various disreputable or nefarious acts. Once caught out, he expects the habitual standard physical punishment; but his commanding officer simply admonishes him and asks him to change his ways. The effect is powerful: 'the soldier was so surprised at this new way of being treated that he changed completely and became a model soldier'.

There is an economic structure that underlies this; and the commanding officer's action calls a prior economy into question and institutes a new one. Crime is no longer 'matched', 'equaled', or economically 'paid for' by punishment, but is instead met by grace or graciousness. Grace rejects an intrinsically shaming economy based on the exercising of corporal punishment for perceived wrongdoing. Tolstoy mocks the idea that there can be a 'calm discussion' of economics, of 'how many rods' are germane and applicable to a specific instance, as if wrongdoing has a rationalized tariff, a hypothetical economic and numerical equivalence between crime and punishment. Any such tariff must be essentially arbitrary; and it therefore lacks the very rationality that it claims as the ground for its legality, making flogging irrational, illegal, and therefore shameful.

The logic here should be followed through: if corporal punishment brings shame upon us, we might equally say, inversely, that shame as such is the condition of our being ruled by the arbitrariness of a law that is based upon the crude power of class (especially if that is legitimized by our ideologies of education-as-social-mobility) instead of reason. Only if we become ashamed at this shame will we do what is required to avoid the legalization of the crime involved in class-based corporal punishment.

Tolstoy establishes a profound link between the claims of an ostensibly positive cultural capital on one hand and the shameful prejudices of arbitrary class-based social order on the other. He is clear on the fundamental illegitimacy and moral worthlessness of the resulting arbitrary law. 'If we have to speak at all of this monstrousness', he writes, 'we can only say that there can be no such law, signatures, or command of the czar that can make a law of a crime, and that, on the contrary, the vesting of such a crime with the form of law proves better than anything else that, where such an imaginary legalization of a crime is possible, no laws exist, but only savage arbitrariness of rude power.'

'Rude power' is essentially unearned authority: an authority that may be legal constitutionally but which lacks any proper legitimacy within modern democratic arrangements, because it has been imposed autocratically or in a quasi-feudal manner. It is power-without-authority: tyranny. The point is that some forms of 'soft power' in cultural capital – such as that of literature within the university institution – will reveal themselves, in fact, to be themselves a form of rude power.

The only way beyond such barbarity, argues Tolstoy, comes not when any individual peasant escapes flogging 'but only when the ruling classes will recognize their sin and meekly confess to it.' Change can only happen when the ruling classes, like the converted soldier in the text, see themselves publicly shamed. The text becomes itself an articulation of the position of the commanding officer, an admonishment of the ruling class; and, like that officer, it acknowledges that change requires patience.[11]

Kafka revisits the motif, in *Zur Frage der Gesetze*, or 'On the Question of our Laws', published in 1931 (though probably written as early as 1920, in the immediate aftermath of the Russian Revolution). Kafka writes: 'Our laws are unfortunately not widely known, they are the closely guarded secret of the small group of nobles who govern us'.[12] From the beginning, according to this account, law divides society, but also establishes class bonds – in this case, the nobility bound together in complicit possession, literal possession, of the laws, laws that are essentially made for the personal interests of the nobility. Further, being in possession of the law, members of the nobility themselves stand 'outside the law, and that is why the laws seem to have been given exclusively into their hands'.

Some dispute the actual existence of these laws, writes Kafka; and those of this disposition 'try to show us that, if any law exists, it can only be this: the Law is whatever the nobles do'. The only way round the paradoxes here would be a revolutionary act through which to effect the overthrow of the nobility – like the Russian Revolution that just preceded the writing of this text. Yet, even though that would be popular, 'no one dares to reject the nobility'. Kafka concludes his short piece with the observation that 'the only visible unquestionable law that has been imposed on us is the nobility, and who are we to rob ourselves of the only law we have?'[13]

This, too, is a shameful condition. Kafka's text laments this cravenness before the nobility, and hankers for a time when the people will own the laws and the nobility will vanish. This is not because of hatred of the nobility. Instead, 'We are more inclined to hate ourselves, because we have not yet shown ourselves worthy of being entrusted with the laws'.

Between Tolstoy and Kafka lies our fundamental question: how do shame, worthiness, dignity, regulate themselves as values? More succinctly, how do we construct value itself – cultural value or cultural capital – from the interplay of shame and dignity? Kazuo Ishiguro explores precisely this terrain.

3

The Remains of the Day establishes value through its explicit opposition between shame and dignity. The key shaming episode relates to Miss Kenton, the housekeeper at Darlington Hall, working alongside Stevens; and the shame is not just moral but also political. Lord Darlington's Nazi sympathies lead him to dismiss two Jewish maids, Ruth and Sarah. Miss Kenton is horrified and threatens to resign if Stevens goes ahead and fires the two young women. She sees the immorality, and is also aware of its politics, in a way that Stevens – deliberately and willfully blind at this point to what he will call the 'errors' of his lord – does not. However, after the two are fired, she stays on, despite her earnest threats. The threat to resign is founded in ideas of dignity and integrity: Miss Kenton does not subscribe to the view that the Jewishness of the maids indicates a lesser worth, as workers or as human beings. Yet she is unable to sustain her dignified position, and to maintain her integrity.

Miss Kenton eventually explains that this was because of her own moral cowardice: 'Had I been anyone worthy of any respect at all, I dare say I would have left Darlington Hall long ago'. So why didn't she? 'It was cowardice, Mr. Stevens. Simple cowardice. . . There,' she concludes, 'that's all my high principles amount to. I feel so ashamed of myself.'[14]

The resignation threat is recognizably consistent with a fundamental principle of all criticism, and perhaps especially of criticism that has serious material high-stakes risks at its core. The dignity of her stance comes from solidarity with those who are wronged, especially those wronged through the exercise of arbitrary and unjustified power by the nobility. Cultural criticism often depends upon the willingness to take similar risks, risks that jeopardize the survival or livelihood of the speaker or critic herself. In this respect, 'free' speech can be a costly business.[15]

In establishing solidarity with the underdog, the critic puts herself willingly in that precarious position, speaking back to the arbitrariness of barbaric 'rude power' the better to expose its lack of reasonable authority, and thus, consequently, its lack of legitimacy. The moral standing of such a speaker rises: she or he foregoes social or personal advancement and financial reward, say, for an increase in *moral capital*. In criticism, moral value is accompanied by this logic of self-sacrifice. Conventional economics would monetize this, based perhaps on a calculation of loss of earnings: Tolstoy's 'how many rods' becoming 'how much profit or loss?' Yet the point is that this critical stance fundamentally rejects conventional monetized economics: its governing principles are not determined by financial considerations, nor indeed by calculation.

Miss Kenton, however, fails to sustain her dignified position: she is aware of the price that her stance might cost; and, afraid of unemployment, with no means of survival, she avoids the risk and fails to bear witness to Darlington's anti-Semitic Nazi politics. Her avowed 'cowardice' is conditioned by the economic demand for self-preservation.[16] When the maids are sacked, there is no recourse to law available to mitigate the 'error' of Darlington. As Stevens acknowledges, it was simply a matter of carrying out their lordship's wishes in a professional manner, for it was 'a task ... that demanded to be carried out with dignity'.[17] As it remains legally permissible for Darlington to sack the maids because they are Jewish, Miss Kenton's only recourse is to morality: 'if you dismiss my girls tomorrow, it will be wrong, a sin as any sin ever was one'.[18]

This is as close as anyone comes to acknowledging how seriously wrong is Darlington's anti-Semitism. When, one year later, Darlington whimsically changes his tune, he too acknowledges that 'It was wrong what happened and one would like to recompense them [Ruth and Sarah] somehow'.[19] Darlington seems also to accept the view that a wrong can be 'recompensed', in terms of the economic logic of the 'tariff' that Tolstoy had exposed as intrinsically irrational and shameful. Money is still key here, for all parties. Miss Kenton loses moral stature because she can't resign, needing the financial security of her job; Darlington thinks that handing over money can right or erase a moral wrong. For the latter, financial capital can eradicate moral shame: you can buy your way into 'justice', like buying religious indulgences in medieval and feudal societies.

Darlington distances himself from responsibility for the action: 'it was wrong what happened', as if 'what happened' did not derive from him. This is precisely the same position as that of Stevens himself, who acts as he does because he regards it as 'dignified' professionally simply to carry out unquestioningly the will of the lord. In the prevailing feudal structure here, responsibility for actions is evaded by being effectively 'outsourced'. The shadowy Mrs. Burnet outsources her anti-Semitism to Darlington, who outsources the responsibility for leaving Ruth and Sarah potentially destitute to Stevens. Behind all this lies the arbitrary 'rude power' of feudal pre-capitalist servility.

Theoretically, then, 'dignity' depends upon a distancing of the self from the material realities of ethical action. Dignity is a matter of establishing and maintaining a 'private self', withdrawn from the struggles of the world, above the bodily materiality of class-struggle or even just rational argument. This is the meaning of restraint and propriety for Stevens. It is important that one does not remove one's clothes in public: it is important that there be a distance between the self and the world. Dignity needs the mediation of a distancing protocol – a veil of sorts – even if that means the refusal to risk changing one's status by entering into a reasoned debate.[20] 'Propriety' becomes intimate with its near cognate, 'property'; and, in this bizarre logic, dignity is the privatization of such property.

The point of class distinctions is to allow those who claim to be inherently superior to distance themselves from social and ethical responsibilities to others. The fundamental issue here is the 'shame of privilege'. In his 1997 'Culture and Finance Capital', Fredric Jameson argued that, in contemporary politics, 'we sense that the problems of ideological analysis are enormously simplified, and the ideologies themselves far more transparent'. If there is a veil here, then it is transparent. Privilege is shamelessly brazen in parading itself, and in establishing greater distances between the privileged class or 1 per cent (Kafka's contemporary 'nobility') and the rest. Jameson goes on: 'Now that, following master thinkers like Hayek, it has become customary to identify political freedom with market freedom, the motivations behind ideology no longer seem to need an elaborate machinery of decoding and hermeneutic reinterpretation; and the guiding thread of all contemporary politics seems much easier to grasp, that the rich want their taxes lowered'.[21]

In the face of this, criticism that relies on moral capital will always fail, because in material terms finance capital trumps moral capital. But what about a more particular form of cultural capital: musical aesthetics? This is the subject of Julian Barnes' 2016 novella, *The Noise of Time*.

4

Barnes depicts Shostakovich, accurately enough, as a composer whose life was often in jeopardy because of his music. What endangered him is the relation between his musical cultural capital and political power, the Stalinist power that governed society through the primacy of fear. For Shostakovich here, 'Fear normally drives out all other emotions as well; but not shame. Fear and shame swilled happily together in his stomach'.[22] As in Ishiguro, shame marks a specific value, allowing us to consider the relation of criticism to cowardice. First, though, it yields a direct link back to Tolstoy. Barnes describes Shostakovich punishing his child, Maxim, for some naughtiness; and 'the boy's shame was often such that it felt as if the punishment were being visited back upon the father'.[23] Corporal punishment, here conditional upon nothing more 'rational' than the supposed superiority of age and experience is, as in Tolstoy, a recipe for the shame we should feel at the very existence of irrational and unjustified privilege which, in the final instance, rests on the threat of violence.

The Noise of Time is structured around Shostakovich's 'conversations with power', conversations shadowed by the threat of a violence that might be perpetrated upon Shostakovich at any time. Power here is not class based but is *institutional*. Stalin has established legal and cultural institutions that operate as vehicles for the maintenance of his own power. Those who operate the institutions are apparatchiks, bureaucrats who function as the instruments of power. It is the simple knowledge of how this system works – a conscience, as it were – that, as in *Hamlet*, makes cowards of everyone, both inside and outside the vectors of the institutions themselves.[24]

This yields the dark inversion of moral capital. Barnes exposes how rude power hi-jacks the soft power of moral capital – the very core component of what makes cultural criticism valuable in the first place – and converts it to a principle of fear. The bureaucratic institution makes cowards of all citizens who live through it. A criticism that wants to produce action and material change becomes almost impossible, certainly stymied. As in the Stalinist State, criticism is mute under compliant conformity.[25]

Shostakovich imagined that he would resist the demands of rude power, figuring himself an ethical critic, able to retain legitimate authority in the face of unearned brutal power. He is mistaken. At a crucial moment, he is given the Russian text of a speech that he must make in America. As he starts to read it out, he realizes that it is an attack on his favourite composer, Stravinsky. By this stage, he has realized that it would be a folly, threatening his own life, if he were to denounce the speech. In despair, he simply stops reading; but his translator continues to deliver the speech, despite Shostakovich's silence. His shame is enormous at this point, worsened when he does denounce Stravinsky in the question-and-answer session, in direct response to a provocation from Nicolas Nabokov.

The denunciation is inevitable; yet it is equally inevitably shaming. Shostakovich ponders the difference between himself and a composer like Prokofiev. Prokofiev thought it possible to make an accommodation with power – to compromise diplomatically, as it were. That, however, is precisely the problem: in believing this, Prokofiev 'completely failed to see the tragic dimension of what was happening'.[26] Far from ethical criticism reaching an accommodation with rude power, the opposite is occurring: even oppositional criticism becomes encompassed by power, such that it is completely neutered, rendered complicit with barbarity.

Shostakovich sees the limits of a criticism based on the cultural capital contained in his music: it is neutered in the face of another form of capital. In this instance – and this is the next stage after Ishiguro's Miss Kenton – it is not financial capital that it loses out to, but *institutional capital*. 'Those words of his,' – words of defiance – he realizes, 'had been at best a foolish boast, at worst a mere figure of speech. And Power had no interest in figures of speech.' There are, in fact, only two types of composer in the face of the forms of Power that are grounded in institutional capital such as that of Stalin's bureaucracy: 'those who were alive and frightened; and those who were dead'.[27]

Shostakovich puts this explicitly in terms of different types of capital. He survives; and he had been good at managing to survive and yet to keep faith with his art. He had been good at doing what was needed, rendering to Caesar that which was Caesar's, but 'Yes, he had been naïve about Caesar. Or rather, he had been working from an outdated model. In the old days, Caesar had demanded tribute money, a sum to acknowledge his power, a certain percentage of your calculated worth. But things had moved on, and the new Caesars of the Kremlin had upgraded the system: nowadays your tribute money was calculated at the full 100 per cent of your worth. Or, if possible, more.'[28] This is, in crude terms, a mode of capitalization that essentially returns us to precisely the feudalism with which I opened this study: a coercive relation, based on a rude power that lacks the genuine capital of cultural and reasoned or consensual authority. This coercion makes a virtue of complicity with institutional rude power, our contemporary version of the 'nobility'. It is based upon fear; and it is yet more 'efficient' in preserving privilege because, in such systems, the apparatchik will always over-comply, doing more than is required by tyrannical power (more than the 'full 100% of your worth').

Yet the institutional apparatchik has also internalized fear; and she or he deals with that fear by becoming someone to be feared. They can shame those who would criticize the institution by informing on them; and while the effect of such shame may not be life-threatening, it can certainly be livelihood-threatening. The apparatchik knows that a certain amount of professional capital is gained by encouraging fear, by a general economics of 'growth', an increase in the 'circulation' not of money but of fear, and its corollary, shame, swilling together in the stomach. In the face of this, the critic's only possible mode of self-preservation is through the acceptance of cowardice as a mode of survival. That cowardice entails, in turn, the production of more fear.

Institutional capital achieves its goal by co-opting the idea of criticism as morally uplifting. *Pravda* articulates Stalin's hint, giving the ethical judgment that *Lady Macbeth of Mtensk* is 'muddle instead of music'. It fails to edify the public, fails to offer the kind of uplift that good art should give. In making this judgement – the judgement that blights Shostakovich's career and life – Stalin's institutional power has quite simply fully co-opted the idea of the critic as a heroic individual standing up for the ordinary underdog. It is a political tactic common to many totalitarian social structures and to many authoritarian institutional structures.

Can there be a way out of this predicament? We can turn to the very central institution of cultural capital, the university, to find out.

5

'Shame makes human beings of us,' says the character of Wunderlich to Coetzee's alter-ego, Elizabeth Costello, in *Lives of Animals*.[29]

It is in Coetzee that we see shame operating most forcefully as a driver of economic relations. Interestingly, the relation between shame and economics, between morality and capital, focuses here on land ownership. It takes us back not just to financial capital (money) outweighing cultural capital (the institutions of knowledge, criticism) and moral capital (ethics); worse than this, it takes us back to an essentially feudal structure in which capital and values are tied intimately and incontrovertibly to the ownership of land.

Most criticism of Coetzee's much-lauded and controversial 1999 novel, *Disgrace*, focuses on issues of personal shame. Almost without exception, the focus is on the shame that accrues around the issues of rape (especially inter-racial rape) and sexual harassment (in the context of the university institution). In this, shame becomes merely a matter of character.[30]

Yet what if we take shame – the shame of privilege and especially the privilege of the writing that constitutes Lurie's employment (and Coetzee's profession) – in terms of capital, or as an issue of value as such, put into an economy with grace or with dignity or honour? This changes our understanding of shame, and it shifts the 'disgrace' issue on to a general idea of value associated with propriety, 'property' and ownership.

The story of Lurie taking advantage of Melanie is paralleled with the story of the burglary that becomes a physical attack on Lurie and his daughter Lucy, who is gang-raped. Lurie is troubled that Lucy will not go public with the story of her rape; and he sees this as the basic demonstration of the rude power of the rapists. The attackers will read the reports of their actions in the newspapers, with no mention of rape, because, for Lucy, what happened to her 'is a private matter'. As Lurie sees it, 'It will dawn on them that over the body of the woman silence is being drawn like a blanket. *Too ashamed*, they will say to each other, *too ashamed to tell*, and they will chuckle luxuriously'.[31]

In contemplating the crime, Lurie thinks that it is 'A risk to own anything ... Not enough to go around, not enough cars, shoes, cigarettes. . . What there is must go into circulation, so that everyone can have a chance to be happy for a day. That is the theory. . . Not human evil, just a vast circulatory system, to whose workings pity and terror are irrelevant'.[32] The circulation of finance has no relation to cultural form such as tragedy and simply ignores it: money and property are absolute. But, above all, what Lucy owns – and what is desired by others, especially Petrus, her worker who will eventually acquire it – is land. As she puts it, in a statement that seeks an understanding of the assault on her, 'They see me as owing something. They see themselves as debt collectors, tax collectors. Why should I be allowed to live here without paying?'[33]

With Lucy pregnant from the rape, running her smallholding becomes almost impossible, physically and spiritually. Petrus assumes increasing importance in running things; and, eventually, she signs the land over and becomes a tenant on what is now Petrus's land. She and Lurie both agree that this reversal of fortunes is 'humiliating', but, for Lucy, 'perhaps that is a good point to start from again . . . With nothing. Not with nothing but. With nothing. No cards, no weapons, no property, no rights, no dignity. . . Like a dog'.[34]

That phrase, 'like a dog', does two things. First, it refers us back to Kafka, whose novel *The Trial* ends with precisely this phrase. *The Trial* is an extended version of *Zur Frage des Gesetze*. Secondly, the phrase refers us to Coetzee's own interest in animal rights. Within *Disgrace*, the dignity of animals is considered insistently. When Lurie first arrives at Lucy's farm, he and Lucy take her dogs for a walk. One of the dogs defecates: 'The bitch continues to strain, hanging her tongue out, glancing around shiftily as if ashamed to be watched'.[35] But the shame of the dog will, in the course of the novel, be transferred to the shame of the human 'owners'.

Just as in Tolstoy, where flogging reflects badly on those in the position of master, so also, here – but with a major political component and inflection. When Petrus takes over the land, we are invited to consider the situation as one in which the revolutions of Tolstoy and of Kafka take place: a revolutionary but feudal reversal of roles between lord/landowner and servant/serf. Coetzee's focus on the dog – recalling not just Kafka but also the cynic Diogenes – will yield a substantial argumentative advance.

Lurie starts to work occasionally at the 'Animal Welfare House' run by Bev Shaw, Lucy's friend. Bev takes care of abandoned dogs. Often, they must be slaughtered. On Lucy's farm, Petrus took care of her dogs, and he was called a 'dog-man', inviting the direct allusion to Diogenes, the cynic. Diogenes, apocryphally, knew no shame; and, by knowing no shame himself, he was able to shame his society. This is how cynical reason works: it is shame converted to cultural and political capital. Not much is known of the historical figure of Diogenes himself; but he was probably involved in economic business, somewhat like banking, as was his father, and he rejected money for the search after knowledge and wisdom, ostensibly therefore prioritizing cultural capital over financial capital.

After Petrus takes possession of Lucy's land, Lurie starts visiting Bev Shaw regularly; and he, now, becomes 'the dog-man'. His task in the Animal Welfare House is chastening. The dogs are victims of their own productivity and copulation: they are – like 'Little Father Time' in Hardy's *Jude the Obscure*, a novel concerned explicitly with the limitations of cultural capital in the face of rude power – 'too menny'. Bev runs the Animal House in terms that explicitly invite comparison with the Nazi death-camps, and Lurie's task is to be with the dogs when they are killed and then to dispose of the corpses. By this point, shame is fully associated with the simple fact of death itself, as if the necessity of dying – for humans as for animals – is a reminder of the shamefully simple physicality of life, *la vita nuda*. As we saw with Stevens in Ishiguro, or with men who 'shat in their pants' in Barnes, embodiment itself becomes a shameful condition.

In debasing pretension, death makes shame the human condition: death is the ultimate bond between the self and the materiality of history. The upper classes find it an impropriety. Stevens, in *Remains*, ignores his own dying father while serving his lord, Darlington. Lurie in *Disgrace* senses that the dogs instinctively turn against him as they go to be killed: 'If, more often than not, the dog fails to be charmed, it is because of his presence: he gives off the wrong smell … the smell of shame … They flatten their ears, they droop their tails, as if they too feel the disgrace of dying'.[36]

Finally, this – the cynicism of the death camp – is the condition of our shame. There is a profound limitation in anything that tries to redeem capital by relocating it to culture and knowledge, both of which serve to fracture the solidarity of class by promising 'social mobility'. Recall Lurie's profession: he is an academic, and one who has become somewhat cynical about the condition of the camp – the campus – or institution of knowledge, the university. He has come to realize the false pretense – the pretensions – of human knowing: there is no form of cultural capital that can outweigh the shame of our dying. Death, as Baudrillard once told us, is the end of any form of exchange, especially that of capital.[37] That is so in a capitalist society; but it is not so in a feudal one. This is our predicament: in a state of affairs where value is inscribed in culture, we drive a wedge between conscience and history, between theory and the world. We hanker after the belief that while financial capital is transitory, knowledge can transcend its moment or occasion of production, giving us a soft power that outweighs the realities of money. Yet what contemporary society also knows is that money itself is increasingly 'soft' too. It has lost its link to labour, for example; and has even lost its link to value as such.[38] Now, capital turns to what it once knew as the sure foundation and cornerstone of superiority and power: the ownership of land, the reality of 'real' estate. We are witnessing a return to feudalism. It is the extreme form of privatization.

Lurie tells his daughter, 'These are puritanical times. Private life is public business. Prurience is respectable, prurience and sentiment. They wanted a spectacle: breast-beating, remorse, tears if possible. A TV show, in fact. I wouldn't oblige'.[39] This – the 'puritanism' that makes private life public – is simply one side of a coin that is minted in privatization. In making a fetish of the private, it also valorizes 'culture' as the marketization of shame.

6

Amartya Sen frequently rehearses J. S. Mill's definition of democracy as 'governance by discussion'. The idea – as in Habermas – is that rational societies seek, through non-coercive discussion, the better argument. We thereby propose and jointly agree on the best solution to predicaments or issues. This ideal is moot, for, in all real-life argument, there is an attempt at persuasion by all parties, and such persuasion can itself be characterized as the desire to make the other party agree. In short, all argument involves the attempt to prove one position to be superior to another, more valuable than another.

It is here that democracy itself can become contaminated and destabilized by shame. The texts I have discussed here, where shame is the instrument by which we can change shameful activity, are all politically motivated by a desire for greater democracy and by making a challenge to unearned and class-based authority. They appeal to the 'better argument'; and, in the end, the better argument is always characterized as an argument based on sound rational thinking. The place where we usually encourage such thought is, in its highest formulation, the University institution. We come now to a concluding observation in this chapter about the now shameful University.

The point of any argument is to prove that 'my' case is better than 'yours'; and, ideally, this is a substantial positive factor, a force that is positive in bringing a society together. However, it is now actually conditioned by shame, and becomes a negative force. How is this the case? Reason becomes conditioned by shame when the winner of an argument shames the loser by demonstrating a superior intellectual grasp of issues in a specific debate. Remember the case of Jacobson's ill-fated Professor Probrius from my previous chapter, accused of 'cognitive condescension'. But under what conditions might I feel such shame at losing? Shame and humiliation occur if and only if I feel myself to be *personally* implicated, *privately* beaten in argument, such that it is not the argument that is lost, but 'I' that am lost. Shame occurs when it is the private individual – and not her or his argument – that is scrutinized and exposed.

Shame, we can therefore say, occurs as a condition of the identification of the individual with an argumentative case: in short, shame is a condition of a reason that has been essentially 'privatized'. In this, reason itself becomes characterized as elitist, demeaning the loser personally and privately through argument.[40] 'The personal is political' is a slogan that is complicit with this privatization of the political as such.

The contemporary university is an institution that is increasingly driven precisely by that privatization of reason, and of all economic, social, moral and political interests. It is also, as a result, a quasi-feudal institution.[41]

As is now well known, UK students are incurring massive personal debts as the new form of tax on knowledge. The debts incurred are linked explicitly to the drive to marketize fully the sector. According to the logic of this, the student is getting whatever commodified version of knowledge it is that she or he pays for. Yet we also know this to be untrue. Many institutions are taking in those massively hiked tuition fee incomes, and using the money to build new parts of their estate. Students now, therefore, are essentially funding a legacy. The buildings are designed to boost further the standing of the vice chancellor or president who builds them, for they stand as an indication of how well funded the institution is under her or his 'leadership'. Cultural capital here is fully enmeshed with the capital of the estate, exactly as in the days of Ben Jonson, Thomas Carew and the others I discussed in my opening chapter. One key source of the income for all this, alongside the domestic UK student debt, is the income from overseas students, whose fees are yet higher than those paid by UK individuals. The estate of Delhi, as it were, is also now being further ransacked by our feudal overlords.

The university, as the site of debate, has itself been fully 'occupied' and claimed, as it were, by its presidential lord. This is tantamount to a situation in which all authority is returned directly to the now neo-feudal 'lord of the manor'. Education now becomes subservient to this, and the language that is rendered legitimate in this is the language of the lord. The criticism of 'literature', which is fundamentally about the arguments that we have regarding wherein authority and capital should lie, has here been undermined fully in the wresting of the estate back into the hands of private ownership: the logic of privatization denies the student of literature the 'right' to ownership of the capital that is to be found in criticism – unless that capital is a direct echo of the authority of the neo-feudal institution. When that institution has become complicit with the privatization of knowledge as such, then cultural capital becomes, purely and simply, the production of human capital. In this, as in feudalism, those who work in the institution and keep it going are rendered subservient to their neo-feudal masters, and are required to become complicit with the values of the institution itself.

We need, as Kafka knew, a revolution to overthrow this new nobility; we need to change the shameful university. One key reason why we need such a shift relates to what is now clearly the increase in the brazen parading of shameful behavior by those in power or those seeking power. The clearest instance comes from the realm of politics, and might be associated more or less directly with the far right political class. Thus it is that Nigel Farage in the UK, Donald Trump in the United States, Marine Le Pen in France, Vladimir Putin in Russia – and many others – feel licensed to make public statements that are properly shameful, yet expressed as if they are shameless.

The epitome of this is the case of Trump, a man who seems almost constitutionally unable to speak the truth, and who is committed to broadcasting mendacious statements through his 'writings' on Twitter. He has managed to turn shame into capital, especially into the political capital that was necessary to take him to the White House as President. In the presidential campaign, many of these shameless remarks were also directed forcefully against Hillary Clinton, with specific reference to her acts of writing (the 'damned emails', as Bernie Sanders called them); and what was at issue was the use of a 'private' email server. If shame is a marker or register of various types of capital, we need to explore the conditions of such shame, in terms precisely of private and public literature. That is the subject of the next chapter.

PART THREE

Institutions and Human Capital

7

The Privatization
of all Interests

1

On the evening of 23 January 1963, the Cold War double-agent Kim Philby boarded the *Dolmatova*, leaving Beirut and heading to Odessa. This was the moment when he defected to the Soviet Union definitively, never to return to the west. He offered a kind of explanation-cum-justification of his activities: 'I am really two people,' he said, adding 'I am a private person and a political person. Of course, if there is a conflict, the political person comes first'.[1] This is an important statement, and it has currency here. Philby makes a fundamental distinction between private life and the public sphere, identifying the public sphere as the arena of politics while maintaining that there is a private sphere that can be kept separate from the political. That position is consistent with spying, with a detachment from the immediacy of an engagement with worldliness, and even with a kind of aesthetic distancing in a human subject that is akin to voyeurism, looking at the world across a veil. Fundamentally, it also raises a serious question about what I will here call the 'privatization of all interests'.

In stating that the political person comes first, Philby suggests that his private life as an individual is a subset of his political life and that it is subservient to it. The essence of the private here is determined, pre-determined, by the political. The logical culmination of this is a position that is summed up in the clichéd phrase that 'the personal is political'. This, however – and notwithstanding the neat rhetoric of Philby's statement or of the cliché – comes close to saying that there is no such thing as a genuinely 'private' life. It essentially eliminates the realm of privacy – even perhaps that of intimacy – from distinctive substantive existence, seeing it only as a particular reflection or instantiation of a more generally applicable political and public stance, an ethereal shadow in the cave reflecting a real world outside.

This, I suggest, is problematic in any number of ways. In terms of the argument of this book, it falls deep into the logic of political and commercial privatization, and in this, it aligns all of life with material and monetary interests. It monetizes the self as such. Furthermore, it consolidates the sense that there exists a kind of veil between the self as a locus of private experience and the material world as the locus of politics. In doing this, it demands a kind of ideological purification of the self, such that there can never be any distance between one's political views and one's personal views: the veil becomes fully transparent. We are at a high noon when shadows disappear and the self stands naked.

In eliminating that distance between one's personal and one's political views, it also eliminates the possibility of genuine criticism, because such criticism must be based upon the idea that an individual can change their mind through dialogue and debate. For that to be a possibility, there must be a kind of permeability between what one *wants* to believe as a private person and what one *ought* to believe given the publicly shared facts of any matter. In simple terms, it is important – if we are to remain worldly at all and if literary criticism is to have any purchase on political realities such as that of capital – to ensure that we do not manipulate empirical facts to suit private theory. The material world – the political realm as such – is not there to be privatized; and this, in fact, is one of the fundamental lessons of our critical engagement with literature. We must be aware, as Paul de Man was aware, that 'the resistance to theory' comes primarily from within theory itself, precisely when the general applicability of a theory steamrollers the particularity of a specific literary (or other) empirical fact. Further, as he put this in terms pertinent to the argument here, 'The resistance to theory ... is a resistance to reading' which 'appears in its most rigorous and theoretically elaborated form among the theoreticians of reading who dominate the contemporary theoretical scene'.[2]

Philby's view is entirely consistent with a profoundly right-wing ideology that tries to establish privatization as a normative politics and philosophy. In exactly the same way as the Reaganomics and Thatcherism of the 1980s harmonized with an economics that saw capital purely and simply as the collapsing of the public sphere into a series of atomized business transactions, each carried out for personal gain and benefit, so also the claim that 'the personal is political' is essentially consistent with a privatization of the self, and of selfhood as such. In short, far from being a critical position, this rhetorical claim conforms completely to the demands of the dominant ideology of the moment of its emergence. The would-be radically critical political stance had already been assumed, as it were, as a founding principle of neoliberal economics, one of the aims of which was to privatize (or personalize) the political economy.

In what follows here, I will explore how it is that criticism itself becomes reduced, in this neoliberal moment of the movement and transformation of capital, to an activity that has been complicit with precisely the ideology that it would prefer to contest.[3] There are dangers lurking in the cult of transparency, especially when we mistake transparency for truth.

This is central to the argument here, which will relate the cult of transparency to the logic of economic privatization; and will then consider that in relation to the primacy of identity and of identity-politics in cultural and literary criticism. The core of the argument will be about how this mode of critique, ostensibly concerned to redress inequalities, becomes complicit with precisely the economic programme that it sets out to critique. It is aided and abetted in this by the institutionalization of literature and of literary criticism that privatizes politics as such, making it a personal or private matter, and subjecting both literature and politics to capitalization. The consequence is the reduction of the human individual to the merest capital resource, available for exploitation.

2

Espionage makes transparent that which is usually kept secret. In Philby's case, the two senses of 'betrayal' – as revelation and as treachery – come together. The comparison with a criticism that claims to unveil or reveal the various occlusions in any text is obvious. We should consider the ethical issues that are at the base of one of the most pressing issues of our time. In a so-called 'transparent society', or in a society of surveillance, what are the limits (if any) of the 'private person'?[4] How do we regulate the claims of privacy with those of participation in a polity or being a 'political person'? The entire Wikileaks phenomenon rests upon a proposition that there is always an intrinsic discrepancy, in the life of politicians above all, between their private belief and their political decision. As an observation on my part, this is banal, of course. However, it has a very specific power, as seen in the 2016 US presidential election.

On 6 October 2016, Wikileaks released a series of email correspondences revealing the content of speeches that Hillary Clinton had made to a number of finance industry professionals, including Goldman Sachs. These speeches were gentler in tone than the statements she was making in public on her campaign, where she was much more critical of the banks in relation to their activities around 2007–8. The release of these emails was extremely damaging to her campaign and they played a part in ensuring the election of Donald Trump to the presidency.

The point of the Wikileaks release was to endorse the view, advanced consistently by Trump through the campaign, that, despite public appearance, Hillary Clinton was secretly, privately, 'crooked'; and that she deserved to be in jail. Her alleged offence was that she had used a *private* server for a good deal of her email correspondence, including correspondence relating to public matters, affairs of State. In the terms I am advancing here, she had essentially 'privatized' her political role in relation to the emails whose content was intrinsically related to matters of State. This, we might say, is a privatization of the State, evidenced in the privatization of a specific act of writing, even if that writing is not yet classified as 'literary'.

The assumption throughout, further, is that things said 'in private' reflect the truth of what one believes, while statements made 'in public' are a hypocritical attempt to manipulate audiences in the interests of gaining power over that audience. On 7 October 2016, the *New York Times* reported the leaks, stating that the 'tone and language of the excerpts clash with the fiery liberal approach she used later in her bitter primary battle with Bernie Sanders of Vermont and could have undermined her candidacy had they become public'.[5] Crucially, the leaks revealed that – rather like Philby – she had stated that it was necessary 'to have both a public and a private position' on politically sensitive issues. This mode of thought – which is not in itself exceptional or controversial – will have substantial consequences for our present argument.

My argument is not related to ethical hypocrisy but is more fundamental than that. What I want to explore is how we have come to capitalize on literature through the privatization of its institutions. I will begin by an immediate turn to a specific literary text and a specific capital – capitalized – letter. On 28 February 1905, Virginia Woolf published a brief essay titled 'The Decay of Essay Writing' in *The Academy and Literature*. Like almost all others with an interest in the form and genre, she dates the invention of the essay back to Montaigne; but in doing so, she adds his name to the list of the 'moderns', claiming him for what she calls the new 'invention of essay-writing'. The key thing that she says about the form, however, is that 'almost all essays begin with a capital I', for they all begin with 'I think' or 'I feel'; and, in doing this, the essayist reveals that what is coming in the writing is 'primarily an expression of personal opinion'.[6]

Woolf is dismayed that there are so many essays now, seeing the popularity of the form as being due to 'the fact that … under the decent veil of print one can indulge one's egoism to the full'. That capital letter from which the essay originates allows for a parading of the personal certainly; yet this is the personal improperly if decorously revealed, 'veiled' by the medium itself. The consequence is that we have writing that is based on opinion and not knowledge; and, further, that we have a form that, while pretending to reveal the I, actually occludes it. 'Confronted with the terrible spectre of themselves, the bravest are inclined to run away or shade their eyes' and we get essays that disguise and hide the subject beneath a prose that operates according to its own laws and its own desire for 'the turn of a phrase of the glitter of paradox'.[7]

This ties a specific capital letter to a specific phenomenon: the emergence of 'public opinion' as a key determinant of social and political value. It is as if the route to cultural capital itself is signaled precisely by the use of that capital letter, the I on which an essay capitalizes, working on the interplay between private opinion and public knowledge. The essayistic I is, in many ways, the purest instantiation of the capitalization of the human itself: it is the realization of the human precisely as capital. The question here relates directly to these remarks regarding the writing of essays, the writing of emails, the issue of espionage and the betrayal of the polity. What is at stake is whether we value private life at all in our time, an age where we demand complete and total transparency in all matters, personal and political – and also institutional and professional. To express the question in its most succinct and apt form here: what does the 'capitalization of I' signify?

In exploring this, we need to consider the relation of writing (and reading) as a 'private' activity, set against the institution of literature as a form of public (and even professional) discourse. 'Publication' here means more than just the business of the mass production of texts. I attempt here to understand publication as a specific set of institutional relations between the capital-I and the capital-city, between the subject of consciousness as a 'private' individual and the city or polity as a 'public sphere'. Virginia Woolf would have thought of it as a question of how to calibrate and regulate the relation between the privacy of 'opinion' and its expression as a constitutive element of the public realm of shared and agreed 'knowledge'. The 'market-value' of an essayist can be measured by the distance and discrepancy between her private opinion and our public knowledge: value is given by idiosyncrasy, eccentricity.

We also need to consider the 'currency' or value of 'public opinion', and of its concomitant in the propagation of a relativistic attitude to truth-telling, such that all interest in truthful knowledge decays in the face of the proliferation of 'points of view'. In one of the founding documents of a key literary institution, the university, we are explicitly warned against this. Newman worried that, as he was inaugurating University College Dublin, he was facing a social situation in which 'viewiness', as he called it, prevailed over truth given by faith. 'Viewiness' is a 'spurious philosophism', which he rejects on the grounds that it would teach students 'nothing better than brilliant general views about all things whatever'. This social phenomenon dates from the nineteenth century, when newspapers started to extend their opinion columns, followed quickly by letters pages.

As Benjamin argued, it was once the case that writers were faced by 'many thousands of readers', but this changes by the end of the nineteenth century. 'With the increasing extension of the press, which kept placing new political, religious, scientific, professional, and local organs before the readers, an increasing number of readers became writers – at first, occasional ones. It began with the daily press opening to its readers space for "letters to the editor"'.[8] Our contemporary equivalent (presciently also foreseen by Benjamin) would be the blog, the vlog, and the 'below-the-line' proliferation of usually anonymized (privatized) abuse in the comment pages of newspapers or journals. When abuse replaces argument, we witness the demise of democratic processes – a series of changes that have become only too apparent with the rise of the opinionated post-truth and post-factual far-right across Europe and the US in recent years.

In this condition, both the State and state of the polity have been reduced to being matters of private opinion, resistant to any serious demand for truthful knowledge. We are encouraged to subscribe to the myth that there is a complete continuity between what we *want* the world to be (opinion) and what it *is* (which is given by shared knowledge). We need not look out from the self to see the truth: it is transparently available, immediately, within the I that regards its own shadow. Fantasist politicians, especially of the political right, provide the key exemplars of this. Our key question here is whether the private person – the individual and the entirety of her or his interests in and engagement with worldliness – is also now not just politicized but also 'capitalized'.

That is to say, in the age of a transparency in which the political has itself been essentially privatized, is the private individual herself or himself – and all of her or his human interests – reduced to the status of 'human capital': is this the real and essential meaning of our validation of our existence as capital?

Transparency has become a pious cult; and, worse, transparency has become our poor substitute for truth. We may no longer care whether a politician tells the truth, as long as she or he is transparent, even *brazen* in their lying, like a double-agent betraying the State. We started out with a project of literature that related to credit and credibility. What happens when credibility is shot, and when credit has been replaced fully by debt, by a sense that the human is herself or himself the capital that is 'owed' or owned by someone else, an entity or polity whose agent or double-agent the human individual is? How does literature sit alongside Othello's great question, his preface to suicide: 'I have done the state some service, and they know't. / No more of that'? What is literature's relation to contemporary ideologies of 'service', service industries and servitude? These are the questions that now call for answers.

3

Political persons are those whose life conditions are essentially public: they exist in 'public life'. However, what constitutes 'the public'? If something is revealed or addressed to 'the public', then it must, almost by definition, address *no one in particular* but *all in general*: 'the public' is of indefinite identity. In principle – but in principle only – it may resemble 'the multitude', in the political reconfiguration of that term as advanced by Michael Hardt and Antonio Negri.[9] However, at this stage, it is important to note that the particular iteration of 'the public' with which I work here is not intrinsically democratic, much less revolutionary, even if it may share some of the characteristics of a multitude that is heterogeneous, anarchic, uncontrolled and uncontrollable, and radically decentred. The clearest way into this will be through an exploration of 'public opinion' in its contemporary forms.

During a debate on 'freedoms of speech', held at the Hay Festival on 27 May 2006, between Shashi Tharoor and Christopher Hitchens, Hitchens began by declaring himself a 'first amendment absolutist'. He argued that, in our times, it is not the case that the State is the greatest enemy of freedom of speech; rather, he said, 'the main threat to freedom of speech comes from public opinion'. Yet this 'public opinion' is of indeterminate identity, except insofar as it defines itself by 'not being an elite', as it were. For Hitchens, if you dare to resist the tacit agreement with this public opinion, 'you will be accused of being elitist'. That is to say, those who have sufficient 'cultural capital' to go against the prevailing ideological grain become, by definition in this state of affairs, intrinsically opposed to 'the community'.

In political terms, this translates into a hatred of expertise, and a dismissal of experts – and thus also, fundamentally, a dismissal of those institutions that establish cultural values through expertise in language and in semantics, such as universities. This goes beyond the 'hatred of literature' that I described earlier, and it takes that hatred to a logical conclusion. This political condition requires that we start to de-value what has become conventionally understood as cultural capital. Our existence itself becomes valued and validated only and precisely to the extent that we ourselves start to undermine any cultural capital that we may have (we express shame at our own elitist expertise), and in the process we start to identify ourselves precisely as 'human capital'. We become efficient purveyors of the non-elite 'ordinary', under the guise of 'public opinion' or 'the popular will'.

In its basest, crudest political form, this becomes a validation of 'the will of the people'. This phrase is typically deployed in populist political rhetoric. It seeks power by manipulating 'the will of the people' that it claims only to serve; and in this it reduces 'the people' to human resources, human capital, fodder for a specific political programme. Those populist politicians who translate cultural capital into human capital in this way are politicians whose incipient despotism is hidden and veiled behind their claimed allegiance with the ordinary, the open and the transparent.

Michael Gove, the then Lord High Chancellor and Tory MP, explicitly dismissed experts during a Brexit debate with Faisal Islam on 3 June 2016. 'I think the people of this country have had enough of experts', he famously said, when confronted by Islam with a monumental list of organizations, governments and individuals who all took the view that it is better for Britain to remain in the EU. The people, he argued – without specifying which people he meant – should 'trust themselves', saying that his view was based in 'a faith in the British people to make the right decision'. In this sentence he at least gave a qualifying adjective to 'the people' describing them as 'British people'; yet, obviously, the people of Britain are many and varied. He went on to claim that 'the majority' of these British people were suffering because of membership of the EU. In short, they were not being permitted to fulfill themselves and to extend their potential – which means, in the terms I am using here, that they were not maximizing their own human capital.

Challenged by Faisal Islam to provide any factual data on the basis of which he could substantiate his claim that over thirty-three million people were thus suffering, he turned to his own personal opinion and private life again: 'I know myself, from my own background, I know that the European Union depresses employment' before going on to make express political use of his own father, whose fishing business – Gove claimed – had been destroyed by the EU Common Fisheries policy. When it became clear that he was unable to answer the case from Islam rationally and truthfully, he resorted to abuse: 'You, Faisal, are on the side of the elites, I am on the side of the people'.[10]

Private sentiment must trump the reason made by publicly debated argument, because reason is an acquisition underpinned by cultural capital; and this, for Gove, must cede place to the intrinsic worth of those whose capital is given to them not by culture, learning or knowledge (or even thinking) but by their own intrinsic private being – *as human capital*. The visceral, physical self here – the 'private' self, unadorned by thought – is to triumph. In such a triumph, any capital that is vested in knowledge – and perhaps especially in any and all forms of humanist knowledge, such as we find it in and through reading literature – must be disowned as being a dangerously subversive cultural capital.

Obvious questions arise. Are Gove's own statements based upon knowledge and expertise? Is he an expert on the EU? If so, then (by his own logic) why should we trust him; and if not, then, equally, why should we have any *reason* to trust him? Yet more pertinently, we might also ask what is at stake when, instead of giving the evidence of the alleged thirty-three million people who are suffering because of membership of the EU, he decides instead to completely personalize and privatize the political matter, by referring to the case of his own father and family? Finally, that last gesture, in which he abuses his interlocutor – 'You, Faisal, are on the side of the elites' – is one in which he is simply saying that he will not engage in the debate, preferring verbal attack over rational dispassionate engagement.

The elites – with cultural capital – are aligned with experts; and if he has dismissed the experts as people from whom we have heard enough, then he is simply telling Faisal Islam to shut up. Against that, he claims for himself the voice of 'the people' or of 'public opinion'; but actually, he is of course expertly constructing public opinion and characterizing it in his own voice through the debate itself. And this public opinion will brook no argument. It will brook no argument in principle; but it will also ensure that no serious argument can be enjoined, through the pious appeal to sentiment. Who, after all, wants to dismiss an old man of the sea whose son sanctimoniously alleges that he has been the poor victim of the acronym-riddled EU? Gove acts in all of this as if he has successfully prized open the hidden secret subversive activities of the EU: he has, as it were, spied on the internal workings of the EU and now acts as our agent-spy. In doing this, however, he claims no knowledge (for that would be to rest his case on cultural capital); rather, he simply tears the veil to reveal to 'the public', what the 'private' EU really is. This is his implicit logic.

It follows logically from these kinds of appeal to public opinion that criticism itself – even in its minimal form as debate or dialogue – becomes intrinsically unacceptable and ruled out of court, for the simple reason that criticism becomes a realization (in the sense of 'making a reality') of inequality with respect to our learning capital, our relative intellectual standing or individual human capital. To differ from whatever is established as an anonymized 'public opinion' – an opinion for which no one individual ever feels any need to take responsibility, nor any need to justify, rationalize, explain – is to mark oneself out as an 'alien' of sorts, even an 'enemy of the people'. It is to condemn yourself to the solitude of a 'private life' in a very specific sense of isolation or internment. It is as if you find yourself in a solitary confinement. It is perhaps because of this that, for Hitchens in that Hay free speech debate, 'part of growing up is to say the community can go to hell'.[11]

The single most important aspect of this is that it sets up an absolute distinction between private and public, such that to be permitted to have access to the public sphere at all means to conform to its norms, to embody 'public opinion'. It thus becomes an absolute constraint on how any writer might ever try to capitalize on her or his letters, her or his 'literature'. It is as if criticism as such – based on dialogue and debate – becomes proscribed, an impossibility, as a simple matter of empirical fact. However, the fact that the acknowledgement of public opinion is substantially accepted and indeed normative – even when we do not know whose actual opinion this is, given the anonymity of 'the people' – means that it places literature itself in an odd position, as an institution that is intrinsically private or privatized, a matter for the forlorn individual forced to return from the public fray to her or his sole private self.[12]

Logically, critical dialogue and debate are permitted to work in this regime if and only if it is 'properly' monetized, or monetized in ways that are accepted or legitimized by 'public opinion'. By contrast, we might now reasonably also ask what is it exactly that constitutes 'the private'? Is it indeed meaningful – or even possible – for anything to be private and yet to have a meaningful and legitimate existence; and, if so, under what conditions might this happen?

4

Transparency can be thought of as that which erases the boundary between private and public; but it can also be considered as that which eradicates the difference, as in espionage, between the secret and the revealed.[13] There may be a relation between transparency as a condition of modernity on one hand, and espionage as the conduct of secret business on the other. A similar structure is broadly construed as operative in basic literary criticism, which sees the meaning or significance of the text as something that requires revelation. What links all these are the issues of confidentiality and trust as social phenomena. We will see that, in modernity, transparency has become the medium through which we eviscerate politics of content and substance, and replace it with the norms of social conformity. Literature, once it becomes institutionalized as a constituent part of the norms of the modern University, serves a similar purpose of consolidating and legitimizing social conformity, a demand to conform to the requirements and norms of 'public opinion', non-specialized 'common sense'.

The contemporary university has become complicit with the ideological positions of Michael Gove. In its attempts to demonstrate that it is no longer the preserve of the hyper-privileged elites – as it was portrayed in popular cultural forms, and as it was seen in Waugh's *Brideshead Revisited*, say – it must appear to be on the side of 'the ordinary'. Although it is ostensibly concerned with 'higher' education, it cannot permit itself to be portrayed as 'elitist'. It circumvents this potential charge and self-contradiction by talking of 'excellence', instead of elitism; and it shows that it is 'excellent' in serving 'the will of the people', at least as that is allegedly represented by the will of an elected government or State. The result is the politicization of the institution, the politicization of cultural capital.

However, this politicization is one that, in serving 'ordinariness', must acknowledge the already existing and intrinsic capital of all citizens, including those who attend a university. That is a mode of capital that exists in them purely by virtue of their human being and not by virtue of their literary (or other) knowledge, or any other form of capital that might be attained or acquired by education, *Bildung*. In short: they are human capital above all. As almost every university (or any other professional institution) will say, our people are our greatest resource. The problem is that they mean it. The private self – the self that exists prior to any engagement with external realities, or culture as such – is seen to be the primary capital that is valued. That is the very meaning of human capital as such; and this goes some way towards explaining how human capital has supplanted cultural capital in our times.

In claiming to foster the advancement of the popular will – public opinion – our educational institutions in fact are depriving people of the very cultural capital that is required to allow that will to engage reasonably with the world and with history: it precludes any effecting of historical material change. Literature – insofar as it plays along with this institutionalization of human capital against cultural capital – becomes complicit in this process. It becomes difficult to critique any right-wing, populist authoritarian political positions. Instead, literature is silently co-opted by a political right-wing that de-values culture and asks all human individuals to rest easy in their sole self, to trust only what is superficial.

This also helps explain the solace that many critics find in identity politics. One unstated proposition underpinning identity politics is a reassurance that the individual is to be valued *as she or he currently is*. This is admirable: it tells the poor, for example, that they must not be disregarded simply because of their poverty; it tells women that they must not be oppressed because they are women; it does the same for working-class people, for those described as differently raced; and so on. However, at the same time, in reassuring me that I am fine already as I currently exist and as I currently identify myself, it does nothing to suggest that I might or should change things in terms of public or class struggle, or that I myself might need to change as part of those struggles. The only serious point of an identity politics in criticism should be as a prelude to a difference-politics, so to speak – a politics of making things (including my own identity) different by learning more.

For this, and to effect any political change or agency, we require the re-validation of cultural capital: we need to know things, not to rest content with our existing intrinsic capital, a capital that is given to us precisely because of our current identity. Identity-politics is a recipe for political quietism; and it is consistent with all those right-wing political ideologies that are suspicious of culture and of cultural capital, precisely because such capital threatens the standing of those who are currently in power.

Our contemporary historical period witnesses the rise of far-right and neo-fascist parties across Europe and elsewhere. We see the rise of various fundamentalisms and the return of isolationist nationalisms – with their disturbing undercurrents of white supremacist ideologies. These have in common one fundamental set of political norms or normative beliefs, and the beliefs in question accept the normality of having an absolute intimacy between the world of government and the world of business. The election of Donald Trump to the US presidency in 2016 is a clear realization of this, for it indicates the underlying belief that a country is itself a business, its people being the capital of that business; and that if someone can run a business then he can, *ipso facto*, be seen as the most qualified person to be the US President.

Naomi Klein's analysis of what happened in the presidential elections in the US in 2016 indicates that, worldwide, we have been living through an economic normalization of neoliberalism. 'Under neoliberal policies of deregulation, privatization, austerity and corporate trade', many people – many members of the public – have lost jobs and lost security for themselves while also foreseeing a worse future for their children. These same people 'have witnessed the rise of the Davos class, a hyper-connected network of banking and tech billionaires, elected leaders who are awfully cosy with these interests, and Hollywood celebrities who make the whole thing seem unbearably glamorous'.

In the specific analysis of the US presidential election, Klein describes Hillary Clinton as an integral part of the Davos set, and thus as part of the problem. Faced with the election of Trump, however, it is not the case that the problems brought about by the triumph of a public opinion that sees neoliberalism as a norm will be solved. If we genuinely wish to address and solve the problems facing many people, Klein argues, we need a new green left, with 'policies that fight institutionalised racism, economic inequality and climate change at the same time. It could take on bad trade deals and police violence, and honour indigenous people as the original protectors of the land, water and air'.[14]

In this, it is not so much the 'public' and their 'opinion' that is at stake, rather it is the very survival of *real* 'human resources' – those of land, water and air – that people need for biological survival in the first place. The entire public sphere is at stake; and it is set against the logic of privatization, as normalized in and through the institutionalization of the Davos phenomenon, that has shaped 'public opinion' for at least four decades. In short, the problem here has been the commercialization of politics as a monetized business, whose net effect is to destroy the public sphere – and the land or general ecology that has been so central to my arguments about literary capital – through an atomization of that public into a series of discrete and atomized individuals. This is, as it were, precisely the 'modernization' of the feudal system of political and economic relations from which we began. Modernity thus may not be marked by historical progress at all, but rather by the return to a new version of feudal social relations, with substantial and significant consequences for capitalizing on literature.

5

Arguments over what constitutes modernity are legion. For Hannah Arendt, modernity is coeval with the invention or emergence of 'society'. I want to introduce what will be a key modification that will add a specific inflection to Arendt's account. In specific relation to 'capitalizing on letters' – and in particular to the question of what I have called the 'capitalization of I' – modernity can be characterized as a movement or moment in which there occurs a very specific reduction of the political, collapsing the political into the personal, even the private. Further, the personal or private realm of *intimacy*, itself often shaped by a 'philosophy of pity', is now seen as being in direct opposition to the social, and to the sociality of norms and normative human behaviours.[15]

The logic is that we have *critique* itself as the site of the problems that accrue around our demand for total political and social transparency. Our questions become: how transparent, how true, how authentic is the self that proposes the criticism? In this, we end up looking for a self that is 'beyond hypocrisy', a self that hides nothing and that reveals all and everything in all and everything that it is and does, and a self whose 'consistency' is, as it were, a register of its complete self-identification and utter transparency. To what extent is I self-evidencing; does the meaning and value of I equate with the capitalization of I; or, to put this in its most succinct form, 'how I is I?'

This produces the self as an anorexic size zero. Not only is it the case that the self becomes axiomatically transparent; but also, sadly, there is nothing left to see. In politics, it yields a Trump figure, a hollow man, a 'cipher of a man [who] has revealed the hidden depths, the ugly unmastered history, of the country he claims to lead', as Adam Shatz puts it.[16] We have obliterated the self – and with it we have obliterated the idea of personal responsibility for history or for any agency. This, as I will show, is one of the central paradoxes governing what we often call 'human capital', the idea that value stems from within the human self-as-agent. As such a 'zero' or Trumpian cipher, we find the real value of the self when cultural capital is reduced to human capital: it is, precisely, zero.

It is in her 1958 study of *The Human Condition* that Arendt offers her highly original definition of modernity. Modernity is characterized by the emergence of 'the social'. Society has not always been with us, and its emergence yields a specific set of political problems. Essentially, the social emerges when the borders between private and public realms become blurred, when 'housekeeping' ('economics', *oikos nomos*, household law) emerges 'from the shadowy interior of the household into the light of the public sphere'.[17] The existence of 'society' is, in short, another way of describing what happens when matters pertinent primarily to the private realm enter the public domain, when 'opinion' goes 'public'.

In my own terms, it is when 'I' utters that we produce the social. 'Uttering' is also literally consonant with 'outering', with crossing a border from a private inside to a public exterior ('utter' and 'outer' are linked etymologically). 'Uttering' is 'ex-pressing' an I. Technically, in legal discourse, 'to utter' is also 'to put money into circulation', and the word has a special sense in law in relation to forged money or what we can call 'false capital'. Uttering is an economic exercise in which the border between the true and the false, between 'I' and my words, becomes blurred. It is the moment when 'I' becomes foreign to itself, becomes other as it becomes outer, so to speak. This, following Arendt, is also an economic moment.

The further consequence of this emergent modernity, for Arendt, is that we start to prioritize and prize the values of intimacy, even systemically to overvalue intimacy as such. She dates this historically, suggesting that it can be seen in '[t]he astonishing flowering of poetry and music from the middle of the eighteenth century until almost the last third of the nineteenth, accompanied by the rise of the novel, the only entirely social art form'.[18]

Things were clearer in antiquity where there is actually no place for what Arendt calls 'the social' at all. The ancient world divides cleanly between the claims of the private realm (household or *oikos*), and the public realm, the *agora* or public place where debate orders the political way in which people organize their world. These are simply different orders of being: they do not constitute the inside and outside of some unified entity. In terms that may be more pertinent for what follows here, this is a straightforward division, then, between economics and ecology, between *oikos nomos*, the law of the household, and *oikos logos*, or talk concerning our environment.

The ancient world's private realm is shaped by the struggle for survival: it is the realm of simple biological survival and sustenance, as opposed to a life lived in actual activity that relates the naked self to all that exists beyond it.[19] As such, the private realm is governed by *necessity*, which grants to the head of the household the right to exercise violence. Such violence is strictly conditioned and does not resemble the kind of 'despotism' that we saw described as a constituent element of the modern in Swift's 'modern author' in his

A Tale of a Tub, or as we see it in Trump's politics. As Arendt puts it, 'force and violence are justified in this sphere because they are the only means to master necessity ... and to become free'.[20] By contrast, the public realm is precisely the realm of freedom, and is characterized as the space or realm in which those whom Arendt describes as 'free men' (by which she means men who have mastered the basic needs of survival) engage in dialogue to establish the polity. In this latter, 'force or violence becomes the monopoly of government'.[21] Individuals eschew violence, preferring talk as a means of resolving dispute; and, if that fails, they have recourse to law which the State or government can enforce, by State-sanctioned violence if need be.

Modernity changes this by blurring the distinction, bringing the two orders of being together, thereby producing 'the social'. Consequently, our very understanding of the private and the public must change. Once conjoined, they may certainly remain as distinct elements, but they are now distinct elements of the one single phenomenon, like two sides of a coin. The private sphere is elevated and magnified to encompass the greater space of the political; and in this, we get a sudden prioritization of the values of the private realm, especially that of 'intimacy'.

A 'blurring' of the distinction between private and public also introduces the idea and even the necessity of a demand for transparency as such. Prior to modernity, there is no relation at all between these two: we do not 'look through' a wall that separates them: they are simply different orders of being. In Arendt's modernity, they become intrinsically related to each other, even integral to each other. They open themselves to deconstruction, as it were, by establishing a structural relation that constitutes 'society' itself.

In this account, modernity establishes intimacy as a secret space, a place secreted away; and this intimate realm is one that, though occluded, can be revealed, however 'veiled' it may initially be. Indeed, the task of modern criticism now becomes precisely one of hermeneutic, 'unmasking' or revealing the essence of an interiority, be it the interior/private meaning of a text, the interior/private psyche of a writer or other individual, the interior/private structure of an ideology and so on. The idea, we might say, is to reach the 'bare I' that stands somewhere naked behind the capitalized I, the I that has what the finance sector would call 'economic exposure'.

Transparency – the structuring of a very specific kind of intimacy – is my equivalent for this kind of modernity. It is fundamentally related to the privatization of the self – *and of ideology* – and to the idea that the 'bare I' has its meaning entirely through its 'exposure' to capitalization, to becoming the locus for what Woolf thought of as the expression of the I, as the I essays itself into the public sphere, testing there the value of its opinions or the capital value of the I itself. We can test Arendt's dating of this phenomenon. In 1759, Voltaire published his little *conte philosophique*, the story of *Candide*. Famously, the ostensible 'message' of the tale is given at the end. Candide and his little group, having submitted to terrible misfortunes, come across an old man. They ask him if he has any detailed news about the recent assassination of the Grand Mufti. He has none:

'J'ignore absolument l'aventure dont vous me parlez; je présume qu'en général ceux qui se mêlent des affaires publiques périssent quelquefois misérablement, et qu'ils le méritent; mais je ne m'informe jamais de ce qu'on fait à Constantinople; je me contente d'y envoyer les fruits du jardin que je cultive' (Voltaire, 148–9)
[I'm completely unaware of the adventure you're telling me about; I presume that in general those who get mixed up in public affairs sometimes perish miserably, and that they deserve to do so; but I don't keep up with what's happening in Constantinople; I'm just happy to send over there the produce that I grow in my garden][22]

From this, Candide derives the message that it is best to withdraw entirely from the public realm. Candide's economic existence is now to be fully governed by ecology: *il faut cultiver notre jardin*. The private realm takes precedence over the public, and requires abandoning any public role. It also confirms the residual idea that the private realm is that where we struggle for bare life: this is how Candide and his little group will survive.

A contemporary version of this is the character of Nathan Zuckerman, in Philip Roth's *The Human Stain*. Nathan reflects on his own withdrawal from the hurly-burly of the world, that world that has ensnared Coleman Silk, the classics professor, in a web of predicaments relating to race and sex. Nathan's view is that 'The secret to living in the rush of the world with a minimum of pain is to get as many people as possible to string along with your delusions'. He himself has rejected this for the past five years, preferring to live alone in a wilderness; and 'the trick to living up here', he suggests, 'away from all agitating entanglements, allurements, and expectations, apart especially from one's own intensity, is to organize the silence, to think of its mountaintop plenitude as capital, silence as wealth exponentially increasing'.[23]

In this privacy and withdrawal from public engagement, Nathan finds capital; but he finds it primarily as something that is realized not just in silence but in its ostensible cultural opposite: music. He listens to music alone in the evening, and, when he does so, he is clear that 'The music I play after dinner is not a relief from the silence but something like its substantiation: listening to music for an hour or two every evening doesn't deprive me of the silence – the music is the silence coming true'.[24] The analogy is clearly invited here: just as music is the realization of the capital wealth that lies invested in silence, so also is literature, as Nathan writes in and from that silence. Yet this is a capital that depends – as in Voltaire – upon a kind of ecological minimizing or reduction to zero of the human footprint – the human stain – upon the public realm.

Such a situation remains, in many ways, the fundamental principle of ecology. Voltaire's mid-eighteenth-century text ostensibly advocates a withdrawal from the world and its public realm, and a concentration on the ecological in the form of the managing of the local concerns of a small household. It re-draws ecology (*oikos logos*) as the ground for an economy (*oikos nomos*). Crucially, it does this by prioritizing the 'privacy' of such ecology: it removes ecology from the worldly environment and makes it an individual and a private matter. The world, as such, is lost. The problem here, if we translate this into our contemporary moment, is that such a withdrawal is tantamount to the demise of the public sphere as a whole. In that demise, we are no longer able to seek out shared and verifiable truth, and we replace that ethical demand instead with what we have been told to call 'post-truth' or 'post-factual' politics. By definition, such an account of politics denies the possibility of our sharing the world at all.

The withdrawal from the public realm in *Candide* is conditioned by a corresponding elevation of the values of intimacy. Candide,

Cunégonde, Paquette, Martin, le frère Giroflée and even Pangloss exist in communal intimacy with each other, as the final paragraph of the tale makes clear. Better to find one's real self in private like this than to concern oneself with the political and the public realm – which here, in an inversion or subversion of Arendt's ancient world, is shaped by violence and tyrannical mayhem.

This is also a return to an earlier sense of the private, and one that is in accord with Arendt's explanation of the etymological root of the word in 'privation' (and this yields more fruit in our consideration of Roth's contemporary version of silence-as-capital, and of the reduction of cultural capital to the ground-zero of the human-as-capital). Arendt points out the link between privacy and privation, which she argues were intimate terms in the ancient world: 'A man who lived only a private life, who like the slave was not permitted to enter the public realm, or like the barbarian had chosen not to establish such a realm, was not fully human'.[25] We have lost that sense of privation because of a kind of reversal: modern individualism has so enriched and monetized or capitalized the private sphere that we often prioritize it over the public. This, in fact, is Candide's end-point; but it is very important to see that, in this emergent modernity, the political is being restricted, being collapsed, as it were, into the private sphere. As with Roth's Nathan, the self is privately capitalized, and grows; but it grows only by addressing and confirming its own identity, leaving material politics to its own devices.

In short, 'the political is personal'; or politics is a private matter. Which means the end of politics as a matter of public concern. Which, in turn, means the end of politics as such, and an endorsement of the ideological view that sustains privatization, with the infamous Thatcherite claim that 'there is no such thing as society'.

6

However, is it unproblematic that the private realm can be thus positively valorized? That question is a fundamentally exacting one, given that I have shown the intrinsic construction of human capital – the privatized self – as one that tends to reduce the human to a base condition of zero-worth in capital terms. Arendt points out that, for

Aristotle, 'man's highest capacity [was] not *logos*, that is, not speech or reason, but *nous*, the capacity of contemplation, whose chief characteristic is that its content cannot be rendered in speech'.[26] In one way, this is the very extreme of the valorization of the private self: a self that is so intimate with itself that it cannot communicate. It sounds something like the fundamental problem that shapes the entirety of Beckett's work; and, in at least this sense, Beckett might come to be seen, controversially perhaps, as our *most* political modern writer, a paradigmatic example of the exploration of what happens to literature when it is related to capital in the twentieth century.

The general logic that needs to be explored here is that literature itself becomes a matter of privatization, in that the *logos* (speech and reason, and, by extension, public writing) cannot be shared any more. The capital letter L of our institutionalized 'English Literature' is essentially supplanted by that other sign, £, which is developed from the writing down of a very elaborate capital L. The *liber* or book has become the *libra* or pound: literature is erased under the sign of capital, and, paradoxically, through its commercial capitalization. L is realized as £, and, as £ it is subject to private ownership. A community is 'deprived' of L in direct proportion to how its reality is measured by £.

That extremist version of the issue of a *logos* or logic that exists in the mode of privation was considered by Wittgenstein, in his posthumously published *Philosophical Investigations*. There, it takes the form of the 'private language' problem. Wittgenstein famously asks: 'could we ... imagine a language in which a person could write down or give vocal expression to his inner experiences – his feelings, moods, and the rest – for his private use?'.[27]

Wittgenstein allows for the complete privacy of sensation – the limit- or test-case is the sensation and experience of pain – but although it may be true that that experience is totally private, it is so in a philosophically trivial sense. It constitutes a test case of his closing proposition in the *Tractatus*: something of which we cannot speak. 'Whereof one cannot speak' – Aristotle's *nous*, the utter intimacy of self-with-self that constitutes sensation, 'thereof one must be silent'.[28] We cannot comprehend this privacy, this intimacy of self-with-self, nor can we communicate it, because comprehension requires a language community.

In my terms here, any comprehension of the text demands the 'worlding' of literature, the act of bringing the world into contact with the literary and vice-versa.

Arendt puts this in different terms, and perhaps even more succinctly: 'No human life, not even the life of the hermit in nature's wilderness, is possible without a world which directly or indirectly testifies to the presence of other human beings'.[29] As in any mode of production, there is a surplus: I produces itself, but in doing so it also produces We and You. This is all the more so when that I, that subject, is a speaking subject, or the agent of a communication that is of the essence of the literary as such. But does it follow from Arendt's account of this that only that which is politics – only that which is transparently available in the public space as the engagement of I-with-You – is constitutive of reality?

In some ways, the institutionalization of literary criticism depends precisely upon the idea that language is the site of obscurity. In even the most banal terms – terms that most professional criticism would now abjure – literature is puzzling, enigmatic; and it needs the mediation of the critic to explain its dark mysteries. In less banal terms – terms that would remain acceptable to most professional critics and readers invested with institutional cultural capital (such as professors of literature) – literature works to the extent that it keeps calling us back for further and further re-engagements and re-readings. To put this anecdotally, it is when a student tells me that she or he feels that they are now beginning to 'understand' some text or other than I call them back to that text to ensure that I, as a teacher, make it yet more difficult for them, to ensure that I re-open it. The point of this is to make clear that 'literature' is not reduced to a commodity – be it the 'grasped' meaning of the text or of the author – that can be circumscribed and assimilated to the culture industry, or to crude forms of privatized capitalization. While books may be for sale, literature resists such a reduction.

7

For Arendt, the key issues are biopolitical. In Arendt's ancient public realm, the presence of the body – the speaking body – was important and central to political life. It was not possible to be political within the private realm, for there we were not freed from necessity, from the demand for biological survival. We can now add to this that modernity, in changing this state of affairs, is also coincidental with changes in technology, and especially with the change in technology and consumerism that produces the modern age, and with it, Habermas's 'public sphere': the technological advances made by print, and the logic of consumerism that is based on the international trading and drinking of coffee.

As Markman Ellis points out, 'coffee's eruption into daily life seems to coincide with the modern historical period', and the first coffee houses in London date from the 1650s, in 'a city gripped with revolutionary fervour'. Samuel Johnson defined a coffee house as 'A house of entertainment where coffee is sold, and the guests are supplied with newspapers'. Ellis points out that 'In the coffee-house, men learnt new ways of combinatorial friendship, turning their discussions there into commercial ventures, critical tribunals, scientific seminars and political clubs'.[30] The drug of caffeine combined with the daily urgency of print helped construct the public sphere.

Coffee has become one of the world's most traded products. In terms of total value of world trades, oil is the only commodity that exceeds that of coffee today. Historically, trade in coffee was related to the ways in which some European countries controlled their overseas colonies; and, today, the prevalence of coffee in our advanced world economies depends still on the continued exploitation of resources among the world's poorest communities and nations. While the coffee-houses of London in the seventeenth and eighteenth centuries brought coffee and newspapers together, our contemporary period retains the coffee (in a massively enhanced consumerist form), but has largely ditched the print for free Wi-Fi. That technological shift combines with the capitalist model of market-choice in significant ways, especially in a culture where literature is also widening its media from print to web, even from language to image.

The 'public sphere' in Habermas is markedly different from Arendt's 'public space'. For Habermas, the technological innovations of print culture, combined with institutions such as the coffee house, produced a less tangible, less physically material instance of the political. It is language itself – texts – that constitute the political; and this is the meaning of a public *sphere* as opposed to a public space, that material place that requires physical bodily presence. The difference is yet more marked when contemporary wireless and 'immaterial' web-based technology brings literature into the coffee-house without the intervening and physically material medium of print. Literature, now, is in the air; and in this sense, it becomes ethereal, airily transparent. As Shakespeare's Theseus has it in *A Midsummer Night's Dream*, 'as imagination bodies forth / the forms of things unknown, the poet's pen / turns them to shapes and gives to airy nothings / a local habitation and a name'. The words are important and precise: the task of the poet is to provide a 'local habitation' for the things of imagination. The coffee-house operates – not just now but also historically – as precisely such a facilitator.

Importantly, neither my body nor I need to be 'present' in the public sphere as envisaged in Habermas to exist or to exert an influence there. The public sphere, in the account advanced by Habermas, can be and often is largely characterized precisely by my personal absence, and the replacement of my physical speaking self with the virtual written or textual self. That textual self can be an airy nothing, but one that exerts an influence. The text becomes a mechanism through which we answer Luc Boltanski's question of how we sympathize 'at a distance' with those who are 'absent'. The text is precisely the site of our issue regarding transparency: what does the text reveal, and what does it conceal? Reading with this question in mind is itself an exercise in finding or making such sympathy, such *souffrance à distance*.[31] These are the questions that now shape the conversation that constitutes politics in the public sphere itself. That is to say: politics becomes an issue regarding textual hermeneutics, regarding those various transparencies that have been at issue throughout. Criticism becomes associated with a book of revelations, revealing meaning, revealing a self, revealing an ideology.

The material force of body language (and its attendant potential for violence) gives way in this public sphere to the abstractions of reason itself, *logos*. However, this – the operation of logic/reason – is what demands transparency. Further, it requires confidential trust, whereas, in body language, all is revealed in its full immediacy, most obviously in physical violence or physical love, in terror or pity. For Habermas, therefore, the public sphere is not a physical public space as such, but instead a somewhat nebulous affair, constituted by speeches, memories, films, literature, newspapers, symbolic forms – but only insofar as these constitute or produce that public sphere as a habitation that is shared, a habitation that is the site for the sharing of communications as such. This public sphere is constructed by and constituted by acts of communication. Sensation is banished from this public sphere, for sensation is a 'purely' personal matter, dependent upon the physical body itself. That is to say: Habermas essentially rejects the importance of sensation as a political matter, replacing sensibility with sense in this domain. One might even go so far as to say – very controversially – that he rejects the value of material experience, and that he prefers instead to prioritize the existence of communicative acts, as in his developed 'theory of communicative action'. At the very least, we can say that, in the distance between Arendt's public space and Habermas's public sphere, we make private life more precarious, more nebulous and less 'embodied'.

Now, our technologies and cultures have changed our world again; and in an age of digitization, private life can become yet more precarious still. Consequently, we are now well on the way towards the evacuation of content and substance not just from the human subject as a ground-zero or nebulous airy nothing, but also indeed from politics itself. The net result is the transference of all properly public values back into the world of interiority. In short, what we now face is a culture in which we have the privatization of all human interests, through the reduction of the subject or I to an existence as 'mere' capital, human capital. When this reaches its logical conclusion, the material world of politics is also evacuated in a parallel reduction of its meaning and significance to zero.

8

Peter Sloterdijk provides the limit test case. He begins *Bubbles*, the first volume of his *Spheres* 'Microspherology' trilogy, with the image of a child blowing a soap bubble (an actual image, the mezzotint called *Bubbles*, by G. H. Every, 1887). He then describes what happens:

> A large oval balloon, filled with timid life, quivers off the loop and floats down to the street, carried along by the breeze. It is followed by the hopes of the delighted child, floating out into the space in its own magic bubble as if, for a few seconds, its fate depended on that of the nervous entity … For the duration of the bubble's life the blower was outside himself, as if the little orb's survival depended on remaining encased in an attention that floated out with it.[32]

The bubble is a useful image for the new transparency that dominates contemporary culture. In Sloterdijk, it describes the fragility of the self when it enters the public terrain; and it maps a disengagement of the self. The child's breath, *psyche* or soul may be 'inside' the bubble; yet it also remains inside the material body of the child. If this is an image of transparent modernity, then the modern self is also now conditioned by fragile precariousness. This is not just the precariousness of the self, already so well documented in contemporary theory and sociology; it is also the precariousness of politics itself, which faces a structural demise or disappearance.[33] Transparency shifts into immateriality, for which Sloterdijk's bubble is a perfect image.

We have here an image of the evisceration of the public sphere, and its replacement with a culture – even a cult – of intimacy, which confuses political truth with personal intimacy. In short, the world collapses into the most intimate part of the human self. This entails the demise of politics, and its replacement with gossipy prurience: a presidential candidate, for one paradigmatic example, assures the world about the size of his penis in staking his claim for political legitimacy.[34]

We dignify this horror by the newer forms of economics: the economics of well-being, of happiness, of the private life. Yet the entire discipline of modern economics has always been based precisely on this consideration of human happiness. Economics sets out simply to measure, through capital monetization, the commodities or services for which individuals are prepared to pay in order to keep them happy.[35] Even the recent commercial fashion of *hygge* is a consumer-driven capitalization of well-being, but it has its roots in eighteenth-century utilitarianism.

The contemporary suggestion that a turn towards the valorization of *hygge* in non-commercial ways is somehow an escape from capitalism and consumerism is, in fact, simply a cover for how our intimate self is always already capitalized, because we are now nothing other than pure human capital, available for financial exploitation and to provide profit to our neo-feudal masters. This contemporary drive is not an escape from capital, but rather the perversion of intimacy into corruption; and the corresponding politics is grounded in espionage: the mistrust that says we are being betrayed, and that demands transparency to reveal that betrayal and thereby to respond to our contemporary political culture of generalized resentment.

Arendt's account offers us a new fundamental distinction: the privacy is *not* the opposite of the political, but of the social:

> The decisive historical fact is that modern privacy in its most relevant function, to shelter the intimate, was discovered as the opposite not of the political sphere but of the social, to which it is therefore more closely and authentically related.[36]

The triumph of 'the social' produces the normative demand for social conformity, such that it is only in the intimate sphere that we can find distinctiveness.

At one level, of course, we have never had such a high degree of transparency in all things. The culture of transparency has led to the production of a huge amount of previously unrevealed information and data. This is so much the case that the analysis of 'big data' has itself become almost a full academic discipline. We can, for the moment, leave aside the simple fact that the body of literature, worldwide, probably constitutes one of the largest single masses of data that has ever been produced. If you want 'big data', enroll in a World Literature class.[37] It is as if there has been a clear correspondence between mass society, mass higher education, and mass data.

Structurally, we have seen similar things before. With the development of what sociologists identified as 'mass society' we had to find new ways of understanding how society worked. The key to this was the elevation of economics as a kind of meta-discipline, and one that has been governed by the regulatory modes of capital. The institutional form of literature, as we have seen, is not immune from this monetization of all values.

On one hand, literature has to be shared if it is to exist at all, which means that it has to be something that is intrinsically public; and, at the same time, we find ourselves now in a political situation in which the public is emptied of meaning and even emptied of being. When there is no such thing as society, it follows that we have essentially privatized all interests; and the consequence of this is that anything, such as literature, that is intrinsically characterized by its public existence has only two possibilities. Either it ceases to exist; or it, too, becomes privatized, and this latter position denies literature any political efficacy or material worldly reality.

The privatization of all interests then leads to the circumscription of the radical and critical powers of the 'event' that is literature, translating the event into the commodity form. 'Literature' becomes the 'Great Books' – the physical and often 'unread' commodities on the shelves – of the neoconservative traditionalist. Such a state of affairs entails the end of criticism, the end of freedom of assembly and, finally, the end of freedom of speech itself. This is where we now are. The economic condition of this needs some further exploration here.

Economics depends upon two things: a lot of information, and a tendency to abstraction; and it works through these on the basis of a presumed equality of all individuals in a society. As Arendt argued, mass society is another way of describing a unified homogeneous social world. Mass society indicates that various social groups have been absorbed into one specific identity, as a mass. Further, as a consequence, 'the social has finally … reached the point where it embraces and controls all members of a given community equally and with equal strength'. It follows that 'society equalizes under all circumstances, and the victory of equality in the modern world is only the political and legal recognition of the fact that society has conquered the public realm, and that distinction and difference have become private matters of the individual'.[38]

When economics becomes the meta-discipline, we establish an entirely new social dynamic. Where the public realm had once been where individuals displayed their individuality and distinctiveness, it is now the space for conformity and an abstract equality, which we often mistake for 'democracy', especially so whenever we confuse democracy with the tyranny of 'public opinion' or with a subscription to neo-Fascist attention to 'the will of the people'. Distinctiveness is now a private matter, such that our initial capital letter, capital I, is governed by its privacy, or privatization. This makes the demand for 'transparency' all the more pressing; but it also means that the demand for transparency has become determinedly complicit with the acceptance of a normative surveillance; and what surveillance is looking for is 'deviant' behaviour, conduct that is at odds with the conformity required by those already in power in our unequal neo-feudal societies.

If economics deals in this way in generalities and abstraction, literature – by contrast – is that which deals in the relations between such general abstractions and particularity. Literature registers the tensions between the public and the private; and the writing that does this is 'the novel'. In considering this specific genre of literature in such a way, we also discover that literature – inasmuch as it is literary – resists commodification under capital. That is to say: first, literature is something that 'happens' and is of the nature of an event; second, literature is that mode of action, event or happening that disturbs the homogenization of society and also of any of its constituent elements. It is thus anathema to all forms of identity politics.

The literary – and its attendant activity of criticism – refuses normalization. It is unruly, it 'misbehaves' with respect to rules; and in doing so, it resists the business and activity of being managed.

9

André Gorz points out that contemporary technology, and especially digitization of industries, has led to the position where work becomes 'the management of a continuous information flow', in and through which it is not the specific knowledge or vocational skill of the worker that is important; what matters is adaptability and 'behavioural skills, expressive and imaginative abilities and personal involvement in the task at hand'.[39] Performance is now measured in terms of the employee's personal commitment to specific forms of 'acceptable behaviour'.

Under contemporary capitalism, cultural criticism faces a similar fate. The institutionalization of literature is precisely the attempt to 'manage' it, to bring it to heel and to make it 'acceptable'. Indeed, the entire apparatuses of modern and contemporary literature – that endless stream of prizes, the publicity, advertising, and lobbying, the resulting celebrity status of some authors – all work to 'domesticate' literature. The corollary is that the subject who reads is also domesticated, given a private self to inhabit. It must, though, be inhabited in approved conformist and appropriately managed fashion, as a managed identity. The logic is precisely the logic from which this study began: feudalism, and not capitalism. The privatization of all interests – established through a demand for a specific version of 'transparency' that substitutes for 'truth' – entails a state of affairs in which the very subject itself is privatized and atomized. Certain problems follow for those who share an interest in how capital works alongside the institutions of literature.

Transparency in contemporary society is vital insofar as it ensures that the citizen *really* commits to determined social conformity. In our behaviour, we must *show* that we are the 'shiny happy people' of the utopian polity. Literary criticism, likewise, is a constituent part of this conformity, precisely because it happens within a system of 'management' in our universities and other social sectors.

In this state of affairs, it is the human subject herself whose bubble has now burst, and has become profoundly *immaterial*, insubstantial and of no consequence. We are now conditioned as immaterial subjects: transparent and precarious, like the child's balloon in Sloterdijk. Worse, however, politics itself has also thus become immaterial. It is nothing more than a contemporary business, a series of transactional relations shaped not by material content but by normative processes, whose legitimacy is governed precisely by mass conformity.

10

It is a commonplace of economics that, in many of the advanced economies, manufacturing of products has given way to the processing of services as the cornerstone of economic activity.

We no longer make doors, but learn to hold them open. Robots or the impoverished in other and poorer exploited nations now make the doors; managers go in procession through them; we are the facilitators of that procession.

This has an effect on our institutions of education. Veblen was right when he wrote, a century ago, that 'the higher learning takes its character from the manner of life enforced on the group by the circumstances in which it is placed'. He is more specific when he adds that 'These constraining circumstances that so condition the scope and method of learning are primarily, and perhaps most cogently, the conditions imposed by the state of the industrial arts, the technological situation', which he identifies as 'the pursuit of business'.[40]

That was 1918. In 2018, there is a very specific metaphor that governs the pursuit of business. It is a metaphor whose source lies in the myth of Hermes, the great messenger or agent of 'delivery'. In the contemporary world, for example, doctors and nurses no longer care for people but rather 'deliver' care, usually in a 'care-package'; law courts do not deliberate but 'deliver' judgments; and, in education, teachers do not teach, but 'deliver' learning.

Given that I opened this book with a consideration of the postal service with its delivery of letters, it is worth making a brief detour here on the contemporary motif of how we 'deliver' literature, or how literature has become part of the service industries. The key question is how literature relates to a culture of service. That issue is itself further shaped by the imminent privatization of higher education in the world's advanced economies.

The privatization of higher education has serious consequences, obviously for the general polity, but also more locally and specifically for the study of literature. The logic is simple, but also simplistic. Reading is a private matter, carried out alone and in silence, withdrawn from material and historical realities. It is not at all related to public life or to the service of the public; therefore, it is essentially a luxury and one in which it would be improper for the state to invest economic interest. As the late Patrick Johnston put it when he was vice chancellor at Queen's University Belfast, 'society does not need a 21-year-old that's a sixth century historian'. Instead, he argued, his task was to 'produce' a 21-year-old who can contribute to society, and who is a citizen with 'the potential for leadership in society'.[41] Behind this lay Johnston's abiding concern, which was that he had to 'produce' citizens who would be 'employable' in the society. We can admire the sense that the university should have a care for the society that subtends it; and we can admire the concern for the future employment of graduates. What makes this uncomfortable is simply the sense that, for all the university's focus on learning and research, it assumes that the world of business that runs the society has already got all the answers. Johnston is not producing citizens who will change things, but citizens who will fit into the existing structures of employment, consolidating the grip that existing capital has on our society as a whole.

Those structures are those of service, rather than of manufacturing or of making (*poiesis*). Service – service delivery or logistics – becomes the key determinant of value and of capital worth in this. But the question is: whom do we serve? If we are to serve the public, then, surely, we must be open and 'transparent' to that public. The privatization of knowledge – with individual students 'buying' it as their private acquisition – is entirely at odds with this, and thus we have a quandary in contemporary ideologies of higher education.

In fact, the university sector today has dealt with this problem by changing, quite radically, the name of the master whom we serve. An example will help explain. In 2013, some students occupied administrative offices in the University of London, as part of a protest in support of ancillary staff. Cleaning and maintenance had been outsourced, with the consequence that cleaners and maintenance workers found themselves being impoverished and exploited. The students wanted to serve these members of the general public better. The VC of the University of London, Adrian Smith, went to law and brought police onto campus to evict (eventually forcefully) the students from the site. He then secured an injunction prohibiting the students and 'persons unknown' from having access to the campus and its estate for any purposes associated with occupational protest.

Brenna Bhandar points out that the injunction was a 'private law remedy', which treated the University as a 'legal person' and 'private property owner'.[42] To compress this simply, Adrian Smith, as VC, claimed the estate as if it were his personal fiefdom.

This is increasingly common practice. It goes well beyond the traditional ways in which individuals are related to the estate of a campus, as when their name goes onto a new building, say, built because of their sponsorship. It is becoming quasi-structural. In the UK, the 'top institutions', it is well known, are in the 'Russell Group'. However, legally, that group contains not a single institution at all: it is a membership organization, comprising twenty-four *individual* vice chancellors, private individuals each paying a subscription from the funds of their own institution. Membership is by invitation only, and there are no published (public) criteria regarding the qualifications for membership. It is essentially secret, secretive, and thus prone to corruption; but what it corrupts is the entire university sector.

The twenty-four individuals arrogate to themselves the right to speak to the world on behalf of their own institutions (without any structural necessity of consulting the members of those institutions: students, faculty, ancillary colleagues), and also to speak on behalf of the 'elite' or leading institutions in the sector. They contend that it is their institutions alone that should receive research funding, the effect of which would be to increase yet further the already clear inequalities of access to knowledge that afflict the society as a whole.

In all of this, they are acting like feudal lords, carrying quasi-baronial titles and, as they see it, the corresponding entitlements. They require conformity to the university's commercial and reputational brand, which is the academic equivalent of an ill-informed and misled 'public opinion'. They demand feu duty, nowadays called 'grant capture'; and, when this is achieved, they take the credit in the form of scandalous personal pay increases. By this point, they have started to behave as if they were owners of the estate of the university: landlords. Academic staff and students become fodder for the position of the estate in competitive league-tables, themselves determining of further capital gains. The higher the league-table position, the greater will be the capital turnover, the general 'economic activity', and the higher the capital rewards for the landlord. This is the new serfdom. The paradox is that Hayekian economics, which was supposed to ensure that we avoided 'the road to serfdom', becomes precisely the vehicle that drives us straight onto that road.

In my final chapter, I will look at some examples of how it is that literature can resist such capitalization and neo-feudalism, and how we might retain the possibility of non-conformity, of criticism, of politics and even of our own subjectivity as citizens, through a consideration of literature's radical geography.

8

Radical Geography

1

Throughout this book, it has become clear that the institutions of literature have some fundamental relation to the ownership or appropriation of land, whether it be in terms of the financial capital that is invested in the ownership of private property, or in the material reality of 'real' estate as in estate poems, for instance. Indeed, we might find that this offers us a useful way of thinking not just about value, but also about culture as such; and it is one that will allow us to relate the very term of 'culture' to its etymological roots in ideas of growth on the organic land itself, or to that kind of 'cultivation' that we associate with 'civility' or civilization. Immediately, of course, we should see the linguistic oddity here: 'culture' seems to involve a relation to the rural land (as in our estate poetry and elsewhere) while also relating directly to civic life and to the developed city (as in Delhi, for example). We will be exploring this antinomy in the pages that follow here.

First, though, we should rehearse some fundamental – and politically emancipatory – positions regarding the operations of culture and of literature. Edward Said argues for the edifying properties of culture, as 'a concept that includes a refining and elevating element'.[1] In writing this, Said is holding to an idea of culture that relates it to moral or intellectual improvement, to some sense of a positive growth of the self, but one that is not crudely materialistic. This is an account of 'growth' that considers it in terms of how it 'refines' the cultured individual, and of how that individual becomes refined and elevated by her or his engagement with the materials of culture. This is close to both the Prussian ideals of *Bildung* or self-development and self-consciousness, and it is also reminiscent of Hegelian notions of a mode of thought that is related to *Aufhebung*, a synthetic transcending of perceived antinomies.

Further – and ostensibly against the logic of my arguments thus far – Said actually begins his definition of culture from an initial premise in which he essentially establishes culture as a kind of anathema to economics. For him, culture means, among other things 'all those practices, like the arts of description, communication, and representation, that have relative autonomy from the economic, social, and political realms'.[2] Such a culture takes 'pleasure' as one of its principal aims, argues Said. The point of this type of argument, I think, is to try to suggest that culture is that which cannot be reduced to commodification and that it is therefore intrinsically opposed to capitalist appropriation. You might own some books, but that does not mean that you have 'literature' or that you are somehow 'in possession of' culture. Culture is not something that you have or own; rather, it is something that – fairly literally – 'becomes' you: it is a form of life that we best describe as a mode of 'becoming someone', someone who is edified through the cultural engagement itself.

In my chapter on 'The Career of English' above, I indicated how Terry Eagleton has argued something similar, in *The Event of Literature*, when he tries to identify literature as a resistance to capital as it emerges as a dominant economic social form: 'One of the most vital functions of the work of art since Romanticism has been to exemplify that which is gloriously, almost uniquely free of a function, and thus, by virtue of what it shows rather than what it says, act as an implicit rebuke to a civilisation in thrall to utility, exchange-value and calculative reason. The function of art on this viewpoint is not to have a function'.[3] And, as I pointed out, Eagleton is really following his teacher, Raymond Williams, in this. For Williams, the concept of a mode of writing that is characterized primarily as 'creative' or related to the workings of imagination, is something that emerged 'in the late eighteenth century as a form of resistance to an increasingly prosaic, utilitarian social order'. Eagleton then construes this to mean that such a mode of writing becomes 'one of the last besieged outposts of transcendent truth in a harshly pragmatic environment', which allows

Eagleton to make the grand claim that 'The transcendent imagination and early industrial capitalism are born at a stroke. Literature and the arts become forms of displaced religion, protected enclaves within which values now seen as socially dysfunctional can take shelter'.[4] This was a key aspect of my argument above regarding how literature becomes institutionalized in the first place. Here, I will take this into the specific issue of 'the place of literature' as such, so to speak. That is to say, in this concluding chapter, I want to show how that early intimacy between land ownership and literature that shaped feudalism is transposed into a new critical disposition, regarding what I will call 'radical geography'.

Under the aegis of a supposed uselessness, literature submits to one of two possible fates: either it is subsumed within the culture industry, or it is institutionalized via education. In the first case, as an element within the culture and leisure industries, literature becomes subject to capital through the production and sale of books, magazines and journals. These can be extraordinarily lucrative, although not necessarily for the actual producers: authors. As in many forms of classical capitalism, it is the intermediaries between producer and consumer who 'make' and take the real profits. Recent (2016) figures for the UK, for example, indicate that a professional author's average annual income is around £12,000, which translates as around half the annual average UK income, and is substantially below the annualized minimum wage (of around £18,000). Most authors who responded to the survey that yields these figures gave a figure of around £7,000 as their annual income from writing. The UK publishing industry that same year registered profits of around £4.4 billion. Further, within this, there are massive inequalities of income among individual authors, replicating the general economy of inequality. The earnings of 0.1 per cent of authors account for more than 13 per cent of the total economy.[5]

In the second case, where literature is institutionalized, the economy is structured around cultural capital, and not on the primacy of such individual incomes. In this latter case, the value of literature is itself instrumentalized: a literary education becomes the means through which an individual progresses – via the claim of cultural capital – to demand or command a higher salary in the workplace. Cultural capital here becomes the means whereby an individual gains financial capital for their private good; but the price that the individual pays for this is that the individual submits herself or himself to the process in which they are reduced to mere human capital.

This – the reduction of the student to the status of mere human capital – is the logical corollary of the ideology that governed the Browne Review of 2010 in the UK, *Securing a sustainable future for higher education*.[6] That Review stated unequivocally the ideological proposition that a higher education is primarily a private benefit, and that any public good that follows from the private gains of the individual as they cash in their cultural capital is really purely incidental to the pursuit of individual profits. It fails to follow through the logic of this position, a logic that drives us to see cultural capital itself as being merely a shadow form of private financial profits. In this, the Review's ideological position is one that thoroughly undermines any tendency that might exist within the study of literature that would lead towards a criticism of the function of classical capitalism itself. Further, it fails to see the extension of that logic, in which the failure to critique the prevailing ideological economic norms of market fundamentalism leads to the re-feudalization of students (and teachers and critics) themselves.

This means that, within the institution that validates culture as capital (the institution of the university, say), literary students, teachers, and critics themselves all become instruments through which the institution itself manages the flow of capital and money. These are all now human capital, employed and deployed by the institution to boost its own cultural standing; and that standing and status is given to it by its corporate size, marked by annual turnover. If the institution is one that is fully and officially, legally, privatized, then the status is given by profit; and if it is at least notionally still a public institution, it nonetheless has to mimic the private model, and to act *as if* it is a profit-making business.

In short, uselessness has its supposedly intrinsic radicalism subverted by the processes and power of capital. The real and genuine decay that is at work in this renewed cultural decadence is the decay of the political itself, shaped to a large extent by the decay in the value of cultural capital. As my argument has shown, the only serious outcome of this, historically, is a situation in which cultural capital itself decays into human capital; and the result of that is the return to a neo-feudal condition, which is sometimes mistaken as the grounds for a revived democracy. The democracy in question is a democracy of the powerless, however: no matter our specific human capital, we are all equally disempowered against the substantive feudal structures that increasingly govern us, reducing us all – equally – to a ground-zero condition.

The ostensibly leftist and critical positions that are advanced in their various ways by Williams, Eagleton or Said, all work with a tacit desire to ennoble literature, in a fairly literal sense. They ensure that literature, like a noble gas, does not mix with other elements, that it somehow stands aloof and above the murky material world of finance capital. Literature 'refines and elevates', in the terms advanced by Said. It obviously does not follow from this, however, that literature escapes the clutches of politics, especially for these three thinkers. On the contrary, their position calls for explicit and detailed political analysis of literature – which is exactly what Williams, Eagleton, Said and others who take this view provide. After all, if literature is identified with a form of 'nobility' (with its shades of Kafka's *Zur Frage der Gesetze*), then it demands critical scrutiny by anyone who might be interested in the relation of literature to a wider polity. Yet the fundamental quandary here also explains why left-wing critics might be suspicious of the avowedly aesthetic qualities of literature, or why they fear that the political dimension that shapes and gives a constituency to literature can be lost under allegedly transcendent qualities that are supposedly immune from historical determination, qualities that are said to arise independently of history, politics and other material realities, including the realities of financial capital or of real estates: money and land.

The position that is outlined here, though – in which literature somehow is of the essence of a resistance to a specific functionalist and utilitarian ideology – is one that does nonetheless establish (or that tries to establish) a distance of sorts between literature and capital; and that is a distancing that I want to contest here. For Eagleton, the emergence of 'literature' is at one with transactional and functional capital; yet in terms of its function, it is opposed to capitalization. The suggestion of self-contradiction in this formulation is dealt with by seeing literature as 'dissonant' with the political moment of its emergence; and it is the more precise understanding of this relation between literature and capital – as one of assent or dissent – that must be explored further. 'No man but a blockhead ever wrote for anything, except money', said Johnson, famously. That is probably not true, especially given the historical fact that effective copyright only dates from the early eighteenth century; yet it does invite us to think seriously about the relation of writing – and, within that, the *institutions* of literature – to capital.

In this concluding chapter, I will pursue the inquiry further into how literature relates to the appropriation of place and thus also of identity, an appropriation that I will argue is a condition of the establishment of the modern nation State. As that nation-State comes under pressure thanks to the globalization of commerce, I will examine the radical geographies that now become possible. By this, I do not simply refer to that tradition of Marxist geography that started in the 1970s, best seen in the work of David Harvey, and that offers great insights still; rather, I take the term in a more literal and precise sense. I am interested in 'writing the earth', in 'earth-writing' (*geo-graphein*), and its relation to the radix or root, and thus once again to land, cultivation and culture.

2

A useful and interesting place to begin is with a text that dramatizes and explicitly visualizes the relation between a 'capital' letter and its less elevated miniscule. The poem I have in mind is one of Edwin Morgan's 'Newspoems', called 'Sick Man'. I quote it here in its entirety:

Sick Man

Say

O

o

1968

Morgan's 'Newspoems' are poems made of words, phrases or passages cut out from newspapers or ephemeral publications, and they are often distinguished by unusual and irregular typography. In calling them 'Newspoems', Morgan recalls Orwell's 'Newspeak', but there is a massive difference. 'Newspeak' in *Nineteen Eighty-Four* is a language designed to narrow the range of possible thought, and to limit or even eliminate entirely any form of dissident thinking or 'thoughtcrime'. By contrast, the 'Newspoems' – partly because of their very brevity – are expansive, calling for expansive and extended thinking in order to read them at all. These extend the possibilities of thought; and, in this respect, they are like Joyce's *Finnegans Wake*, while being more 'economical' than that text, at least in terms simply of linguistic brevity. The point of the Newspoems depends almost entirely on the dissonance or discrepancy between what might have been intended in the original use of the words or phrases and what can be invented or 'found' in the texts as they appear. Morgan deliberately plays on this – an intrinsic structural dissidence – to establish a large space for inventive engagement and interpretation.

He is clear about this in his Prefatory Note to the Newspoems, where he points out that 'most people have probably had the experience of scanning a newspaper page quickly and taking a message from it quite different from the intended one'. This was how he 'composed' the poems, in this act of 'cut-out-and-photograph' that is reminiscent of the aleatory techniques of William Burroughs or of John Cage.[7] In addition, though – and this is hinted at in the fact that the texts are photographed once they have been cut and pasted together – Morgan selected those that 'had some sort of arresting quality, preferably with the visual or typographical element itself a part of the "point" '. It is in this way that the poems become 'inventions', in both senses: 'the old sense of "things found" and in the more usual sense of "things devised" '.[8]

How, then, to read 'Sick Man'? How to 'invent'? After the title, the poem opens with someone saying 'Say O'; and the response is 'o'. It starts with what looks like a voiced (and inflated) 'capital letter'. Immediately, given the title, we might reasonably surmise that this is a poem about a sick man, which suggests that we have here a scene in a doctor's surgery. There, we hear two voices, one the doctor and the second a patient. The doctor – or the doctor's capitalized voice – towers over that of the patient, which looks and sounds like a faint shadow or echo of the voice of the doctor. The capital letter leans over the patient in his lower case not only visually, but also in terms of a literal standing that is measured metaphorically. It is more active, more the voice of an agent against that of a passive and echoing patient to whom it gives a lesser voice. It looks and sounds louder, more authoritative, more autonomous in that it is this voice that initiates the poem, with the patient merely echoing it or 'repeating after me', as it were.

Are we therefore not just in a doctor's surgery, but also in some kind of scene from Ovid, that of Narcissus and Echo? Given that the metamorphosis associated with that tale in Ovid turns Narcissus into a flower, does the poem therefore recall another text about a specific floral illness, like Blake's 'Sick Rose'? That, too, is a minimalist text whose very minimalism invites the reader to maximize possible worlds of meaning, in turn evoking an entire history of literature associating love with sickness, for instance. Some of this dates not just from Petrarch and other medieval courtly love traditions but also from the ancient world of Greeks and Romans. Yet perhaps the reference is to something in the Scots tongue, as in 'A Red Red Rose' by Burns, a poem also built around some structural repetitions, and a poem that is also a farewell poem, a poem about a lover leaving but being followed, and about the health of faring well or travelling well.

In 'Sick Man', we also have – literally 'literally' – a big O and a small o; or, were we speaking Greek, 'omega' and 'omicron'. If so, then the key initial word, the 'omega' as the last letter of the Greek alphabet, comes here before the omicron; and it suggests a reversal of the Greeks and perhaps even of Greek culture itself. Of course, the more conventional situation in which the doctor urges the patient to speak is one where she or he says 'Say Ah', not 'O'; but here, the A or alpha, or beginning, is missing. Instead of the alpha and omega, we have omega and omicron, an ending and a middle with no beginning, other than the word 'Say': so, in the beginning, therefore, is the word, 'say'; and we are in the realm of John's Gospel, the world of Revelations. This takes us back to the source of the text, which is 'revealed' in the newspaper cutting, as a revelation.

Morgan was adamant that the visual element in these poems was central. And, once we consider it visually, 'Sick Man' becomes also a fairly clear representation of money: it looks like a *penny-farthing* bicycle, with the 'Say' as the handlebars, the capital 'O' as the front wheel and the lower-case 'o' as the back. We might now therefore add that all of the foregoing – the medical aspect, the intertextual references, cyclical traveling, and the reversal of the Greeks – are all tied up with the look of money.

I begin here partly to show the richness – the 'wealth', as it were – of Morgan's poetry; but also to show that his poetry is never merely local. Its deep weaving of intertexts makes the reader move – perhaps even cycle – from the local to the peripheral. Indeed, this is actually at the heart of Morgan's aesthetic: he takes us 'from Glasgow to Saturn', as in the title of his 1973 collection, from the local space and land of Glasgow and Scotland, all meticulously described in his verse, through to the more-than-global, the cosmic that so fascinated him, as in 'In Sobieski's Shield', say, where 'we had been / dematerialized . . . / / . . . and here we are now rematerialized / . . . on a minor planet / of a sun in Sobieski's Shield'[9].

Interviewed several times in 2015 about his novel published the previous year, *Perfidia*, the American writer James Ellroy repeatedly stated that 'Geography is destiny'. In his case, the specific geography in question is that of Los Angeles, and he describes the city succinctly: 'LA: Come on vacation, go home on probation. LA is a life sentence for me; it's where I go when women divorce me; I need to live here in order to scrounge movie moolah to pay off my numerous ex-wives!' He goes on to reinforce his tie to LA as a place of his birth: 'I'm from LA. I'm obsessed with LA because I'm from here. My parents hatched me in a cool locale; geography is destiny – and I simply got lucky in that regard'.[10]

Edwin Morgan was 'hatched' in Glasgow and, notwithstanding the fact that he was multi-lingual, much of his poetry is determined by the language of Glasgow. This is his 'root', and his rooted tongue, as it were; and in his case, the root is a very radical geography indeed and one that is constantly 'displaced'. He became the laureate of Glasgow, and Scotland's Makar. It is convenient to think of him as a poet of place, a poet whose writing describes a place. However, as the 'Sick Man' analysis shows, it is a subjectivity that is revealed through the words: the words are what locate the speaker. Morgan's 'I' is not in control of his land; rather, he 'emerges' from the land; in the same way that his equally idiosyncratic 'emergent poems' emerge from a phrase.[11]

Yet what land is this? At one level, it is of course the local space of Glasgow. His Glasgow Sonnets, for example, delineate Glaswegian life: its streets, cafes, railway stations, the starlings in George Square in the city centre, the City Chambers, the Glasgow people. It is apposite to consider more fully the relation here between the tongue and the location: that is, to look at some poems that dramatize the giving of voice to the location of Scotland within the institution of literature as such. One key text here must be the poem that gives us 'The Loch Ness Monster's Song', which appears for the first time in the middle of the collection *From Glasgow to Saturn* in 1973 – almost as if this song fits into some median space between the intimacy of the location in Glasgow and the displacement of the self to Saturn.

The poem is often described as a 'sound-poem', and it looks rather difficult to read:

> Sssnnnwhuffffll?
> Hnwhuffl hhnnwfl hnfl hfl?
> Gdroblboblhobngbl gbl gl g g g g glbgl.
> Drublhaflablhaflubhafgabhaflhafl fl fl –
>
> gm grawwwww grf grawf awfgm graw gm.
> Hovoplodok-doplodovok-plovodokot-doplodokosh?
> Splgraw fok fok splgrafhatchgabrlgabrl fok splfok!
> Zgra kra gka fok!
> Grof grawff gahf?
> Gombl mbl bl –
> blm plm,
> blm plm,
> blm plm,
> blp.

Again, the question here is how to engage, how to 'invent'? The poem is explicitly written in the singing voice of the Loch Ness Monster, and so we might not expect it to be immediately available to us. It is foreign, coming from the depths of one of the deepest lochs in Scotland. But the Monster is moving between its media: from the water to the air. What is it saying as it emerges in this way, as we witness the emergence of this new Scottish voice, a voice that ties a tongue to a place and that dramatizes how geography becomes destiny?

As was the case with 'Sick Man', this poem too is replete with repetitions or with near repetitions. It opens with two questions, which seem to generate a response that is first fluent before degenerating into what looks like a stammer of sorts: 'gbl gl g g g g glbgl'. Clearly (clearly?) the Monster is trying to speak to us but is having difficulty in finding – or inventing – a voice. In the second line of the second stanza, it suddenly looks as if the Monster might have heard some Russian being spoken, or might have heard itself referred to as being related to a diplodocus. Yet there are also some terms that look as if they may be derived from Polish or Hungarian: 'Splgraw', 'Zgra' and so on. In response to fresh questions, the Monster seems to speak with a certain urgency or impatience, perhaps even trying to approximate to the language that it has heard, including some obscenities: 'fok fok … fok splfok!' Yet it still sounds not quite clear, though we are now perhaps approximating to a condition of communication, for fuck's sake (or 'fok splfok!').

As if desperate to be heard, the Monster utters three variants on the same basic sound: 'Grof grawff gahf' and the question-mark indicates that this is in a tone that is seeking a response of some kind, or that is unsure of how best to speak the word. It is as if the Monster is trying various ways of uttering our own language, whatever that may be. The sounds approximate to a more or less standard English-sounding phrase: 'get off'. First, it is as if abbreviated into an almost Glaswegian pronunciation 'gerroff!', itself uttered yet more gutturally as 'Grof'. Next, the Monster tries a much posher, almost standard English variant, in which the 'off' of Glasgow-English mutates into something close to 'awrf'. Finally, it becomes even more high-falutin' as we lose the 'r' entirely, and the 'o' of 'off' changes to an English Received Pronunciation as 'ah'. In short, what we see here is the Monster speaking a Scottish tongue but having to translate it into upper-class English in order to become audible. At this point, it gives up and submerges itself again.

The poem, in short, is about the emergence of a specific Scottish writing that has been submerged and considered a fantasy by the proclaimed 'norms' of a 'standard' English. It asserts an identity that differs from that which is given to Scottish writing by the institution of a standard and standardized 'English'. Perhaps needless to say, standard English is scandalized by this, finding it 'monstrous', especially given its hints of infiltration by foreign tongues, like that of Russians, Poles, Hungarians: communists all at the time when Morgan wrote the poem. Morgan's own interest in these languages was also shaped by his interest in dissident voices, such as that of Attila Jószef or of Mayakovsky, both writers whose work he translated.

The Loch Ness Monster thus sings, in a condition of dissidence and dissonance, and in a voice that we might think of as being tied intimately to a place, confirming the Ellroy view that 'geography is destiny'. However, given that this 'Scottish' voice is contaminated by snippets of words that sound like an odd combination of Russian, Hungarian or Polish tongues, we cannot simply conclude that Ellroy's aphorism is correct in its applicability to Morgan's case. Rather, it is the case that Morgan is demonstrating a voice that is travelling, that is very definitely *not* to be identified purely and simply with a specific patch of land.

This is a kind of 'deterritorialized' poetry, and to that extent – and to the extent also that it resembles the Joyce of *Finnegans Wake* – it is anathema to a feudal and also to a capitalist relation to the land. This is a song, then, of deracination and of a more general deterritorialization; and the same applies to the poetry of Morgan more generally. The claim of poetry upon the intimate relationship between land and identity is one that is not shaped by ownership or propriety or property; rather, it is about the mixing of tongues, the refusal to claim the land itself. In this regard, it is the very opposite of imperialist appropriation of an other land. It is, as Seamus Heaney might put it, an 'opening' of the ground itself.

In Joyce's own wake, in Ireland, perhaps the greatest example of this is indeed Heaney. For many, this will be counter-intuitive, given Heaney's obvious concern with the land, with the archaeological demand to dig for one's ancestry, through which much literary criticism sees him as the bardic inheritor of the mantle worn by Yeats. Yet, if we look closely at how Heaney thinks the 'language of the land', as it were, we see that this is also 'the lie of the land'. The kind of authenticity he seeks is not one of a fixed rootedness and an ethnic claim for a kind of intrinsic Irish autochthonous identity.

Morgan built a poem, as we saw, on the capital letter O; and Heaney frequently comments on the 'vowel meadow' that forms the ground for a good deal of his own poetry.[12] A more or less random, if typical, selection of moments in his poetry makes the case clear. 'Broagh' gives us 'the shower / gathering in your heelmark / was the black O // in *Broagh*', where we also hear of the '*gh* the strangers found / difficult to manage'. In 'Gifts of Rain', we have 'Moyola ... // breathing its mists / through vowels and history'. The Glanmore Sonnets – coming just after 'The Guttural Muse' – opens with 'Vowels ploughed into other: opened ground'. 'A New Song' tells of how 'our river tongues must rise // ... To flood, with vowelling embrace / Demesnes'. 'The Skunk' sees the poet writing love letters, and the key letter is a vowel: 'broaching the word "wife" / Lie a stored cask, as if its slender vowel / Had mutated into the night earth and air // Of California'. 'Field Work', where we might expect a concentration on land, turns instead to 'your vaccination mark ... / an O that's healed'.[13]

It is perhaps in 'Alphabets' that we see this focus on individual letters most fully deployed. In this poem, letters are re-described precisely as visual and material entities, with a Y being a 'forked stick', an A (whose pronunciation is contested) being 'Two rafters and a cross-tie on the slate', and so on. The letters themselves become first homely, describing elements that are familiar and based in the childhood home and school; but then they become increasingly 'unhomely', *unheimlich*, as they translate the familiar into the strange or foreign. The way into this is through 'a wooden O' where the poet stands, after the globe of the earth in the window – itself already described as 'a coloured O' – has spun. Standing in that wooden O, the poet alludes directly and explicitly to Shakespeare, for whom the world itself was a stage wherein we find our identity precisely through a series of changes, disguises, 'antic dispositions', differences and dissident modulations of selfhood.

The point of these engagements with Heaney or Morgan is that they show how fully tied to letters the poets are. They 'capitalize' on the letters, and are – perhaps paradoxically – unfailingly 'literal' in the sense that they re-map the world as language. In this sense, they are genuinely 'world poets', engaging with what we must call a 'worlding' of literature, and a worlding that takes us away from a sense of national identity towards a more internationalist sense that the self is given through a translation, and through a transfiguration of identity into difference.

3

In returning us to Shakespeare – as he has also done in his early poems such as 'Viking Dublin', where 'I am Hamlet the Dane' – Heaney invites us also to look at the importance of letters historically. Here, I am not referring to letters as missives, important though they are in Shakespeare; rather, my focus is on how letters engage a worldliness, in this same worlding of literature that I have outlined in both Morgan and Heaney above. In a trope relatively common in late sixteenth- and early seventeenth-century poetry, Shakespeare maps the globe onto a woman's body, and does so by way of a play on words, involving crucially a word that sounds like a letter. In *The Comedy of Errors*, Dromio of Syracuse is being pursued by the kitchen maid, and, when asked her name, he replies: 'Nell, sir; but her name and three quarters / That's an ell and three quarters, will not measure her from hip to hip ... she is spherical, like a globe; / I could find out countries in her'.[14] Following this, he satirizes various countries by aligning them and their classic characteristics with the material form of her body. 'An ell' is, of course, a unit of measure; but, spoken in the theatre, it sounds exactly the same as 'an L'; and that is, indeed, what the kitchen maid is, a Nell, an L. Indeed, she is an L and three quarters, or £1¾: she is herself (L) and three-quarters more of herself again, her body the site of an economic inflation.

Shakespeare also applies a similar trope in his mapping of the land itself in *King Lear*. In Act 1, scene 4, we find the Fool engaging Lear in a deliberately ambiguous language. His first substantive speech is a song that he proposes to teach Lear; and it is a song about making profit:

> Have more than thou showest,
> Speak less than thou knowest,
> Lend less than thou owest,
> Ride more than thou goest,
> Learn more than thou trowest,
> Set less than thou throwest;
> Leave thy drink and thy whore,
> And keep in-a-door ...

And then, finally, we arrive at the moral of the song:

And thou shalt have more
Than two tens to a score.

This is followed by the description of a commercial transaction, when Lear says that 'This is nothing, fool', to be countered by the Fool's 'Then 'tis like the breath of an unfee'd lawyer; you / gave me nothing for't'. Can you make no use of / Nothing, nuncle?' The capital O, this time as a capital zero, 0, returns here to haunt and provoke Lear; but the Fool is not yet finished. When Lear answers that 'nothing can be made out of nothing', the Fool turns to Kent and tells him 'Prithee, tell him, so much the rent of / his land comes to'. Lear's capital, tied to the land of the nation, is here reduced to nothing.

Yet the Fool has more. He proposes a mercantile transaction: 'Give me an egg, / Nuncle, and I'll give thee two crowns'. Two crowns are ten shillings; and, in Shakespeare's time, this would have often been written in lower-case Roman letters, thus: xs – or 'excess'. Yet, when Lear tries to keep up with the fooling and asks 'What two crowns would they be?' he is again met by a zero, a nothing: 'Why, after I have cut the egg i' the middle, and eat / up the meat, the two crowns of the egg' – or, in other words, another empty spherical O. In these Shakespearean examples, we see that authority is again tied to land and to money: this is where capital itself lies, but this time it is tied firmly to a kind of autochthony, a feudal sourcing of the self in the soil and land at one's feet. That soil now roots the individual's capital in the nation-state. It is, literally, a radical geography, a writing of the roots of a self as located in a place; and here is the source of a national and nationalist polity, as the basis of an economy.

We know this kind of trope more familiarly through its use by Donne, who famously sexualizes geography, and genders imperialism and colonization, as in the much-discussed example of 'The Sun Rising', which locates the poet and lover at the centre of all that exists. We have been very accustomed to a conception of globalization that places Europe – and indeed Britain and France – at the centre of the world. That tendency has been somewhat corrected since the mid-1980s, especially in the wake of Said's pioneering work

on *Orientalism*. Prior to the emergence of such work on colonialism
and imperialism, we had more or less unquestionably accepted the
silent geo-politics of a reading of John Donne that placed this English
poet at the centre of the world. This, however, was controversial even
when Donne was writing.

In 1543, Copernicus radically de-stabilized the world in his
De Revolutionibus: no longer was the earth at the centre of the
universe. However, such a destabilization was in turn really a means
of re-centring the world, on the European subject or self, and
above all on the speaking subject, the voice that says 'I'. This had
a philosophical component, as I showed earlier in this study, in the
work of Descartes some years after Donne, for Descartes radically
doubts the existence of the entire world before re-generating it,
centred upon the 'thing that thinks', the Cogito and the subject; and
in both the *Meditations* and the *Discourse on Method*, that subject
is the 'I' who utters the words 'cogito ergo sum'. This is the tongue
at the centre of the world – the tongue that we have seen as both
the subject and object of 'government'. It has also a cultural corollary,
such as we see it when Donne collapses the entire world into the
space of his lover's body in 'The Sun Rising'. In that play of space,
the woman herself becomes the centre of an entire world, whose
east and west bearings are taken from the relation between the
lovers and the space in which they make love, a space of a privatized
intimacy.

At the centre of this world is, again, a single letter: I. In this case,
the letter is the foundation of the meaning for the poem and for the
world – or at least that is the conceit. 'She's all states, and all princes, I,
/ Nothing else is'. This is the key to the text as a whole, partly because
of its ambiguities, ambiguities that are nonetheless re-stabilized by
the centrality of the letter I itself. The poet has collapsed the entirely
of the world into the figure of the mistress, and it is this that translates
her into the materiality of 'all states'. However, there are two ways
of reading the following phrase 'and all princes, I, / Nothing else is'.
In the first place, we can read this as meaning that, given that the
mistress is 'all states' and that the poet is the master of the mistress,
then, logically, he is 'all princes'; and, further, there is nothing outside
that text, 'Nothing else is'. However, we can also hear 'Nothing else
is' in its contemporary sense as 'Otherwise, nothingness will come

into being'; or 'nought' – like O, like 0 – becomes the totality of the world – the position claimed by I.[15]

More recent understandings of the relation of literature to land have helped change this kind of account. One way of thinking about Donne's famous conceit is to see it as a metaphysical and metaphorical attempt to control an environment, or to 'contain' the very fact of space and distance. That is also one way of describing the movement of colonization and of imperialist expansion that had its origin in a moment more or less contemporaneous with the time of Donne's writing. To be sure, also, such containing of the world is directly related, as in Donne, to the growth and appropriation of material wealth: 'both th'Indias of spice and mine', as Donne writes it.

Travel is now much more widely available, thanks to all sorts of advances in technology. Further, it has also become something that is increasingly privatized, through ownership of cars. As we saw, it is this that has shaped the ecology of modern Delhi, for example; but it is not just a local phenomenon there. Paul Beatty's satirical novel, *The Sellout*, catches something of what is at stake in this. The novel is set in the fictional town of 'Dickens', near Los Angeles. It is fictional precisely because it no longer actually exists: it had been so synonymous with degradation that the very name of the place gets erased. The narrator, 'Me', wants to reinstate and to re-draw the boundaries of Dickens, but is constantly being hampered by the character of Hominy, who adopts Me as his 'owner', in an attempt to reinstate black slavery. Me finds that Hominy has managed to reintroduce racial segregation on the bus that is driven by Marpessa, the woman whom Me would like as his girlfriend. The situation provokes a meditation on transport in LA.

Me claims that 'There are more cars in Los Angeles County than in any other city in the world'.[16] However, about half of these cars are completely immobile, as they 'sit on cinder blocks in dirt patches passing for front yards'. Me can't think what is the point of these wrecks, but notes that, for each car that is immobile, it means 'one less car on the road and one more rider on the bus of shame'. In Los Angeles, the car relates directly not just to wealth but also to private ownership of the mode of transport. The car indicates how one can pass through the world safe within a privatized sphere; and to be excluded from that privatized wealth and status reduces one to having to ride with others on public transport. The bus is the site of shame because it is a shared space, not owned by those inside it.

Why is this shameful? The answer is 'because L.A. is about space, and here one's self-worth comes from how one chooses to navigate that space'. There is a class hierarchy established: 'Walking is akin to begging in the streets. Taxicabs are for foreigners and prostitutes. Bicycles, skateboards, and Rollerblades are for health nuts and kids, people with nowhere to go'. And, no matter how bad the car, it is always better than taking the bus.[17] It is better precisely because it is the appropriation of private space, but this time of a private space that is mobile and not restricted to a single plot of land. It enables the subject to be mobile, not tied to any single place; and, in this regard, it is a clear symbol of the way in which capital and wealth can melt even the solidity of a place into air.

We should recall here that Rana Dasgupta is also profoundly aware of the importance of the car, not in a fictional world but in the real historical city of Delhi, which he describes as a city that is built around the car. Like LA, it is dominated by what the car signifies, which is the mobility of wealth itself, the very mobility of capital that is increasingly 'global'.

This brings us to the crux of the antinomy from which I began in this chapter. Raymond Williams famously considered the country and the city to exist in a kind of dialectical relationship. The readings I have been advancing, however, modify this. Culture is at once related to the rootedness of the rural landowner and also to the mobility and explicit unrootedness of life in the city. It is the site wherein one is tied to the land for one's identity, while also being simultaneously an uprooting of any such fixed identity. One resolution of the antinomy here is to be found in the formation of the modern subject as property developer or real estate speculator. Such a resolution involves a migration of rural landowning proprieties into the heart of civic life; and it is here that we can return to Delhi.

4

Dasgupta repeatedly points out that Delhi was born of what he calls 'the catastrophe of India's partition'; and he argues that the 'ravages' of partition 'turned its culture towards security and self-reliance'. It follows from this – and here we see the very idea of the privatization of space and of mobility harnessed – that 'the compounds in which its richest citizens take refuge from society are only the most extravagant manifestations of a more widespread isolationist ethos'.[18]

For Dasgupta, Delhi was built from partition itself, in that 'Partition refugees, who had been denuded of their assets, were magnetically drawn to the consolations of property, and they acquired as much of it as they could'.[19] Initially, people were reluctant to live in the city, preferring the countryside with which they were more familiar and where they felt more rooted and at home. A plan was needed in order to bring people into Delhi itself, so 'the administrators offered them large plots of land [in the city] at a greatly reduced rate.' The first people to come on these terms were contractors who 'snapped up sites in the centre of the city for their own mansions, and also bought up large areas of city land as investments'. It is in this way that the contractors, already made rich through payment for the work they did in building the city, become fabulously wealthy as property prices rose, especially in the boom. They are now, as Dasgupta says, 'Delhi's new aristocracy' whose families are guaranteed 'wealth and prestige for a century to come'.[20]

There are massive consequences that follow from this. Uprooted from rural life, the people also disengage from the language that tied them to those places, adopting instead the primacy of English (as I argued in 'The Career of English' above). Further, this linguistic displacement went hand in glove with a further displacement, from communal living to privatized ownership and the increasing isolationism of high bourgeois individualism, predicated on the privatization of land and the establishment of a rentier society. After the establishment of Delhi, contractors do not stop appropriating land: they move back out from the city. More and more land – more and more rural land – in India is appropriated by rich individuals, large multinationals, and corporate businesses; and they do this with the connivance of government, argues Dasgupta. This is part of that too intimate alliance between government and business that is leading to the rise of Fascism across the world. When it happens in India, we get a situation where, 'in the first decade of the twenty-first century, some 15,000 Indian farmers committed suicide every year.

The only way out' – out of a spiral of debt into which they have been forced by conglomerates.[21]

In his outstanding study of postcolonial environments, Pablo Mukherjee has traced this horrific phenomenon in more detail; and has been able to tie it firmly to the shifts in capital, land ownership, and the influence of large conglomerates more directly. Mukherjee draws on the research of Somini Sengupta to reveal the full horror. The figures bear repeating here: in 2003, more than 17,000 farmers killed themselves, most of them doing so by poisoning themselves. The poison they used was the pesticide that they were supposed to use in order to produce high-yielding crops for corporations like Monsanto.[22] Mukherjee goes on to show that these figures, however, are drastically under-calculated. In one decade, between 1997 and 2007, the figure is in fact closer to 182,936 farmers who killed themselves, yielding a statistic for the period 2002 to 2007 of one suicide every thirty minutes. Yet it does not stop there, because there are also a series of corollaries of this state of affairs, inhibiting the life chances of the rural poor, impoverishing Indian people more generally, and establishing that structure of massive inequalities that have started to cause enormous social and political problems worldwide.

There is, then, a clear way of evaluating culture in this. The rural life of an Indian can be sacrificed every thirty minutes in a structure that essentially requires that death in order to sustain the rentier economy that helps sustain the city of Delhi; and the city of Delhi is, in turn, being built upon the capital not just of property but also of symbolic capital such as that of a writing that is done in English and that forms a part of the institution of 'English Literature' as a site of value itself. It is on this sacrifice of human life that the culture of the city of Delhi rests. In this regard, however, Delhi is not an exception: it is, instead, the exemplary manifestation of the rule of contemporary capital. Within that rule, there is the constant danger that literature will find itself capitulating to a coerced acceptance that it, too, exists for money. The key mechanism that facilitates this is the University that converts itself into a shell company whose purpose is the growth of GDP and of turnover. Such an institution routinely now sees itself as 'global'; and its influence globally determines this degradation of human life, reducing the individual to mere bio-capital for exploitation, exploitation unto death.

In Dasgupta's view, Delhi is a manifestation of the ravages of partition; and he writes that the 'spirit' of the place is dominated by a 'sense of living in the aftermath', and that this particular attitude 'has dominated the city's literature until our own time'. It is not just a spatial division between city and countryside that is at work in all this, therefore; it is also the historical sense of there being a division between the present moment and one's historical roots. He writes 'The capital of a fast-growing and dizzyingly populous nation it might be, but Delhi's writers have consistently seen it as a city of ruins and they have directed their creativity to expressing that particular spiritual emaciation that comes from being cut off from ones' own past'. This is itself consistent, we might add, with the oddly neo-Trotskyist attitude adopted by neoliberal economics that there is no past at all, that every moment is a new beginning, and that we are always only in Year Zero. For Dasgupta, the situation in Delhi is one where it is 'as if everyone becomes, by virtue of being in Delhi, a survivor, someone living on after the loss of everything they held dear'.[23]

The very polity itself is now shaped and stratified by this antinomy between the priorities of the city's civic culture and those of rural agri-culture; and it casts Delhi's culture in the shape of an existential crisis. Literature, we might say here, is a matter of life and death, a matter of the survival of humanity as such. And, as it is for Delhi, so it is for any and all places worldwide that are structured according to this new form of capital. In the past, we have often considered literature to be about a kind of survival, certainly; but we have usually cast that as a form of historical transcendence. We have argued, like the Shakespeare of the Sonnets, that literature is where we hear the continuing voice of those who are corporeally dead. In this way, literature has been construed precisely as a 'medium' that allows the living to communicate with the ghostly voices of those who have gone before, and to memorialize their words in various ways.

5

This will no longer suffice, in our contemporary structural organizations of capital. It is the case now that culture itself and culture as such – and within a general understanding of culture, we can take literature as a paradigmatic example – is the site of a particular life-and-death struggle. Writing, as and when it helps formulate and consolidate its own institutionalization in the form of 'literature', is a matter of life and death. Contemporary capital works by putting a price on that, and calibrating the value of a text, say, against the value ascribed to a human life, the life of an Indian farmer, for example. There is indeed, as Benjamin pointed out to us in a time of similar financial crisis to that which we are undergoing in these first decades of the twenty-first century, 'no document of civilization that is not also and at the same time a document of barbarism'.[24]

Benjamin also famously argued that the aestheticization of politics would lead to only two things: first, war, and then fascism. This, I think, can now be modified in a small yet significant way. In our time, we can suggest that it is the commercialization of politics – and with it the concomitant commercialization of aesthetics – that will lead to war and to fascism. That is to say: aesthetics and politics are now both subject to the laws of commercialization – the laws of these new forms of capital, in which finance, land, and writing all coalesce in the deep antinomy that shapes this argument – and, being thus combined and thus subjected to commercial capital, the resulting attempt to resolve the antinomy leads only to conflicts. We can see this in the recent rise of the dispossessed worldwide against the managerialist classes, those managers who have themselves commercialized culture to the point where it becomes a pure commodity. Like the Indian farmer, those who are systematically excluded from this find that their very livelihood is in danger; and they have recourse to various forms of extremist politics, as in the rise of the political far right across Europe and the United States, or the rise of various forms of religious fundamentalisms elsewhere.

The great paradox here, of course, is that the institutionalization of literature, as a site of value or capital as such, is intrinsically linked to the barbarism that says we can sacrifice human beings for its very existence. This may help explain why it is the case that we began from a criticism that desperately tries to see literature as edifying, for the reality – that it is a matter of a human struggle for survival in which the poor will be sacrificed – is a matter not of edification but rather of shame.

A radical geography is now required if we are to avoid this. We have seen here some examples of this, in the mode of reading that I have adopted to engage with some modern and contemporary writing in this chapter. It is a matter of Morgan's 'invention': a literary practice and activity that takes its task to be the discovery of language itself, and an imagining of how we might survive, living on through a mode of inhabiting the earth, an earth that must, now, be re-written. Our survival depends on it.

Notes

INTRODUCTION: LITERAL CAPITAL

1 'June 1657: An Act for setling the Postage of England, Scotland and Ireland', in *Acts and Ordinances of the Interregnum, 1642–1660*, ed. C. H. Firth and R. S. Rait, (London: HMSO, 1911); available at: http://www.british-history.ac.uk/no-series/acts-ordinances-interregnum/pp1110-1113. The Act also standardizes prices for all different types of correspondence, under the head of one Postmaster General. Interestingly, it also makes it clear that one part of the activity will be to intercept mail 'to discover and prevent many dangerous, and wicked Designs' against the Commonwealth; and so it bears comparison with the 'Investigatory Powers Act' of 2016: http://www.legislation.gov.uk/ukpga/2016/25/contents/enacted/data.htm

2 For an outstanding discussion of 'the public' in constitutional terms, see Claire Westall and Michael Gardiner, *The Public on the Public* (London: Palgrave, 2015).

3 Karl Marx and Frederick Engels, *The German Ideology*, ed. C. J. Arthur (London: Lawrence and Wishart, [1846] 1989), 42.

4 Samuel Richardson, *Pamela*, in 2 volumes (London: Dent, [1741] 1924); vol. 1, 2–3. In the revised Oxford edition (2001), edited by Thomas Keymer and Alice Wakely, Pamela tells her parents what they must already know in fact – that she has been regularly sending them money.

5 Samuel Richardson, *Clarissa*, in 4 vols. (London: Dent, [1748] 1962), vol. 1, 3–4.

6 Mary Poovey, *Genres of the Credit Economy* (Chicago: University of Chicago Press, 2008), 104.

7 Montesquieu, *Lettres persanes*, repr. (Paris: Garnier-Flamarion [1721] 1964), 229 [translation mine].

8 Ibid., 231 [translation mine].

9 See Michael Lewis, *The Big Short* (London: Penguin, 2011). Famously, in 2008, when faced with the enormity of the financial crisis in the United States, George W. Bush said that 'If money isn't loosened up, this sucker could go down' (as reported at: http://www.nytimes.com/2008/09/26/business/26bailout.html). We can compare this with the anonymous epitaph written for John

Law: 'Ci-gît cet Écossais célèbre, / Ce calculateur sans égal
/ Qui, par les règles de l'algèbre, / A mis la France à l'hôpital'
(see *Dictionnaire historique, critique, et bibliographique* vol. 9
(Paris: Mame Frères, 1811), 571).

10 Montesquieu, *Lettres persanes*, 242 [translation mine].

11 Arjun Appadurai, *Banking on Words* (Chicago: University of Chicago
Press, 2015), 1, 4.

12 Ibid., 9.

13 See Michael Sandel, *What Money Can't Buy* (London: Penguin,
2012). Joseph Stiglitz has also spoken often of market
fundamentalism; but his argument is that 15 September
2008 'marked the end of market fundamentalism', because that
was the day when the US government 'made clear that it did not
believe that markets by themselves worked'. See Stiglitz, 'Moving
Beyond Market Fundamentalism', *Annals of Public and Cooperative
Economics*, 80: 3 (2009), 345. See also Paul Krugman, 'Why
Zombies Win', *New York Times*, (19 December 2010): 'Free-market
fundamentalists have been wrong about everything – yet they now
dominate the political scene more thoroughly than ever'.

14 Georg Simmel, *The Philosophy of Money*, trans. Tom Bottomore
and David Finlay (London: Routledge, 1978), 66. See also Appadurai,
Banking, 11, on this dissociation in markets.

15 Simmel, *Philosophy of Money*, 128–9.

16 Ibid., 130.

17 Blaise Pascal, *Oeuvres completes* (Paris: Seuil, 1963), 550 [all
translations mine]. The passage comes from pensée number 418 (in
the Lafuma numbering, 233 in the Brunschvicg edition).

18 See Stefan Collini, *That's Offensive!* (Calcutta: Seagull Books, 2010);
and cf. Steven Connor, 'On the Offensive', in which the giving and
taking of offence is fully captured as a capitalist relation. See: http://
www.stevenconnor.com/offence/.

19 Jacques Derrida, *The Gift of Death*, trans. David Wills (Chicago:
University of Chicago Press, [1992] 1996), 34.

20 Ibid., 34.

21 Matthew Arnold, *Culture and Anarchy*, ed. J. Dover Wilson
(Cambridge: Cambridge University Press, [1869] 1971), 51, 52.

22 Ibid., 109.

23 See Pierre Bourdieu, *Distinction*, trans. Richard Nice
(London: Routledge, [1979] 1984), especially 23–4, on the academic
aristocracy and its entitlements.

24 E. M. Forster, 'George Orwell', in *Two Cheers for Democracy* (London: Edward Arnold, [1950] 1951), 74.

25 Forster, 'What I Believe', in *Two Cheers*, 78.

26 Ibid., 78. Forster is referring to *Inferno*, Canto 34, where Dante sees the three-headed Lucifer, each head chewing on a sinner who is characterized by the betrayal of a friend: Judas in the middle mouth, and Brutus and Cassius, who betrayed the individual Caesar in favour of the State, on each side.

27 Ibid., 78.

28 Ibid., 79.

29 Ibid., 82.

30 Ibid., 83.

31 Ibid., 80.

32 Ibid., 84.

33 Ibid., 85.

1 CAPITAL AND THE EMBRACE OF LETTERS

1 See Edward Luce, *The Retreat of Western Liberalism* (New York: Atlantic Monthly Press, 2017). Admittedly, the focus of this book is mostly on the United States, and so it is not as all-encompassing as Oswald Spengler, *The Decline of the West*, abridged edn, trans. Charles Francis Atkinson (Oxford: Oxford University Press, 1991).

2 Shakespeare, *Twelfth Night*, 2:3: Toby Belch asks Malvolio, 'Dost thou think, because thou art virtuous, there shall be no more cakes and ale?'.

3 The reference here is to the systematic destruction of the ancient sites of Palmyra by IS militants. See reports at: https://www. theguardian.com/world/2017/jan/20/isis-destroys-tetrapylon-monument-palmyra-syria and at: http://www.independent.co.uk/news/world/middle-east/isis-destroy-palmyria-central-syria-ancient-city-roman-amphitheatre-antiquities-islamic-state-a7536686.html. For the attack on 'experts', see Michael Gove, interviewed by Faisal Islam on Sky News, 3 June 2016, available at: https://www.youtube.com/watch?v=GGgiGtJk7MA.

4 I am especially indebted here to the work of my colleague, Graeme Macdonald, for making these connections clear to me. See, especially, his extraordinary introduction to his edition of John McGrath, *The Cheviot, the Stag, and the Black, Black Oil* (London: Bloomsbury, 2015).

5 Richard Ford, *Between Them* (London: Bloomsbury, 2017), 55.

6 See Naomi Klein, *This Changes Everything* (London: Allen Lane, 2014); and see also Rudolf Bahro, *From Red to Green*, trans. G. Fagan (London: Verso, 1984) and Daniel Cohn-Bendit, *Que Faire?* (Paris: Tapage, Hachette, 2009).

7 Oscar Wilde, 'The Portrait of Dorian Gray', in *Complete Works* (London: Hamlyn, 1985), 376.

8 Edward Skidelsky and Robert Skidelsky, *How Much is Enough?* (London: Penguin, 2013), 5.

9 David Marquand, *Mammon's Kingdom* (London: Penguin, 2015), xiv.

10 See Mary Poovey, *Genres of the Credit Economy* (Chicago: University of Chicago Press, 2008).

11 Gérard Genette, *Figures III* (Paris: Seuil, 1972), 75

12 Virginia Woolf, 'Modern Fiction', in *Selected Essays*, ed. David Bradshaw (Oxford: Oxford University Press, 2009), 7, 9

13 For the full account of this argument, see my *New Treason of the Intellectuals* (Manchester: Manchester University Press, 2018). I have written a critique of the corrupt nature of the presiding norms of the University institution in two other books, *For the University* (London: Bloomsbury, 2011), and *Universities at War* (London: Sage, 2015).

14 Wilde, *Complete Works*, 30

15 Percy Bysshe Shelley, 'A Defense of Poetry', in *English Critical Essays: Nineteenth Century*, ed. Edmund D. Jones (Oxford: Oxford University Press, [1916] 1971), 138

2 ON THE CREDIBILITY OF WRITING: MATERIAL PROMISES

1 Rana Dasgupta, *Capital* (London: Penguin, 2014), 8.

2 Ibid., 9.

3 Ibid., 9.

4 On the fundamental importance of 'circulation' to modern fiction, see David Trotter, *Circulation: Defoe, Dickens and the Economies of the Novel* (London: Palgrave, 1988). See also W. H. Auden, 'In Memory of W. B. Yeats': 'poetry makes nothing happen; it survives / in the valley of its making where executives / would never want to tamper.'

5 The use of GDP as a measure of a national economy is of recent date. Simon Kuznets is usually credited with its initial formulation in

1937; and it becomes accepted and widely deployed internationally after Bretton-Woods in 1944.

6 See David Marquand, *Mammon's Kingdom* (London: Penguin 2013; repr. 2015), 1 and *passim*; and cf. Paul Mason, *Postcapitalism* (London: Penguin, 2015), 200, 241, 222, 258, respectively.

7 Mason, *Postcapitalism*, 240. He derives the observation from E. L. Eisenstein, *The Printing Revolution in Early Modern Europe*, 2nd edn (Cambridge: Cambridge University, 2005).

8 Thomas Piketty, *Capital*, trans. Arthur Goldhammer (Cambridge, MA: Harvard University Press, [2013] 2014), 238 ff.

9 Ian Rankin, *Even Dogs in the Wild* (London: Orion Books, 2015), 95.

10 Piketty, *Capital*, 241.

11 In some ways, this is the mirror version of those works of literary criticism that made what we called 'the economic turn' that began in the final decades of the twentieth century. The work of Regenia Gagnier is a good example of this turn and its subsequent development into globalization studies. See, for examples, her *Idylls of the Marketplace* (Stanford: Stanford University Press, 1986), and *The Insatiability of Human Wants* (Chicago: University of Chicago Press, 2000).

12 John Lanchester, 'When Bitcoin Grows Up', *London Review of Books*, 38: 8 (21 April 2016), 3.

13 Colin Nicholson, *Writing and the Rise of Finance* (Cambridge: Cambridge University Press, 2004), 4.

14 Ibid., 6.

15 Jonathan Swift, *Gulliver's Travels and Other Writings*, ed. Louis A. Landa (Oxford: Oxford University Press, 1976), 74, 90. It would be interesting to compare these with present-day images related to capitalism, in which artificially pneumatic female breasts are aligned, in advertising, with wealth and masculinist success. There is a further story to be told relating contemporary capital with pornography, and with control of the human body in its very material shape. I will address some of this in subsequent chapters here.

16 William Wordsworth, *Poetical Works*, ed. Thomas Hutchinson, revised by Ernest de Selincourt (Oxford: Oxford University Press, 1975), 163.

17 Jean-François Lyotard, *The Inhuman*, trans. Geoff Bennington and Rachel Bowlby (Cambridge: Polity Press, 1991), 66.

18 Dasgupta, *Capital*, 49.

19 If we are looking for a recognizable literary analogy here, we might consider the poetry of Keats who, trained in medicine, writes his own medical diagnoses into his verse, referring to the 'purple-stained mouth'; and giving credibility to the meaning of the verse in his self-critical Letters.

20 Dasgupta, *Capital.*, 48.

21 Ibid., 62.

22 Ibid., 63.

23 Ibid., 59.

24 Nicholson, *Writing*, 7.

25 Ibid., 8–9.

26 Adam Smith, *The Theory of Moral Sentiments*, ed. D. D. Raphael and A. L. Macfie, repr. (Indianapolis: Liberty Fund, [1759] 1984), 184–5.

27 See Mary Poovey, *Genres of the Credit Economy* (Chicago: University of Chicago Press, 2008), 175 (for Hume and Elibank), 94 ff. (for Defoe).

28 See G. R. Hibbard, 'The Country House Poem of the Seventeenth Century', *Journal of the Warburg and Courtauld Institutes,* 19 (1956), 159–74. See also Alastair Fowler, ed., *The Country House Poem* (Edinburgh: Edinburgh University Press, 1993). Given that Fowler included Pope's translation of Homer, it might reasonably be argued that the tradition long pre-dates this specific English language tradition; and is of much larger extent than was ever imagined by Hibbard in his original identification. It may also be related to 'world literature', which will become of increasing importance in this present study.

29 Hibbard, 'Country House Poem', 163.

30 Ibid., 163.

31 Ibid., 164.

32 Fowler, *Country House Poem*, 8.

33 Ibid., 8.

34 Hibbard, 'Country House Poem', 164.

35 Raymond Williams, *The Country and the City* (Oxford: Oxford University Press, 1973), 32.

36 Stephen Duck, 'The Thresher's Labour', in *Poems on Several Occasions* (1936), available at: http://quod.lib.umich.edu/e/ecco/004857010.0001.000/1:11?rgn=div1;view=toc

37 Fowler, *Country House Poem*, 8–9.

38 Kari Boyd McBride, *Country House Discourse in Early Modern England* (Ashgate: Aldershot, 2001), 4.

39 Ben Jonson, *The Complete Poems*, ed. George Parfitt (London: Penguin, 1975), 96.

40 Virginia C. Kenny, *The Country-House Ethos in English Literature 1688–1750* (New York: Harvester/St Martin's, 1984), 1–2.

41 J. G. A. Pocock, *The Machiavellian Moment* (New Jersey: Princeton, 1975), 450–51; cited in Kenny, *Country-House Ethos*, 2.

42 Kenny, *Country-House Ethos*, 3.

43 The most important foundational work in this area is that done by Edward Said, in *Culture and Imperialism* (New York: Vintage Books, 1993), and Javed Majeed, *Ungoverned Imaginings* (Oxford: Oxford University Press, 1992).

44 Dasgupta, *Capital* 167.

45 The more commonplace version of this Europeanization is that associated with Cairo, described as 'Paris on the Nile' when Khedive Ismail bankrupted the city after he tried to Europeanize its planning, having seen the 1867 'Exposition Universelle' in Paris that year. For an excellent investigation of the real substance behind this myth, see Mohamed Elshahed's online account, 'Paris was never along the Nile' available at: http://cairobserver.com/post/14185184147/paris-was-never-along-the-nile#.V9andksTFZi

46 Dasgupta, *Capital*, 167.

47 Ibid., 167.

48 Ibid., 19.

49 Ibid., 20.

50 In a mode that is almost self-parody, the upper classes in this TV series are perplexed at the idea of 'a job' (instead of 'running the estate'), and the Dowager Countess famously does not even understand the concept of 'a weekend'. See: https://www.youtube.com/watch?v=zhfpBW-nUWk. There are also precursors of this series, also focused on the estate: the TV series *Upstairs, Downstairs* 1971–75, or *The Forsyte Saga* of 1967–78 based on John Galsworthy's Edwardian-era novels.

51 This was the refrain used rhetorically by George Osborne, Chancellor of the UK Exchequer 2010–16, in order to justify his austerity policies that disproportionately hit poor people in the UK, those without land and property.

52 In passing, note that it is always positive value that is thus allegedly inherited: royalty rarely lays claim to the inheritance of various forms of psychological disorder or pathological political positions.

53 John Lanchester, *Capital* (London: Faber and Faber, 2012), 15.

54 Jonathan Coe, *Number 11*, (New York: Viking Press, 2015), 235. For the actual economics of this in terms of housing in London, see Danny Dorling, *All that is Solid* (London; Penguin, 2015).

55 Dasgupta, *Capital*, 267. The European parallel is perhaps that figured in Roddy Doyle's *The Commitments*, the story of deeply impoverished north Dublin youth seeking to make a living from playing soul music. As the film's publicity blurb had it: 'They had absolutely nothing; but they were willing to risk it all.'

56 Ibid., 268.

57 Inequality is the subject of Chapter 5, where I explore its significance in more detail.

3 THE CAREER OF ENGLISH

1 In passing, it is useful to recall that one dominant theory of the beginnings of writing as such suggests that cuneiform writing was an aide-memoire for financial transactions: writing and accountancy go together. This intimacy of writing with accounting – not the main issue for this present book – is explored in some detail in my study of *Complicity* London: Rowman & Littlefield International, 2016).

2 Fredric Jameson, *The Antimonies of Realism* (London: Verso, [2013] 2015), 27.

3 This is an extremely large and complex topic (too large to be able to do full justice to it here), to do with the extent of free speech, freedom of expression, the power of language to shape material realities and similar issues. It will be the subject of another book, provisionally titled *Speaking in, Acting out*. For a good exploration of some of the fundamental issues, see, for example, Timothy Garton Ash, *Free Speech* (London: Atlantic Books, 2016). See also the essays included in Cheryl Hudson and Joanna Williams, eds., *Why Academic Freedom Matters* (London: Civitas, 2016), and Stefan Collini, *That's Offensive!* (Calcutta: Seagull Books, 2010).

4 J. M. Coetzee, *Disgrace* (London: Vintage Books, [1999] 2000), 117.

5 The predicament here recalls that which is also described by James Joyce in 'The Sisters', the opening story of *Dubliners*, mapping the paralysis of a nation as a condition of language and political occupation.

6 Coetzee, *Disgrace*, 117.

7 Dasgupta, *Capital*, 169.

8 Ibid., 174–5.

9　Gayatri Chakravorty Spivak, 'The Burden of English', in *The Lie of the Land: English Literary Studies in India*, ed. Rajeswari Sunder Rajan (Oxford: Oxford University Press, 1993), 276.

10　Bentick would immediately after this return to Britain, where he took up a seat as MP for Glasgow. There, he furthered relations, especially trade relations, between India and Scotland, and found a controversial but at times warm welcome from the increasingly radicalized population. He was a somewhat reluctant MP, desperate to stand down partly for personal family reasons (related to his wife's health, which necessitated living in Paris), but party politics required him to retain the seat.

11　'Minute by the Honorable T. B. Macaulay, dated 2nd February 1835', available at: http://www.columbia.edu/itc/mealac/pritchett/00generallinks/macaulay/txt_minute_education_1835.html. Subsequent references to this text will be given by paragraph number.

12　Macaulay, although ignorant of Arabic and Sanskrit, claims that he is not at all ill-informed: he has acquainted himself with the best work in both literatures through translation. Interestingly, of course, this 'Western literature' is itself also best known through translation – specifically of the ancient classics of Greece and Rome, as the Minute makes clear. The issue of translation will become important later in this chapter as we turn attention directly to 'world literature'.

13　Matthew Arnold, *Culture and Anarchy*, ed. J. Dover Wilson (Cambridge: Cambridge University Press, 1971), 6.

14　F. R. Leavis, 'A Sketch for an English School', in *Education and the University* (London: Chatto & Windus, 1943), 74. I explore this more fully in relation to Leavis and twentieth-century institutionalizations of 'English' in my *Criticism and Modernity* (Oxford: Oxford University Press, 1999), especially pp. 230–42.

15　Gauri Viswanathan, *Masks of Conquest* (New York: Columbia University Press, 1989), 3.

16　Viswanathan dates the introduction of English Literature in England to 1871, when 'it consisted of memorizing of passages of poetry and testing knowledge of meaning and allusions' (Viswanathan, *Masks*, 171 n4).

17　Viswanathan, *Masks*, 6. For a fuller exploration of the philosophical paradox here, especially in relation to the formation of the modern University institution, see my *Criticism and Modernity* (Oxford: Oxford University Press, 1999), 205–45.

18　Viswanathan, *Masks*, 7.

19 Lionel Grossman, 'Literature and Education', *New Literary History*, 13: 2 (1982), 345.

20 Viswanathan, *Masks*, 18; and see also p142, were Viswanathan describes the irony whereby the gradual secularization of literary education in India coincides more or less with the moment when 'the moral motive was slowly gaining ground in English studies in England'.

21 Declan Kiberd, *Inventing Ireland* (New York: Vintage, [1995] 1996), 1.

22 Ibid., 5.

23 Ibid., 4.

24 Ibid., 4.

25 For an interesting complement to Kiberd, see Robert Crawford, *The Scottish Invention of English Literature* (Cambridge: Cambridge University Press, 1998).

26 Kiberd, *Inventing Ireland*, 6.

27 Johann Peter Eckermann, *Gespräche mit Goethe* (Berlin: Aufbau-Verlag, 1982), 198 [translation mine]. See also ibid., 227–8, where Eckermann records a conversation some six months later, in which Goethe again claims for world literature the ability to allow Germans, French and English to 'correct' [korrigieren] the isolated views they hold of each other; and this, he suggests, is the primary usefulness of World Literature.

28 Seamus Heaney, 'From the Frontier of Writing', in *Opened Ground: Poems 1966–1996* (London: Faber and Faber, 1998), 297–8.

29 The key text exploring the issues of translation and translatability for 'world literature' is Emily Apter, *Against World Literature* (London: Verso, 2013).

30 Heaney, *Opened Ground*, 3.

31 David Damrosch, *What is World Literature?* (New Jersey: Princeton University Press, 2003), 4.

32 Ibid., 6.

33 Thomas Piketty, *Capital*, trans. Arthur Goldhammer (Cambridge, MA: Harvard University Press, 2014), 8.

34 Marx and Engels, *The Communist Manifesto*, ed. A. J. P. Taylor (London: Penguin, 1967), 83.

35 Ibid., 84.

36 Damrosch, *What is World Literature?*, 3–4.

37 Marx and Engels, *Communist Manifesto*, 85.

38 See Stefan Collini, *Absent Minds* (Oxford: Oxford University Press, 2006); and, especially in relation to Burke, see Seamus Deane, *The French Revolution and Enlightenment in England* (Cambridge: Harvard University Press, 1988), about which I say more later. See also Richard Bourke, *Empire and Revolution: the Political Life of Edmund Burke* (New Jersey: Princeton University Press, 2015).

39 See Lennard J. Davis, *Factual Fictions* (Philadelphia: University of Pennsylvania Press, 1983; repr. 1997) for the relation between newspapers and the emergence of the modern novel form, linked by a popular interest in crime.

40 Raymond Williams, *Resources of Hope* (London: Verso, 1989), 82.

41 Piketty, *Capital*, 8.

42 See Seamus Deane, *French Revolution*. For an excellent commentary on this work, and its implications for our understanding of modernity in Ireland and England, see Conor McCarthy, 'Seamus Deane: Between Burke and Adorno', *Yearbook of English Studies*, 35: *Irish Writing since 1950* (2005), 232–48.

43 Deane, *French Revolution*, 12.

44 Walter Bagehot, *The English Constitution* (1867; repr., London: Collins, 1963), 262–3. The question addressed here is really about the possibility of maintaining a private life, which is the subject of chapter 6.

45 Raymond Williams, *Keywords* (London Fontana, 1976), 185.

46 Terry Eagleton, *The Event of Literature* (New Haven: Yale University Press, 2012), 24.

47 Ibid., 89–90.

48 John Guillory, *Cultural Capital* (Chicago: University of Chicago Press, 1994), 303.

49 Martin Wolf, *Fixing Global Finance* (Baltimore: Johns Hopkins University Press, 2010), 31.

50 Ibid., 31.

51 Ibid., 31.

52 Arjun Appadurai, *Banking on Words* (Chicago: University of Chicago Press, 2016), 13.

53 Ibid., 126.

54 Ibid., 149.

55 Wolf, *Fixing Global Finance*, 32

56 Appadurai, *Banking on Words*, 127.

57 Dasgupta, *Capital*, 216.

58 Ibid., 216.

59 Ibid., 246.

60 Ibid..

61 See George Soros, *Open Society: Reforming Global Capitalism* (New York: Little, Brown, 2000).

62 Upamanyu Pablo Mukherjee, *Postcolonial Environments: Nature, Culture and the Contemporary Indian Novel in English* (London: Palgrave, 2010), 1; and cf. Dasgupta, *Capital*, 262.

4 GOVERNING THE TONGUE

1 George Orwell, 'England Your England', in *Inside the Whale*, repr. (London: Penguin, [1957]1972), 63.

2 Interestingly, in the First War, Paul Valéry asked similar questions about the relation of war to civilization as such. See his 'Two Letters to the Athenaeum', published in 1919 as *La Crise de l'Esprit*, available at: http://classiques.uqac.ca/classiques/Valery_paul/crise_ de_lesprit/valery_esprit.pdf and see also my commentary on this in my *Universities at War* (Sage, 2015).

3 He notes his own troubling tendency to elide the difference between 'England' and 'Great Britain', but casts any anxiety about that aside rather brusquely.

4 Orwell, 'England', in *Inside the Whale*, 66.

5 Stefan Collini, *Absent Minds* (Oxford: Oxford University Press, 2006), 138. One precursor for this inward turn is to be found in Virginia Woolf's 'high modernist' advice, in her essay on 'Modern Fiction', in *Selected* Essays, ed. David Bradshaw (Oxford: Oxford University Press, 2008), 9, to 'Look within!' for the realities of life. There is a more recent manifestation of this mentality, such as we find it in the determination of a figure like John Carey to valorize a kind of English no-nonsense 'middle-brow' literature and criticism, over against an ostensibly 'foreign' or European 'high theory'. It would be interesting to trace a route from this anti-theory moment in the UK to the vote for Brexit in 2016.

6 Orwell, 'England', in *Inside the Whale*, 75. This kind of position has been at the heart of some of the most important contemporary theoretical discussions regarding the status of world literature and translation. See, especially, the work of Emily Apter, *Against World Literature: the politics of untranslatability* (London: Verso, 2013), and Barbara Cassin, *Vocabulaire européen des philosophes: dictionnaire des intraduisibles* (Paris: Seuil, 2004).

7 Orwell, 'England', in *Inside the Whale*, 66.

8 Ibid., 174.

9 Ibid., 73.

10 Ibid., 74 It is worth pointing out, in passing, that this political phenomenon remains alive and well in England (and elsewhere) in 2016. It formed an essential component of the 'Vote Leave' campaign to persuade the British electorate to leave the European Union: Brexit. It remains the abiding characteristic of the United Kingdom Independence Party, UKIP, and helps explain its otherwise inexplicable centrality in British politics, as a party that has managed to shape the national debate with only one elected MP (Douglas Carswell), who defected to UKIP from the Tory party, only to defect again a short time later.

11 Orwell, 'England', in *Inside the Whale*, 75. In the US presidential election of 2016, the situation is even worse, in that Donald Trump and 'Trumpism' trumps anything resembling coherent thought.

12 Orwell, 'England', in *Inside the Whale*, 77.

13 For a brilliant examination of enthusiasm as a key determinant of a specifically American literature, see David Herd, *Enthusiast!* (Manchester: Manchester University Press, 2007).

14 John Galsworthy, *The Man of Property,* repr. (London: Penguin, [1906] 1967), 24; Montpellier Square is described by Swithin as a ' "capital position" '; Irene will also be described as having a 'capital' figure physically (p. 28).

15 Ibid., 32.

16 Ibid., 35.

17 We might recognize this privatization of truth in its more recent guise, as the so-called 'post-truth' politics of politicians who appear to be not just consummate but also constitutional liars.

18 Orwell, 'Prevention' in *Inside the Whale*, 161.

19 For an outstanding extended examination of the stakes of this, in both politics and culture, see Claire Westall and Michael Gardiner, *The Public on the Public* (London: Palgrave, 2014). My argument here also helps explain why the publishing world has capitalized massively on the increase in interest in personal biography and autobiography, especially of 'celebrity' figures: behind the supposed 'public' and celebrated figure, we get the 'reality', which is a private self. That interest coincides historically with the triumph of economic neo-liberalism.

20 Essentially, it is as if the UK government 'lobbies' the BBC here. Viewed in this way, this becomes part of a wider phenomenon

that corrupts government through an over-intimate relation to commercial business. See Tamasin Cave and Andy Rowell, *A Quiet Word: Lobbying, Crony Capitalism and Broken Politics in Britain* (New York: Vintage, 2015).

21   Orwell, 'Prevention', in *Inside the Whale*, 164. For Mandelson's phrase, see Alwyn Turner, *A Classless Society* (London: Aurum Books, 2013), 334.

22   I have written more extensively on this in *Universities at War* (London: Sage, 2015).

23   Howard Jacobson, *Pussy* (London: Jonathan Cape, 2017), 6.

24   Its contemporary formulation in English politics in 2016 is encapsulated in the phrase 'Brexit means Brexit', which was actually Prime Minister Theresa May's way of retaining an absolute power for herself, by the 'restraint' of saying nothing while seeming to say something substantial. The phrase is fully and totally 'balanced': a pleonastic palindrome, full of sound and fury, signifying nothing. See my essay, 'Brexit: thinking and resistance', in *Brexit and Literature*, ed. Robert Eaglestone, (London: Routledge, 2018).

25   For a critique of the institutionalization of economics on a mathematical model, see Joe Earle, Cahal Moran, and Zach Ward-Perkins, *The Econocracy* (Manchester: Manchester University Press, 2016); and cf. also the work of Ha-Joon Chang.

26   Edward Skidelsky and Robert Skidelsky, *How Much is Enough?* (London: Penguin, 2013), 5. In this regard, see also Richard Wilkinson and Kate Pickett, *The Spirit Level,* revised edn (London: Penguin, 2010); and cf. Paul Mason, *Postcapitalism* (London: Penguin, 2016).

27   For the full and detailed background argument about this, see my *For the University* (London: Bloomsbury, 2011), and my study of *The New Treason of the Intellectuals* (Manchester: Manchester University Press, 2018).

28   Geoffrey M. Hodgson, 'The Great Crash of 2008 and the Reform of Economics', *Cambridge Journal of Economics,* 33: 6 (2009), 1205–21. The quoted passages come from page 1209. For an account of this making the argument clear for non-specialists, see the 'Knowledge@Wharton' comment, 'Why Economists Failed to Predict the Financial Crisis', available at: http://knowledge.wharton.upenn.edu/article/why-economists-failed-to-predict-the-financial-crisis/

29   There are numerous accounts of the formation of 'Comparative Literature' as a historical and institutional phenomenon. For a fuller

discussion of the key texts (by Haun Saussy, Franco Moretti, Gayatri Spivak and many others), see chapter 5, 'For a Literature that is without and beyond compare', in my study of *The English Question* (Brighton: Sussex Academic, 2008). The account that I prioritize here is that of Gayatri Spivak, from her *Death of a Discipline* (New York: Columbia University Press, 2003).

30 Erich Auerbach, *Mimesis,* trans. Willard R. Trask (Princeton: Princeton University Press, 1968), 552. I have examined this passage in detail in my *English Question,* 83.

31 See Anthony Howard, 'We are the Masters Now', in *Age of Austerity 1945–1951,* ed. Michael Sissons and Philip French, (London: Penguin, 1964), 16.

32 With the most extraordinary series of paradoxes here, the original melody of the Tory song derives from a French song, though the language here is very characteristically upper-class English; and the words of the Red Flag were composed by an Irishman, Jim Connell.

33 Howard, in Sissons and French, *Age of Austerity,* 21. The identification of propriety with restraint in the House of Commons persists to the present day, though it is coming under increasing pressure. The group of 56 Scottish Nationalist MPs elected in 2015 were reprimanded by a (Scottish) Deputy Speaker for applauding; but the whole House was essentially permitted to applaud Tony Blair when he gave his last Prime Minister's Questions session, and, more recently, they applauded – especially the Tory benches – when Hilary Benn, a Labour MP, made an impassioned speech supporting the Tory-planned extension of air-strikes against Islamic State militants in Syria.

34 Orwell, 'Prevention' in *Inside the Whale,* 159.

35 Brian Leveson, *An Inquiry into the Culture, Practices and Ethics of the Press,* vol. 1 (November 2012) Executive Summary, introduction, paragraph 5, p 4. See https://www.gov.uk/government/uploads/system/uploads/attachment_data/file/229039/0779.pdf

36 Ibid., paragraph 9, p. 5.

37 Orwell, 'Prevention', *Inside the Whale,* 160.

38 Ibid., 160.

39 I mean here to refer not only to the First and Second Iraq Wars, but also to a general disposition towards war itself in our political discourse. Clear examples of this would include the so-called 'war on terror', and the language of the Brexit campaign in 2016, which reveled in nostalgic images of the plucky British set against a European enemy. There is, in historical research, a further argument that suggests that not only have we never fully surfaced from the

Second War (1939–45), but that war was itself a continuation of the Great War of 1914–18. If this is so, then we have been living through a new 'hundred years war'.

40 James Joyce, *A Portrait of the Artist as a Young Man*, ed. Richard Ellmann (London: Granada, 1982), 171.

41 Ibid., 171.

42 Ibid., 172.

43 Ibid., 178, 179.

44 The fine distinction here, between cultural capital and cultural capitalism is taken from Robert Hewison, in *Cultural Capital* (London: Verso, 2014). Cultural capitalism is what we have when cultural capital is monetized and commodified as product for sale.

45 Orwell, 'Prevention', in *Inside the Whale*, 171.

46 Ibid., 171–2.

47 Ibid., 172.

48 Needless to say, most colleagues within those programmes may well not teach mechanistically at all; but my point is about the structural – and therefore ideological – similarity between these programmes and the schools attacked by Orwell on the grounds of their incipient intimacies with totalitarian modes of thought, modes that are subtended by bureaucracy. Others might see the growth of 'creative writing' as a mechanism for supplying the advertising industry and, with that, extending the reach of the culture industry itself. This would then be complicit with the monetization of culture, and the transfer of such capital into crude financial capitalism: the 'bought writer', in Orwell's phrase.

49 Orwell, 'Prevention', in *Inside the Whale*, 172.

50 Ibid., 162. Lying and totalitarianism go together for Orwell; it is not that lying is simply a matter of political expediency, but is structurally integral to totalitarianism. On this, see the nuances in two essays by Hannah Arendt: 'Lying in Politics', in her *Crises of the Republic* (New York: Harcourt Brace, 1972); and 'Truth and Politics', in her *Between Past and Future*, ed. Jerome Kohn (London: Penguin, 2006). I explore this in more detail in *Complicity* (Lanham: Rowman & Littlefield, 2016), 77–103.

51 Orwell, 'Prevention', in *Inside the Whale*, 164.

52 Robert Harris, *Conclave* (London: Hutchinson, 2016), 70.

53 Ibid., 70. Tedesco, here, rehearses the well-worn Sapir-Whorf hypothesis; but the important aspect of that, in my argument here, relates to the politics of place and nation, the politics of national identity.

54 Harris, *Conclave*, 71.

55 For a fuller exploration of this, see my *Reading (Absent) Character* (Oxford: Oxford University Press, 1983). In 1972, Gabriel Josipovici, from whose work some of this argument derives, noted precisely this 'paranoia' in his explanation of the 'rise of the novel' in England. In *The World and the Book* (London: Penguin, 1972), he advances an argument that links the rise of novelistic fiction explicitly with Protestantism.

56 Orwell, 'Prevention', in *Inside the Whale*, 161.

57 This long pre-dates some structuralist and post-structuralist accounts of Marxism, such as we see it in the work of Pierre Macherey or Louis Althusser; and is expressed by Orwell in his much more 'plain style' prose. That difference in mode of presentation is itself worthy of fuller exploration.

58 Fredric Jameson, *The Antinomies of Realism* (London: Verso, 2015), 6.

5 INEQUALITY, MANAGEMENT AND THE HATRED OF LITERATURE

1 The classis inaugural exposition of all that is at stake here is found in Hans Ulrich Gumbrecht, *Atmosphere, Mood, Stimmung*, trans. Erik Butler (Stanford: Stanford University Press, 2012). Gumbrecht's proposition is that such mood, such *Stimmung*, is not in the least ethereal but actual and material: literature makes mood 'present', and thus 'presents' the world. My claim is that, on the contrary, such a 'presenting' or 'presencing' is always 'otherworldly', imaginary, an idea and an ideal. I owe almost all that I know of this subject to Birgit Breidenbach.

2 Karl Marx and Frederick Engels, *The German Ideology*, ed. C. J. Arthur (London: Lawrence and Wishart, 1989), 42.

3 See W.K. Wimsatt, *The Verbal Icon*, repr. (London: Methuen, [1954] 1970), and Cleanth Brooks, *The Well-Wrought Urn*, repr. (London: Methuen, [1947] 1968).

4 See Wolfgang Iser, *The Implied Reader* (Baltimore: Johns Hopkins University Press, 1974).

5 The classic history of Russian Formalism is Victor Erlich's *Russian Formalism*, 3rd edn. (New Haven: Yale University Press, 1981).

6 The classic texts are gathered in Theodor Adorno et al., *Aesthetics and Politics*, with foreword by Fredric Jameson, trans. ed. Ronald Taylor; repr. (London: Verso, [1977] 1990).

7 For another view of our current economic condition, see Paul Mason, *Postcapitalism* (London: Penguin, 2015). Rigorous in his analysis of current crises, Mason nonetheless finds cause for optimism in a hypothetical future where technology and ecology are embraced for general human survival and well-being. David Marquand, in *Mammon's Kingdom* (London: Penguin, 2013), has an equally bleak analysis, and a different prescription for the re-establishment of a shared public realm, taken back from the privatized culture of individualist acquisitiveness or greed. See also Michael McKeon's magisterial *Secret History of Domesticity* (Baltimore: Johns Hopkins University Press, 2005), and Walter Benn Michaels, *The Gold Standard and the Logic of Naturalism* (Berkeley and Los Angeles: University of California Press, 1987).

8 Michael Sissons and Philip French, eds., *The Age of Austerity* (London: Penguin, 1964), 10.

9 Thomas Piketty, *Capital*, trans. Arthur Goldhammer (Cambridge, MA: Harvard University Press, 2014), 264.

10 Primo Levi, *The Drowned and the Saved*, trans. Raymond Rosenthal (London Abacus Books, 1989), 17.

11 Piketty, *Capital*, 275.

12 In passing, it is worth noting that the Grenelle Accords were discussed and agreed (though never signed) in the Ministry of Labour (Ministère du Travail) in the Rue de Grenelle. The Ministry building had previously been the seat of the Archbishop of Paris between 1849 and 1905, during which time it housed four Archbishops. Medieval and feudal culture is in the very brickwork of Grenelle.

13 Piketty, *Capital*, 289.

14 David Kynaston, *Austerity Britain 1945–51* (London: Bloomsbury, 2007), 605.

15 Jerry Z. Muller, *The Mind and the Market: Capitalism in Western Thought* (New York: Random House, 2002), 323.

16 Ibid., 323; see also John Kenneth Galbraith, *The Affluent Society*, repr. (New York: Houghton Mifflin, [1958] 1998).

17 See Theodor Adorno and Max Horkheimer, 'The Culture Industry' in *Dialectic of Enlightenment*, trans. John Cumming (London: Verso, [1944] 1979), and Theodor Adorno, *The Culture Industry*, ed. Jay Bernstein, repr, (London: Routledge, [1991] 2001).

18 See: http://www.woodyguthrie.org/Lyrics/This_Land.htm for the lyrics. A variant of this stanza exists, in which Guthrie sings 'As I went walking In saw a sign there / And on the sign it said "No Trespassing" / But on the other side it didn't say nothing, ' That side was made for you and me'.

19 For the full details of this, see 'English Housing Survey: Households 2013–14', available at: https://www.gov.uk/government/uploads/system/uploads/attachment_data/file/461439/EHS_Households_2013-14.pdf. See also Danny Dorling, *All that is Solid* (London: Penguin, 2015).

20 If one wants a crude example of how popular publication exemplifies such a monetization of aesthetics, one only has to consider the explosive growth of both style magazines and celebrity magazines in this period.

21 See Danny Dorling, 'Know Your Place', available at: http://www.dannydorling.org/wp-content/files/dannydorling_publication_id0460.pdf

22 Piketty, *Capital*, 289–90 and see also ibid., 278–81 for more of the detail on this phenomenon. The two figures lying behind this rise of the managerial class are Peter Drucker, who is sometimes credited with inventing 'management studies' as a scholarly discipline, and Tom Peters, whose rise to worldwide prominence in the 1980s helped to realize some of Drucker's ideas but, more importantly, raised the profile of the 'manager' to almost guru and celebrity status.

23 Piketty, *Capital*, 278.

24 Ibid., 278. Piketty also emphasizes these huge differences in social stratification, even within the wealthy top 10 per cent, as he outlines what he calls the 'Different Worlds of the Top Decile'.

25 I mean 'irresponsibility' here in a literal sense: the manager refuses to accept responsibility for any of her or his actions and decisions. For a full exploration and explanation of this, see my *Complicity* (London and New York: Rowman & Littlefield, 2016).

26 Hannah Arendt, *Responsibility and Judgment*, ed. Jerome Kohn (New York: Schocken Books, 2003), 31.

27 Christopher Newfield, in *Unmaking the Public University* (Cambridge, MA: Harvard University Press, 2008), has shown how the 'theory wars' were, in fact, a straightforward political war conducted by conservatives and neoliberals against the academy. Those conservatives had fundamental aims to sustain a social order that subtended massive inequalities, and feared the power of cultural capital to overcome finance capital.

28 Moira Weigel, 'Invention of Political Correctness', *Guardian* 30 November 2016, available at: https://www.theguardian.com/us-news/2016/nov/30/political-correctness-how-the-right-invented-phantom-enemy-donald-trump. Interestingly, D'Souza has since been found guilty of political campaign finance law regulations.

Bloom is allegedly the model for Saul Bellow's *Ravelstein*
(New York: Viking Press, 2000).

29 John Guillory, *Cultural Capital* (Chicago: University of Chicago Press,
1993), xi.

30 Ibid., 56.

31 Ibid., ix.

32 The best single analysis of Managerian is to be found
on the blogging site of Liz Morrish: available at www.
academicirregularities.com . Morrish analyzes the language of
management and, yet more importantly, analyzes how it
functions in universities. Essentially, she points to its fundamental
vacuity, its emptying of substantive semantic content; but
she then indicates that it works like a Ponzi scheme, in that
individuals join up and benefit – at least temporarily – from
doing so.

33 See: https://www.gov.uk/government/uploads/system/uploads/
attachment_data/file/97976/prevent-strategy-review.pdf, 2

34 Ibid., 3.

35 Ibid., 4. We might also note, in passing, the by now entirely
characteristic Managerian rhetorical coercion here: people
'should welcome' this 'opportunity'. Such language and rhetorical
manoeuvres breed piety (at best) and Stalinist complicity
(at worst).

36 Ibid., 11 (subsequent references to the document will be in the
form of paragraph numbers and will be given in the main body of
the text).

37 Part of the point of the argument, however, is that the avowed
'neutrality' is itself simply compliance with a rather extreme right-
wing political position. For more on this, see my *For the University*
(London: Bloomsbury, 2011), *Universities at War* (London: Sage,
2015), and *Complicity* (London and New York: Rowman & Littlefield,
2016); and cf. Tariq Ali, *The Extreme Centre* (London: Verso, 2015).

38 Orwell, 'The Prevention of Literature', in *Inside the Whale*
(London: Penguin, 1972), 166.

39 Ibid., 167.

40 Ibid., 168.

41 For more on this, see Frank Furedi, *What's Happened to the
University?* (London: Palgrave, 2016). Furedi relates the focus
on 'safe spaces' to a larger and compelling argument about the
infantilization of contemporary educational culture. My own point

is that the safe space agenda is consistent with the institution's control of what can be legitimately thought.

42 For the idea of a 'community of interpreters', see Stanley Fish, *Is There a Text in this Class?* (Cambridge, MA: Harvard University Press, 1982). For the relation between a politics of democracy and a primacy of 'listening', see Andrew Dobson, *Listening for Democracy* (Oxford: Oxford University Press, 2014).

43 Walter J. Ong, *Ramus: Method and the Decay of Dialogue* (Cambridge, MA: Harvard University Press, 1958), 121.

44 This is, in raw form, the setting of university tuition fees.

6 CULTURAL CAPITAL AND THE SHAMEFUL UNIVERSITY

1 A clear exception to the supposed 'consensus' is in the 1989 crushing of the Tiananmen Square protests. The 'consensus' remained largely a 'western' proposition.

2 See: http://derstandard.at/2920415/ Im-Wortlaut-Das-Waldheim-Vermaechtnis

3 Kazuo Ishiguro, *The Remains of the Day* (London: Faber & Faber, 1989; repr. 1990), 243.

4 Ibid., 5.

5 Ibid., 185–6.

6 Ibid., 194.

7 Ibid., 210.

8 See Giorgio Agamben, *Homo Sacer* (Torino: Einaudi, 1995), *passim*. In his characterization of 'la vita nuda', Agamben owes much to Hannah Arendt's work, but see, especially, her *The Human Condition*, repr. (Chicago: University of Chicago Press, 1998).

9 For the contemporary exploration of this, see Owen Jones, *Chavs* (London: Verso, 2011); and cf. also, Lynsey Hanley, *Estates* (London: Granta, 2007), and *Respectable* (London: Penguin, 2016). See also Robert Hewison, *Cultural Capital* (London: Verso, 2014), on the perversions of cultural capital into cultural capitalism.

10 See: http://www.nonresistance.org/docs_htm/Tolstoy/Shame.html for the full text of 'Shame' in English. All subsequent quotations are from this web version.

11 It is worth noting dates. Tolstoy writes in the early years of the reign of Tsar Nicholas II, who retained the idea of autocratic rule. Just two years after the publication of 'Shame' (and, despite Lenin's 1895 exile, and in the face of decrees banning the formation of

political parties), the Russian Social Democratic Workers' Party was formed, endorsing fundamentally Marxist principles. 'Shame' sits at the centre of a period when the class system itself is coming under extreme pressure from within the class system itself; and 'Shame' plays its part in shaming and thus undermining the claims to authority of a ruling class.

12 Franz Kafka, 'On the Question of our Laws', trans. Michael Hofmann, *London Review of Books*, 37: 14 (16 July 2015), 23. All subsequent references are from this source.

13 We have a word for our own contemporary 'nobility': the 1 per cent.

14 Ishiguro, *Remains*, 152–3.

15 It is interesting to consider 'free' speech in such economic terms, for it brings into question a play of 'values' other than freedom-as-such. See, for interesting discussions, Anthony Lester, *Five Ideas Worth Fighting For* (London: Oneworld, 2016), chapter 3, and Timothy Garton Ash, *Free Speech* (London: Atlantic Books, 2016).

16 This is also the position of individuals such as Kurt Waldheim. Hannah Arendt pointed out that some Nazis exculpate themselves by suggesting that, in doing as they did, they 'saved' others from having to do terrible deeds.

17 Ishiguro, *Remains*, 148.

18 Ibid., 149.

19 Ibid, 151.

20 This is the logic of the 'aristocracy of culture' in Pierre Bourdieu, *Distinction,* trans. (Routledge: Richard Nice, 1972).

21 Fredric Jameson, 'Culture and Finance Capital', *Critical Inquiry*, 24: 1 (1997), 247.

22 Julian Barnes, *The Noise of Time* (London: Jonathan Cape, 2016), 61.

23 Ibid., 73.

24 The reference here is to Hamlet's most famous soliloquy, in which Shakespeare pits a critical conscience against action; and the consequence is the critic as cowardly procrastinator of action. It is a lesson we are still learning.

25 Many academics will recognize the contemporary university behind this: an institution that demands social conformity and political compliance. For more on this, see my *Complicity* (London and New York: Rowman & Littlefield, 2016).

26 Barnes, *Noise*, 104.

27 Ibid., 48.
28 Ibid., 55.
29 J. M. Coetzee, *Lives of Animals*, (New Jersey: Princeton, 1999), 40.
30 See, for examples, Derek Attridge, *J. M. Coetzee and the Ethics of Reading* (Chicago: University of Chicago Press, 2004), 178, 187; Myrtle Hooper, ' "Scenes from a Dry Imagination": *Disgrace* and Embarrassment', in Graham Bradshaw and Michael Neill, eds., *J. M. Coetzee's Austerities* (London: Ashgate, 2010), 143; Katherine Hallemeier, *J. M. Coetzee and the Limits of Cosmopolitanism* (London: Palgrave, 2013), 113.
31 J. M. Coetzee, *Disgrace* (London: Vintage, [1999] 2000), 112; 110.
32 Ibid., 98.
33 Ibid., 158.
34 Ibid., 205.
35 Ibid., 68.
36 Ibid., 142–3.
37 See Jean Baudrillard, *L'échange symbolique et la mort* (Paris: Gallimard, 1976). On shame as a fundamental human condition, related to the Nazi death camps, see Giorgio Agamben, *Remnants of Auschwitz*, trans. Daniel Heller-Roazen (New York: Zone Books, [1999] 2002).
38 See André Gorz, *L'Immatériel* (Galilée, Paris, 2003) for a good discussion of this.
39 Coetzee, *Disgrace*, 66.
40 In relation to this, witness UK former Justice Secretary and former Education Secretary, Michael Gove, explicitly decrying education during the 2016 Brexit debates: 'the people of this country have had enough of experts'. See: http://www.ft.com/cms/s/0/3be49734-29cb-11e6-83e4-abc22d5d108c.html#axzz4Cry2n3QQ
41 I have written about the neo-feudal nature of this in *Universities at War* (London: Sage, 2015); and I explore its consequences more fully in my study of *The New Treason of the Intellectuals* (Manchester: Manchester University Press, 2018).

7 THE PRIVATIZATION OF ALL INTERESTS

1 See, for example, Charlotte Philby, *Independent*, 6 January 2010, available at: http://www.independent.co.uk/news/world/europe/the-spy-who-loved-me-charlotte-philby-returns-to-moscow-in-search-of-her-grandfather-kim-philby-1915508.html; and cf. Neil

Tweedie, *Telegraph*, 23 Jan 2013, available at: http://www.
telegraph.co.uk/history/9818727/Kim-Philby-Father-husband-traitor-
spy.html

2   See Paul de Man, *The Resistance to Theory*
(Manchester: Manchester University Press, 1986), 17–18. The
argument here is prefigured some two decades previously, by
Jacques Derrida in his review-essay 'Force and Signification' (1963),
in *Writing and Difference*, trans. Alan Bass, (London: Routledge,
1981), an essay that might be said to be the founding text of what
became known as deconstruction.

3   This is not to deny the actual political gains that were made by
feminist movements in their use of the claim that the personal is
political. Those gains have been substantial, but my argument is
that there are also significant losses and impasses that derive from
the potential that the phrase offers for simple reversal, and for the
privatization of politics.

4   I borrow the phrase 'transparent society' here from Gianni Vattimo,
La società trasparente (Milano: Garzanti, 1989). Vattimo's argument
is about how our media of communication and representation have
become 'im-media', as it were: the speed of our contemporary
mediatic representations blurs the distinction between the real
and its representation, since the representation is in 'real time',
unmediated or immediate. I have explored the specific politics
of this in *After Theory*, 2nd edn (Edinburgh: Edinburgh University
Press, 1996). Here, I concentrate more fully on the idea of the
blurring of private and public.

5   See report by Amy Chozick, Nicholas Confessore and Michael
Barbaro, available at: http://www.nytimes.com/2016/10/08/us/
politics/hillary-clinton-speeches-wikileaks.html?_r=0

6   Virginia Woolf, *Selected Essays* ed. David Bradshaw (Oxford: Oxford
University Press, 2008), 4. For an excellent consideration of
the genre of the essay as such, see Brian Dillon, *Essayism*
(London: Fitzcarraldo, 2017).

7   Woolf, *Selected Essays*, 4, 5. In 1952, Emil Cioran suggested
something similar: 'Les "sources" d'un écrivain, ce sont ses
hontes; celui qui n'en découvre pas en soi, ou s'y dérobe, est voué
au plagiat ou à la critique' (A writer's 'sources' are to be found
in her or his shames; whoever fails to discover such shames in
themselves, or who hides from them, is given over to plagiarism
or criticism). See Cioran, 'Syllogismes de l'amertume' (1952)
in *Oeuvres* (Paris: Gallimard, 1995), 748. This should be placed
alongside my arguments regarding the value of shame above.

8   See J. H. Newman, *The Idea of the University*, ed. Martin J.
    Svaglic (San Francisco: Rinehart Press, [1852] 1960), xliv; and see
    also Walter Benjamin, 'The Work of Art in the Age of Mechanical
    Reproduction', in *Illuminations*, ed. Hannah Arendt, trans. Harry
    Zohn (1973), 233–4.

9   See Michael Hardt and Antonio Negri, *Multitude* (London: Hamish
    Hamilton, 2005). Interestingly, in the present context, Tom Nairn,
    in 'Make for the Boondocks', a review of *Multitude* in *London
    Review of Books*, 27: 9 (5 May 2005), writes that 'Hardt and
    Negri are in the Redemption business, door-steppers rather
    than private eyes'. See: http://www.lrb.co.uk/v27/n09/tom-nairn/
    make-for-the-boondocks

10 The interview is available at: https://www.youtube.com/
    watch?v=GGgiGtJk7MA. The story Gove told about his father
    was itself dismissed as untrue the following day, pointing out that
    he had sold the business as a going concern by his own volition.
    See: https://www.theguardian.com/politics/2016/jun/15/michael-
    gove-father-company-eu-policies-fish-processing-aberdeen. Faisal
    Islam, faced with Gove's irrationalities, accurately characterized his
    position as based on 'Oxbridge Trump'.

11 The Hitchens-Tharoor debate is available at: https://www.youtube.
    com/watch?v=jw3dDbc1BHE

12 The allusions here are to John Keats, 'Ode to a Nightingale',
    where the poet wishes that he might 'leave the world unseen',
    like a spy.

13 For more detail on the philosophy underpinning this, see my
    Confessions: the Philosophy of Transparency (London: Bloomsbury,
    2015). See also Emmanuel Alloa and Dieter Thomä,
    Transparency: from the Panopticon to the Selfie (forthcoming,
    London: Palgrave, 2018).

14 Naomi Klein, 'It was the Democrats' embrace of neoliberalism
    that won it for Trump', *Guardian*, 9 November 2016, available
    at: https://www.theguardian.com/commentisfree/2016/nov/09/
    rise-of-the-davos-class-sealed-americas-fate

15 See Luc Boltanski, *La Souffrance à distance,* repr. (Paris: Gallimard,
    [1993] 2007) for a gloss on what I refer to here as a 'philosophy
    of pity'. Boltanski's concern is related to the emergence of pity as
    a political issue in the latter half of the eighteenth century, when
    it is forged mostly through aesthetics and literature; and the key
    question he asks is how we can translate into action our moral
    sentiments of pity when we see suffering happening elsewhere
    in the world, or when 'the world' is 'at a distance'. How can a

mediatized 'representation' of suffering provoke an action that has an effect on those who are 'absent'?

16 Adam Shatz, 'Wrecking Ball: Adam Shatz on Trump's Racism', *London Review of Books*, 39: 17 (7 September 2017), 17.

17 Hannah Arendt, *The Human Condition*, 2nd ed., (Chicago: University of Chicago Press, [1958] 1998), 38.

18 Ibid., 39.

19 See Giorgio Agamben, *Homo Sacer,* trans. Daniel Heller-Roazen (Stanford: Stanford University Press, 1998), 1 and *passim.* It is worth noting that he credits both Foucault and Arendt with their separate explorations of the 'biopolitics' that derive from this distinction.

20 Arendt, *Human Condition*, 31.

21 Ibid., 31.

22 Voltaire, *Candide* ed. J. H. Brumfitt (Oxford: Oxford University Press, 1968), 148–9; translation mine.

23 Philip Roth, *The Human Stain,* repr. (London: Vintage, [2000] 2016), 44.

24 Ibid., 44.

25 Arendt, *Human Condition*, 38.

26 Arendt, *Human Condition*, 27; and the references are to Aristotle, *Ethics*, 1142a25 and 1178a6ff.

27 Ludwig Wittgenstein, *Philosophical Investigations,* trans. G. E. M. Anscombe (Oxford: Blackwell, 1992), 88, §243.

28 Ludwig Wittgenstein, *Tractatus Logico-Philosophicus,* German text with English translation by C. K. Ogden (London: Routledge, 1992), 188/189, §7.

29 Arendt, *Human Condition*, 22.

30 Markman Ellis, *The Coffee-House: A Cultural History* (London: Phoenix, 2005), xi, xii.

31 See Luc Boltanski, *La Souffrance à distance* (1993; repr. Paris: Gallimard, 2007).

32 Peter Sloterdijk, *Spheres, vol. 1: Bubbles*, trans. Wieland Hoban (Cambridge, MA: Semiotext(e), [1998] 2011), 17.

33 See Judith Butler, *Precarious Life* (London: Verso, 2004).

34 See, for example, the report at: http://uk.businessinsider.com/ donald-trump-hands-no-problem-marco-rubio-2016-3

35 For an excellent and succinct explanation of this in a historical context, see Justin Fox, 'The Economics of Well-Being', *Harvard*

Business Review, (Jan-Feb 2012), available at: https://hbr.org/2012/01/the-economics-of-well-being

36 Arendt, *Human Condition*, 38.

37 Essentially, this is the ground on which the entirety of Franco Moretti's work, post-2000, has been based.

38 Arendt, *Human Condition*, 41.

39 André Gorz, *The Immaterial*, trans. Chris Turner (London: Seagull, 2010), 6–7.

40 Thorstein Veblen, *The Higher Learning in America* (New York: B. W. Huebsch, 1918), 3–4.

41 See: http://www.belfasttelegraph.co.uk/news/education/queens-university-vicechancellor-patrick-johnston-can-we-put-my-history-blunder-in-the-past-34763168.html

42 See Brenna Bandhar, 'A Right to the University', *London Review of Books* blog, 10 December 2013, available at: http://www.lrb.co.uk/blog/2013/12/10/brenna-bhandar/a-right-to-the-university/; and see also her interview with Olivier Chassaing, 'Droit et colonialité' in *Période*, 29 September 2016, available at: http://revueperiode.net/droit-et-colonialite-entretien-avec-brenna-bhandar/, which helps justify the appropriateness of founding my case in the examination of Delhi.

8 RADICAL GEOGRAPHY

1 Edward W. Said, *Culture and Imperialism* (New York: Vintage Books, 1994), xiii.

2 Ibid., xii.

3 Terry Eagleton, *The Event of Literature* (New Haven: Yale University Press, 2012), 24.

4 Ibid, 90.

5 See reports at: https://www.theguardian.com/books/2016/oct/19/uk-authors-annual-incomes-below-minimum-wage-survey-average-earnings and at: https://www.theguardian.com/books/2016/jan/15/earnings-soar-for-uks-bestselling-authors-as-wealth-gap-widens-in-books-industry. See also the European Commission Report on 'the remuneration of authors', available at: https://ec.europa.eu/digital-single-market/en/news/commission-study-remuneration-authors-books-and-scientific-journals-translators-journalists-and

6 See Browne Review, available at: https://www.gov.uk/government/publications/the-browne-report-higher-education-funding-and-student-finance

7   For an argument exploring how Morgan had a deep affinity with
    Cage, see my *Complicity* (London and New York: Rowman &
    Littlefield International, 2016), 106–10.

8   Edwin Morgan, *Collected Poems* (Manchester: Carcanet, 1996),
    118; 'Sick Man' is in ibid., 121.

9   Morgan, *Collected Poems*, 196.

10 See Ellroy in interview with Waterstone's bookshop, available
    at: https://www.waterstones.com/blog/fiction-book-of-the-month-
    q-a-with-james-ellroy-author-of-perfidia and see also the interview
    in Time magazine, available at: http://time.com/3907690/james-
    ellroy-los-angeles-lapd-1953/. Note also Ellroy's home as that of the
    'capital letters' L and A.

11 Morgan's 'emergent poems' take a phrase, and repeat it over
    many lines. However, each line erases numbers of letters from
    the phrase, to reveal other words and phrases 'hidden' within
    the presiding and guiding original phrase. See Morgan, *Collected
    Poems*, 132–6. The examples here take phrases from German,
    Italian, Scots, and (transliterated) Russian. The classic example of
    this kind of poem is 'Message Clear', in *Collected Poems*, 159. It is
    interesting to note a similarity between the emergent poems and
    Saussure's interest in cryptic messages: see Jean Starobinski, *Les
    mots sous les mots* (Paris: Gallimard, 1971).

12 Seamus Heaney, *Opened Ground: Poems 1966–1996*
    (London: Faber and Faber, 1998), 46: '*Anahorish*, soft gradient / Of
    consonant, vowel meadow'.

13 Heaney, *Opened Ground*, 54, 50, 163, 58, 176, 178.

14 Shakespeare, *Comedy of Errors*, 3: 2.

15 In relation to this, see J. Hillis Miller, 'The History of 0', *Journal
    for Cultural Research*, 8 (2004), 123–39, and his 'Zero among
    the Literary Theorists', ibid., 165–81; and cf my response to this
    in Thomas Docherty, 'One', in ibid., 141–54. For an expended
    engagement with this, see also my *Confessions* (London
    Bloomsbury, 2012), esp. 110–44. I have worked through the
    specifics involved in the John Donne example here in my *John
    Donne, Undone* (London: Routledge, 1986; repr. 2015).

16 Paul Beatty, *The Sellout* (London: Oneworld, 2016), 116.

17 Ibid., 116, 117.

18 Rana Dasgupta, *Capital* (London: Penguin, 2014), 3.

19 Ibid., 216.

20 Ibid., 169.

21 Ibid., 262.

22 Pablo Mukherjee, *Postcolonial Environments* (London: Palgrave, 2010), 1.

23 Dasgupta, *Capital*, 154.

24 Walter Benjamin, Thesis VII in 'Theses on the Philosophy of History', in *Illuminations*, ed. Hannah Arendt, trans. Harry Zohn (London: Fontana, 1973), 258.

Index

Adorno, Theodor W. 130, 135, 138
Agamben, Giorgio 155
Agricola, Rudolph 150
Amis, Kingsley 102
Appadurai, Arjun 9–11, 93–4
Apter, Emily 246 n.6
Arendt, Hannah 20, 140–1, 189–93, 195–200, 202–3, 256 n.16
Arnold, Matthew 16–17, 19, 26, 73, 76, 86, 91
Attlee, Clement 114, 134
Auden, W. H. 38, 238 n.4
Auerbach, Erich 112–13, 115
Austen, Jane 49

Bagehot, Walter 89–90
Bahro, Rudolf 27
Balzac, Honoré de 40–1, 49, 82–3, 144
Barbie, Klaus 153
Barnes, Julian 32, 155, 162–5, 168
Barthes, Roland 65
Baudelaire, Charles 15
Baudrillard, Jean 169
Beckett, Samuel 196
Bennett, Arnold 31
Beatty, Paul 227–8
Benjamin, Walter 138, 181, 232
Benn, Hilary 249 n.33
Bentinck, William 70, 243 n.10
Beveridge, William 134–5
Bhandar, Brenna 207–8
Blair, Tony 249 n.33
Blake, William 218
Bloom, Allan 141, 254 n.28
Boltanski, Luc 199, 259 n.15

Booth, Wayne C. 128
Bourdieu, Pierre 17
Brooks, Cleanth 128
Browne, John 24, 214
Burke, Edmund 85, 88–91
Burns, Robert 218
Burroughs, William 217
Bush, George W. 235 n.9

Cable, Vince 4
Cage, John 217
Cameron, David 145–6
Carew, Thomas 50, 171
Carey, John 246 n.5
Carlile, Alex 146
Casanova, Pascale 79–81
Cassin, Barbara 246 n.6
Chamoiseau, Patrick 25
Chaucer, Geoffrey 82, 84
Churchill, Winston 114
Cioran, Emil 258 n.7
Clifton-Brown, Douglas 114–15
Clinton, Hillary 172, 178–9, 189
Coe, Jonathan 33, 58, 60–1, 138
Coetzee, J. M. 66–8, 155–6, 165–9
Cohn-Bendit, Daniel 27
Collini, Stefan 79, 85, 102
Copernicus, Nicolaus 226
Craig, Cairns 79
Crawford, Robert 79

Damrosch, David 79–82, 84
Dante Alighieri 18, 144
Dasgupta, Rana 37–9, 41, 43, 45–7, 50–51, 55–8, 61, 67–8, 95–6, 228–31

Deane, Seamus 79, 88–90
Defoe, Daniel 40, 48–50, 58
Delors, Jacques 134
De Man, Paul 176
Demjanjuk, John 153
Derrida, Jacques 15–16
Descartes, René 123, 226
Diogenes of Sinope 167–8
Disney, Walt 119
Donne, John 225–7
Dorling, Danny 137
Doyle, Roddy 242 n.55
Drucker, Peter 253 n.22
Dryden, John 86
D'Souza, Dinesh 141, 253 n.28
Duck, Stephen 52–4, 61

Eagleton, Terry 79, 90–1,
    212–13, 215
Eckermann, Johann Peter 79–80,
    244 n.27
Edgeworth, Maria 33
Ellis, Markman 198
Ellroy, James 219, 222
Elshahed, Mohamed 241 n.45
Empson, William 128
Engels, Friedrich 5–6, 83–4, 128

Farage, Nigel 172
Ford, Richard 26
Forster, E. M. 17–20
Fowler, Alastair 50–3
French, Philip 132

Gagnier, Regenia 239 n.11
Galbraith, John Kenneth 135
Galsworthy, John 31, 105–6
Gardiner, Michael 79
Genette, Gérard 31
Goethe, Johann Wolfgang 79–82,
    84, 144, 244 n.27
Gorz, André 204
Gove, Michael 24, 183–6
Grossman, Lionel 76

Guillory, John 92, 95, 141–3
Gumbrecht, Hans Ulrich 130–1
Gutenberg, Johannes 40
Guthrie, Woody 136–7

Habermas, Jürgen 169, 198–200
Hardt, Michael 182
Harris, Robert 120–1
Harvey, David 216
Hayek, Friedrich 208
Heaney, Seamus 80–2, 84, 222–4
Herder, Johann Gottfried 90
Herrick, Robert 50
Hess, Rudolph 153
Hitchens, Christopher 182, 185
Hibbard, G. R. 50–2
Hodgson, Geoffrey M. 111
Hume, David 49

Ishiguro, Kazuo 153–6,
    159–64, 168
Islam, Faisal 183–4
Ismail, Khedive 241 n.45

Jacobson, Howard 109, 170
Jameson, Fredric 64–7, 82,
    89–90, 124–5, 130, 162
Jefferson, Thomas 115
Johnson, Samuel 11, 86, 90, 123,
    198, 216
Johnston, Patrick 206–7
Jonson, Ben 29, 50–4, 58,
    117, 171
Josipovici, Gabriel 251 n.55
József, Attila 222
Joyce, James 31, 117–20, 149,
    217, 222, 242 n.5

Kafka, Franz 156, 158–9, 162, 167,
    171, 215
Kant, Immanuel 86
Keats, John 11, 240 n.19
Kenny, Virginia C. 54–5
Keynes, John Maynard 135

Khrushchev, Nikita 153–4
Kiberd, Declan 77–9
Kimball, Roger 141
Klein, Naomi 27, 188–9
Koch Brothers 141
Krugman, Paul 236 n.13
Kuznets, Simon 238 n.5
Kynaston, David 135

Lanchester, John 33, 39, 42,
  58–61, 138
Larkin, Philip 102
Law, John 8–9, 11, 235 n.9
Lazarus, Neil 130
Leavis, F. R. 73–4
Le Pen, Marine 172
Leveson, Brian 115–16
Levi, Primo 133
Lewis, Michael 9
Luce, Edward 23
Lutyens, Edwin 56, 68
Lyotard, Jean-François 45

Macaulay, Thomas Babbington
  70–4, 77–8, 91, 103–4, 118
McBride, Kari Boyd 53–4
Macdonald, Graeme 237 n.4
McGrath, John 25
McLuhan, Marshall 40
Mandelson, Peter 108
Marquand, David 28, 39–40
Marvell, Andrew 50
Marx, Karl 5–6, 24–5, 54, 83–4,
  93, 128
Mason, Paul 40, 252 n.7
Mauroy, Pierre 134
Mayakovsky, Vladimir 222
Mill, John Stuart 169
Milton, John 17, 115–16
Mitterand, François 134
Montaigne, Michel de 179
Montesquieu, Charles-Louis
  8–9, 11
Moretti, Franco 79

Morgan, Edwin 216–24, 233
Morrish, Liz 254 n.32
Mukherjee, Upamanyu Pablo
  96–7, 230
Mulhearn, Francis 79
Muller, Jerzy Z. 135
Murray, Patrick 49–50

Negri, Antonio 182
Newfield, Christopher 253 n.27
Newman, John Henry 180
Nicholson, Colin 42–3, 48

Ong, W. J. 40, 150
Orwell, George 17–18, 101–8,
  110, 112, 115–16, 118–20,
  123–5, 132, 134, 146–8, 217,
  250 n.48, 250 n.50
Osborne, George 4, 132–3
Ovid 218

Pascal, Blaise 13–14, 20
Patočka, Jan 15
Pessoa, Fernando 144
Peters, Tom 253 n.22
Petrarch, Francesco 218
Philby, Kim 175–9
Piketty, Thomas 39–42, 49, 82–3,
  87–8,132–4, 138–40, 143
Pocock, J. G. A. 55
Poovey, Mary 7, 30, 49–50, 72–3
Pope, Alexander 34, 50, 86
Proust, Marcel 31
Putin, Vladimir 172
Puttenham, George 85–6

Rankin, Ian 40–1
Reagan, Ronald 134, 177
Richardson, Samuel 6–7, 40
Roth, Philip 193–5

Said, Edward 211–12, 215, 225–6
Sandel, Michael 11
Sanders, Bernie 172, 179

Sen, Amartya 169
Sengupta, Somini 230
Shakespeare, William 199, 223–5, 231
Shatz, Adam 190
Shelley, Percy Bysshe 35, 86
Shostakovich, Dmitri 32–3, 162–5
Showalter, Elaine 41
Sidney, Philip 85
Simmel, Georg 12, 18
Sinclair, Upton 25
Singh, Manmohan 46–7
Sissons, Michael 132
Skidelsky, Edward 27–8, 110
Skidelsky, Robert 27–8, 110
Smith, Adam 48–9, 140
Smith, Adrian 207
Sloterdijk, Peter 200–1, 205
Soros, George 96
Spengler, Oswald 23
Spivak, Gayatri 69, 71
Stalin, Joseph 32, 154, 162–5
Stiglitz, Joseph 236 n.13
Swift, Jonathan 30, 44, 49, 191–2
Swinburne, Algernon Charles 19

Taine Hyppolite 86
Tate, Allen 128
Tharoor, Shashi 182

Thatcher, Margaret 106–7, 134, 136–7, 177, 195
Tolstoy, Leo 156–61, 163, 167
Trump, Donald 109, 172, 178, 188–90, 192, 201, 247 n.11

Valéry, Paul 246 n.2
Vattimo, Gianni 258 n.4
Veblen, Thorstein 206
Viswanathan, Gauri 74–6, 91–2
Voltaire 193–5

Waldheim, Kurt 153–4
Waugh, Evelyn 186
Weber, Max 122
Weigel, Moira 141
Wells, H. G. 31
Whitney, Geoffrey 50
Wilde, Oscar 27, 32–4, 61, 93
Williams, Raymond 19, 52, 84, 86–8, 90–1, 212, 215, 228
Wittgenstein, Ludwig 196
Wolf, Martin 92–4
Woolf, Virginia 31, 113, 179–80, 193, 246 n.5
Wordsworth, William 30–1, 44–5

Yeats, W. B. 222

Zola, Emile 49